NAZI SEX SPIES

NAZI SEX SPIES

TRUE STORIES OF SEDUCTION, SUBTERFUGE AND STATE SECRETS

AL CIMINO

PICTURE CREDITS

Getty Images: page 8, 12, 14, 20, 26, 31, 58, 70, 72, 82, 96, 122, 128, 130, 133, 138, 141, 164, 178, 200, 208, 225, 236

Shutterstock Editorial: 94, 118

Alamy: 94, 170

We have made every attempt to contact the copyright-holders of the illustrations within this book. Any oversights or omissions will be corrected in future editions.

This edition published in 2024 by Arcturus Publishing Limited
26/27 Bickels Yard, 151–153 Bermondsey Street,
London SE1 3HA

AD006670UK

Printed in the US

CONTENTS

INTRODUCTION

THE BLONDE BATTALION

All's fair in love and war. At least that's what the Nazis thought – they deployed sex like a weapon to try to achieve their goal of world domination. There was even a spy school in Germany where prostitutes were taught the tricks of the trade. Other sex spies were enthusiastic amateurs, while a surprising number were attractive young Jewish women who went undercover for the Nazis – even betraying other Jews – to save their own lives.

STRIPTEASE

One of the early casualties of World War II was a woman prepared to use her allure in the service of the Third Reich. Austro-German dancer and actress La Jana, born Henriette Niederauer, was famed for her comic striptease performed to bring a knight in armour to life in the movie *Es leuchten die Sterne* (*The Stars Shine*). Although she had olive-brown skin, she was often seen in the company of Nazi dictator Adolf Hitler and was on friendly terms with *Luftwaffe* chief Hermann Göring and propaganda minister Joseph Goebbels. Her dark beauty meant that she was regarded as an exotic and atypical distillation of German womanhood. She went on to take over the 'primitive' stage roles performed by African-American dancers such as Josephine Baker after they were forcibly removed when the Nazis seized power.

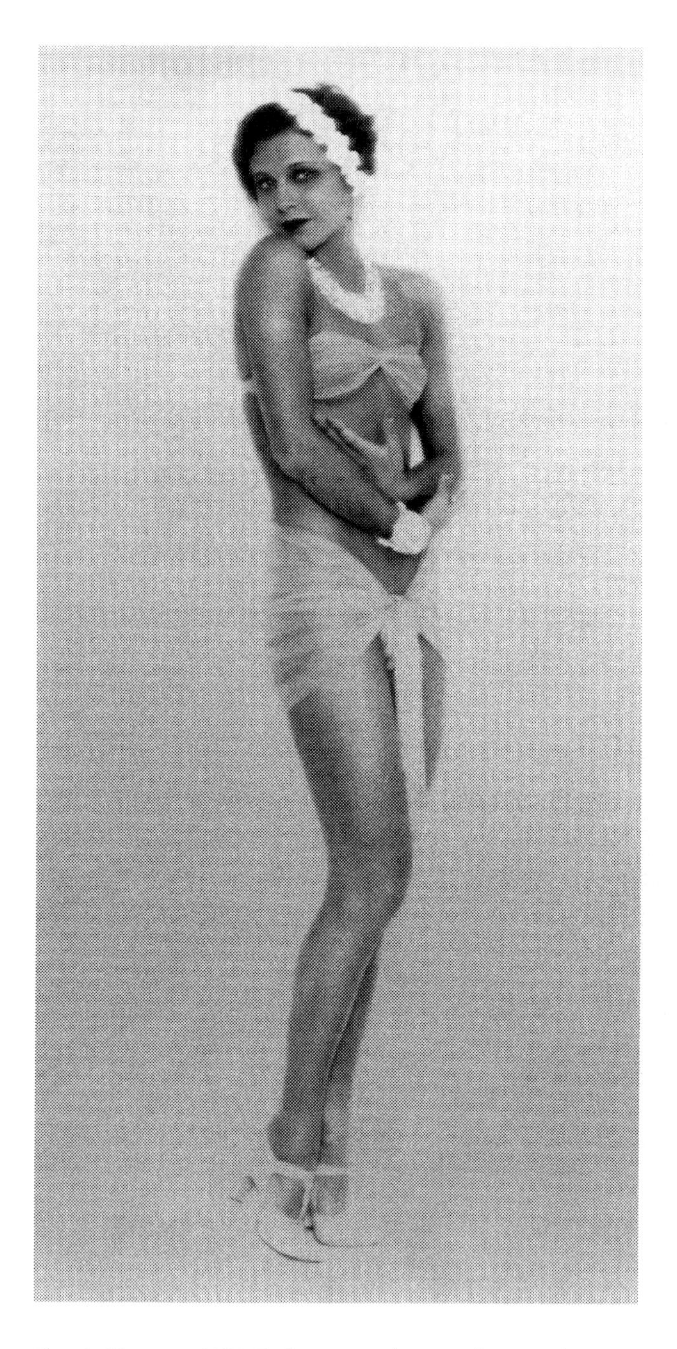

Born in Vienna in 1905, La Jana was a dancer and actress who spearheaded the Nazis' attempts to replicate Hollywood musicals.

In 1938, La Jana visited London to meet impresario Charles B. Cochran. After watching a Test match at Lord's, she invited Cochran to stay with her in Germany where she would introduce him to Hitler.

'You must teach him the game of cricket,' she said. 'He loves sport.'

She fell ill and died in 1940, aged 35, on a mission to Poland for Goebbels.

Another of Hitler's favourites, Princess Stephanie Juliane von Hohenlohe, was Jewish though the head of the SS Heinrich Himmler made her an 'honorary Aryan'. In England, she used her intimate relationship with Lord Rothermere to encourage the *Daily Mail* newspaper to support the Nazis. In 1937, she arranged for Lord Halifax, later foreign secretary, to visit Germany. She also helped to organize the visit of the Duke of Windsor and his wife Wallis Simpson that year. Now Duchess of Windsor, Wallis seems to have been the source of many Allied secrets that found their way to Berlin both before and during the war.

SECRETS AND SEDUCTION

For the purposes of espionage, the Nazis ran an upscale brothel in Berlin called Salon Kitty. German dignitaries, foreign diplomats and other important clients were encouraged to visit, while highly trained girls coaxed them into disclosing secrets or expressing compromising opinions. Meanwhile in New York, there was a gay 'house of assignation' in Brooklyn where German spies hired American servicemen with the hope of gleaning indiscreet pillow talk from wealthy clients. One of its visitors was a US senator who had opposed America's entry into World War II.

The Nazis sent alluring German women to spy in the United States and Britain. There were also home-grown American spies whose allegiance to the Nazi regime was rooted in the German American Bund, a pro-Nazi league of Americans of German extraction. In the UK, some members of the British Union of Fascists were prepared to go to any lengths to betray their country in the pursuit of a German victory. And there were, of course, double agents who were prepared to use their charms to work for either side.

Clearly members of this battalion of secret agents weren't all blondes. But that was how the sons and daughters of the master race who laid down their lives – or just laid down – for the *Führer* came to be portrayed. However we may judge them, after all these years it is difficult to second-guess the decisions people make in moments of murderous political upheaval or all-consuming war. Those were very different times.

CHAPTER 1

SALON KITTY

Hitler's spymaster Walter Schellenberg and his boss Reinhard Heydrich were two of the most notorious Nazi officials. As head of the *Sicherheitsdienst*, or SD – the Reich Intelligence Service – *SS-Obersturmführer* Schellenberg was convicted of war crimes at the Nuremberg Trials, while *SS-Gruppenführer* Heydrich was one of the architects of the Holocaust. He was the infamous head of the Reich Main Security Office that controlled the Gestapo, the SS Intelligence Service and the Criminal Police, and was deputy head of the SS under *Reichsführer* Heinrich Himmler.

The two men had a complex relationship. In 1931, Heydrich had married the cool Nordic beauty Lina von Osten. She had cultural aspirations. The intellectual Schellenberg gave Lina the entrée into cultivated society that she craved and the three of them went to concerts and the theatre together. While Heydrich was flagrantly unfaithful to his spouse with numerous mistresses and prostitutes, Schellenberg became Lina's discreet lover.

They would spend the afternoon or evening playing bridge in what Heydrich called the 'dear intimacy of the family circle' where he would enact 'the part of the devoted husband'. However, according to Schellenberg: 'The very next evening I would get a telephone call from him – his voice now assuming a suggestive leer

Reinhard Heydrich played the part of the devoted husband, but he was unfaithful to his wife with numerous mistresses and prostitutes and regularly visited Kitty Schmidt's brothel.

– saying, "This evening we must go out together – in mufti. We'll have dinner somewhere and then 'go places'."'

HEYDRICH'S BRAINWAVE

Heydrich was already a patron of the establishment then known as Pension Kitty. The madam of this high-class brothel, Kitty Schmidt, kept four or five prostitutes on the premises. Clients could also select a partner from a number of photographic albums, then have their choice for the evening summoned by taxi.

'During dinner his conversation would become obscene,' said Schellenberg. 'He would try to make me drunk as we prowled from bar to bar, but I always excused myself on the grounds of not feeling quite up to the mark, and he never succeeded.'

It seems that Schellenberg strove to be faithful to his mistress, Heydrich's wife, a compliment he extended to neither of his own wives. The first he divorced after one year in 1939. He married again shortly after, though this union was not much more successful.

In 1939, Heydrich was investigating the source of a high-level leak that threatened to give the Allies advanced warning of Germany's plan to attack through the Ardennes to take Belgium, the Netherlands and France. Any strengthening of the defences at this vulnerable point could prove disastrous to the invasion.

During one of his evening peregrinations with Schellenberg, Heydrich came up with the idea of infiltrating a brothel patronized by officers, government officials and other high-flyers, where pretty women and alcohol might loosen an informer's tongue. Schellenberg was ordered to put this plan into action. As a result, he took on an unusual assignment.

The SS – *Schutzstaffel* or 'Protection Squad' – with their black uniforms designed by Hugo Boss, started out as Hitler's bodyguard and went on to become a murderous state within a state. But they had little experience of running brothels. Fortunately, someone who did had already fallen into Schellenberg's hands – it was Kitty Schmidt.

Pension Schmidt in Giesebrechtstrasse in Charlottenburg, a wealthy part of Berlin, became Salon Kitty. It was Heydrich's idea to take over this high-class brothel and install listening devices. He himself made a number of 'inspection tours' to the site, during which the microphones were discreetly turned off.

THE MADAM

Born Katherina Zammit in a working-class district of Berlin in 1882, Kitty changed her name to Schmidt, quit her job as a hairdresser's assistant and became a prostitute. She did well and was seen at the opera and out dining in fashionable restaurants. A brief marriage resulted in the birth of a daughter.

In 1922, at the age of 40, she opened her first brothel. On the advice of wealthy clients, she banked her profits in London, escaping the worst effects of hyperinflation under the Weimar Republic and the Depression. The mass unemployment that swept through Germany during the 1920s made it easy to recruit to her establishment and, as an expert in her trade, Kitty trained her girls well.

After a couple of changes of address, Pension Kitty settled in a large house at 11 Giesebrechtstrasse in the affluent Charlottenburg district where it became the most successful whorehouse in Berlin. Kitty took little interest when Hitler came to power in 1933 and business continued as usual, although several of her Jewish friends left for London. She visited them and they managed her financial affairs there as she continued sending large sums of money to England from Germany.

By 1937, the Nazi authorities began to crack down on money being transferred out of the country and Kitty resorted to sending girls on errands to London with cash sewn into their corsets. Although not interested in politics, she learned about the worsening situation from her clients and in March 1939 decided to quit the country.

Her flight was hastened by a visit from the police, who wanted to use her brothel as a front for the surveillance of her clientele. But the telegrams she had sent making arrangements for her trip were intercepted at the post office and she was arrested at the Dutch border. After two weeks in a police cell, she was handed over to the SS and taken to Schellenberg's office. He pointed out that she had illegally procured foreign currency, sent money out of the country and helped Jews escape. At the very least she was looking at a long stretch in a concentration camp. To avoid that fate, she agreed to do anything Schellenberg wanted and was forced to sign a secrecy agreement.

Kitty was released and returned to Giesebrechtstrasse on 14 July 1939, eight weeks before the outbreak of World War II. On 27 July, Schellenberg put his top-secret operation into action. He would take over Pension Kitty and transform it into Berlin's most notorious brothel – Salon Kitty.

BUGGING THE WHOREHOUSE

Untersturmführer Karl Schwarz was put in charge of the day-to-day running of Operation Salon Kitty and he and Schellenberg visited Giesebrechtstrasse to inspect the premises. Schellenberg then bought the building through an apparently innocuous businessman and brought in an architect to supervise alterations. The place was closed down for ten days, ostensibly for renovation, while microphones were concealed behind double walls. The wires were run down to the basement where a listening station was installed with recording equipment using wax discs.

Next, the Nazis had to recruit reliable girls. On 16 November 1939, senior SS and police officers received a top-secret memo requesting: '*Frauen und Mädchen, die intelligent, mehrsprachig, nationalistisch gesinnt und ferner mannstoll sind*' – 'Women and girls, who are intelligent, multilingual, nationalistically minded and furthermore man-crazy.' This was unproductive, so Schellenberg approached Arthur Nebe, the chief of police. For many years Nebe had worked in the vice squad so he knew a great number of working girls.

'From all the great cities of Europe, he recruited the most highly qualified and cultivated ladies of the *demi-monde*,' said Schellenberg, 'and I regret to say that quite a few ladies from the upper crust of German society were willing to serve their country in this manner.'

The selection board consisted of psychologists and psychiatrists, doctors, university lecturers and interpreters. The recruits had to be single, self-supporting with few family ties, between the ages of 20 and 30, and loyal to National Socialism. Initially 20 were selected and inducted into the *SS*, where they were required to swear a vow of secrecy along with an oath of allegiance to Hitler. Then they were sent to the cadet school at Ordensburg for training, where they received lectures on contraception, sexually transmitted diseases, hairdressing, cosmetics, social etiquette and the art of conversation, and were taught marksmanship, unarmed combat, first aid, foreign languages and the recognition of uniforms. There were also courses on intelligence techniques, including coding and de-coding. All the instruction was delivered within the framework of Nazi ideology and the Party's take on wartime economics.

'I COME FROM ROTHENBURG'

Back in Berlin, the girls were not told that the bedrooms they would be working in were bugged. Instead they were told to make a written report after every encounter with a subject of interest. That way, their reliability could be assessed.

New photo albums were produced showing the recruits in provocative poses. Special customers sent by the SS were given a password. If a client said, 'I come from Rothenburg', they were shown the books so that they could take their pick of (what they believed to be) the best on offer. Word of this specialist service was circulated in diplomatic and other official circles.

The SS kept the newly re-opened Salon Kitty well supplied with food and liquor, despite wartime shortages. In early April 1940, the intelligence operation was put to the test. The guinea pig was *Obersturmführer* Wolfgang Reichert, who had distinguished himself in Poland with the *Waffen-SS*. Schwarz had met him at a social function and tipped him off about Salon Kitty, telling him to say that he was from Rothenburg.

When Reichert did so, he was shown the albums and made his selection; the girl was phoned and arrived soon after. Schwarz was on hand in the basement to overhear their conversation. Reichert let slip that he was being posted to Flensburg on the Danish border. On 9 April, Germany invaded Denmark and Norway.

Soon after, the Italian ambassador and a senior official of the German foreign office were recorded in Salon Kitty's drawing room discussing Count Gian Galeazzo Ciano, Italy's foreign minister and son-in-law of Italian dictator Benito Mussolini, who was visiting Berlin and might be interested in visiting the Salon. After attending meetings with Hitler, Himmler and German foreign minister Joachim von Ribbentrop, Ciano visited Salon Kitty and was recorded criticizing Hitler. Clearly Salon Kitty was going to be an invaluable source of intelligence

– or at least counterintelligence. On 20 April – Hitler's birthday – Schellenberg was promoted to *Sturmbannführer* (major).

The operation was expanded with two dozen SS men listening in around the clock. They were forbidden to discuss anything they overheard. The girls were forbidden to contact one another outside Salon Kitty. They were given a medical examination once a week and a briefing once a month. They were also given additional training in languages and Nazi policy, and the contents of their reports were compared to the recordings for discrepancies. The girls knew, if they put a foot wrong, they faced dire consequences as they were privy to top-secret information.

Heydrich continued making his visits, insisting on the listening equipment being turned off when he was present. In his memoirs, Schellenberg records: 'After one such inspection he sent for me and accused me of failing to comply with his directive. He had, he said, already complained to Himmler about it. The *Reichsführer* was extremely annoyed and wanted me to submit a written explanation. I at once sensed that Heydrich was hatching a plot against me – possibly because he suspected me of conducting an illicit affair with his wife. He declined to accept my explanation that the apparatus could not be switched off that evening because the electric cables were being transferred, whereas Himmler at once pronounced himself satisfied.'

Heydrich ordered Schellenberg to move the listening post to SD headquarters in Prinz Albrechtstrasse where he had his office. This led to a shocking breach of security.

LJUBO KOLCHEV

Another visitor to Salon Kitty was British agent Roger Wilson, who had infiltrated Nazi Germany as a deputy press attaché at the Romanian embassy. He usually went under the name of Ljubo Kolchev, borrowed from a Romanian refugee in exile in London, but at Salon Kitty he used the grander alias Baron von Itty. On his initial visits as a regular client his suspicions were aroused when he noticed that the girls were all remarkable linguists and well-versed in current affairs. He then observed that new cables were being laid in the street outside as the listening post in the basement was being moved on Heydrich's orders. Wilson reported back to London and was told to continue his investigation to see what else he could discover.

In order to dig deeper, Wilson decided to get close to one of the girls and began to favour a young woman named Brigitta. Under her gentle prompting he admitted he was not really a baron and that his real name was Ljubo Kolchev. The SS quickly checked this out and found that Kolchev's diplomatic credentials were registered with the German foreign ministry. The Romanian ambassador was contacted and he vouched for his deputy press attaché. Summoned by the ambassador, Wilson explained the situation. The girl he had encountered at Salon Kitty must have been an SD agent, he said. While a warning went out to other diplomatic staff, Wilson convinced his boss to allow him to continue frequenting Salon Kitty otherwise, he argued, the Germans would realize their secret had been discovered.

On studying the rooms at Salon Kitty, Wilson found circular depressions high up in the wallpaper. These, he concluded, hid microphones. The new cables he had seen being laid in the street outside, he realized, carried the electrical signals from these microphones to an external listening post. He reported this to his superiors in London and technicians were sent who, under cover of darkness, managed to tap a couple of the circuits. Now the British set up a listening post of their own.

LISTENING IN

Joseph 'Sepp' Dietrich, the highest-ranking officer in the *Waffen-SS*, visited Salon Kitty but gave little away. Hitler's propaganda minister Goebbels also revealed little when he turned up to watch two Rothenburg girls staging a lesbian display. Nevertheless, the recordings were piling up. In due course the listening post was updated when wire- and subsequently tape-recorders were used to replace the wax discs.

When the Spanish foreign minister Ramón Serrano Suñer visited Berlin for talks with Hitler in September 1940, Ribbentrop took him to Salon Kitty. (Serrano Suñer was brother-in-law to the dictator General Francisco Franco.) The two

Sepp Dietrich was an old friend of Adolf Hitler who played a prominent part on the Night of the Long Knives and was later sentenced by the Allies to 25 years in prison for his part in the Malmedy massacre.

men discussed plans to take Gibraltar from the British; this would give the Axis powers dominion over the Mediterranean and Britain's western approaches. The covert action was codenamed Operation Felix but was cancelled when Franco, fearing that the British would seize the Canary Islands in retaliation, asked too high a price for his co-operation.

When a Japanese diplomat paid a visit to Salon Kitty, Frau Schmidt panicked, fearing she might fall foul of the Nazi racial purity laws if she admitted the man. She phoned Schwarz for advice and he gave permission for the diplomat to pick one of the Rothenburg girls. Although he was in Berlin as part of the delegation to negotiate a tripartite pact, sealing a military alliance between Germany, Italy and Japan, the diplomat kept his secrets to himself.

In February 1941, an Italian embassy official confided to one of the girls that he feared the war would ruin Italy, as Mussolini had been badgered and bribed into siding against Britain. The Italian advance into Greece was going particularly badly and Germany was forced to go to their aid, delaying a planned attack on Russia. The official also revealed the extent of Italian reverses in North Africa; again, Germany sent in the Afrika Korps the same month.

Schellenberg noted that neither Soviet nor US diplomats patronized Salon Kitty. This was about to become a problem as both nations would soon be at war with Germany. Following Germany's attack on the Soviet Union in June 1941, Salon Kitty was full with jubilant Nazi officers and diplomats. As more indiscretions poured in, Schellenberg was promoted *SS-Standartenführer*, or full colonel, and promoted to head of Department VI, the SD foreign intelligence service. This time, he made a personal inspection of the operation himself, getting Schwarz to inform Frau Schmidt of his arrival. Again, the monitoring equipment was switched off. After two hours spent in the brothel, he left.

When the girl Schellenberg had been seeing fell pregnant, Kitty reported the matter to Schwarz. He arranged for her to be transferred to the *Lebensborn* – an association dedicated to a programme of breeding 'Aryan' children by encouraging SS men to impregnate 'racially pure' unmarried women.

In November 1940, Romania joined the military alliance that had been set up by the signing of the Tripartite Pact. The British agent Roger Wilson feared that the information he had been leaking to keep himself in good standing at Salon

Kitty might get back to Bucharest via the German foreign ministry. He went to see Schellenberg and told him he knew his previous indiscretions at the brothel had been overheard, and that this had been deliberate. Wilson confessed his admiration for Hitler and the Nazis and asked Schellenberg for protection for himself and the girl he had been seeing. But at this point the SS discovered that the real Ljubo Kolchev was in London. Wilson was arrested, interrogated and tortured, then sent to Sachsenhausen concentration camp.

BOMB STOPS PLAY

As the war dragged on, the clientele of Salon Kitty dwindled. As more and more men disappeared off to the front, there were fewer clients left in Berlin. The women they left behind were more willing to take the remaining men to bed for free, if only to dispel their loneliness as few wanted to risk going out at night because of the Allied air raids.

On 17 July 1942, a bomb hit 11 Giesebrechtstrasse, destroying the top floors. Schwarz quickly ordered Salon Kitty to be sealed off and the microphones removed. Two days later, it re-opened, but activities were confined to the ground floor which meant the SD had to depend on verbal reports submitted by the girls. The listening team was sworn to secrecy and dispersed, though a close watch was kept on its members for any breach in security.

Although the tide of war was turning against Germany there was an upturn in Salon Kitty's trade, largely as a result of men returning from the front. Ribbentrop and Admiral Wilhelm Canaris, chief of the *Abwehr* or military intelligence service, heard that the SD had been gathering information from the brothel, so men from their ministries shunned the place and the trickle of information began to dry up. Schellenberg began to rely more on his network of agents spread across Europe, while Schwarz, deprived of transcripts of the recordings, began to mistrust the reports from the girls. As discipline slackened, the girls started having all-night parties.

As Salon Kitty was no longer a valuable intelligence asset, Schellenberg decided to close down the operation. Kitty Schmidt had to return to making her money from regular clients rather than from the SS budget. For the sake of security, the girls were kept on and required to continue providing regular reports. The recordings and transcripts were archived. Kitty was forced to sign another secrecy agreement and ordered to report if any of the girls went missing.

With the closure of the Salon Kitty operation, Schellenberg began to make peace overtures to the Allies on behalf of Himmler. These included a plan to use the fashion designer Coco Chanel, rumoured to be a Nazi spy, to contact Winston Churchill.

When Berlin fell to the Soviets, they tried to use Salon Kitty for their own advantage, as did the British and Americans when it came into their zone of occupation. But Kitty Schmidt kept her vow of silence, dying at the age of 71 in 1954.

Schellenberg was captured in Denmark and sent for trial at Nuremberg, where he was convicted of membership of the SD – declared a criminal organization by the Nuremberg tribunal – and found guilty of involvement in the murder of Soviet prisoners of war. He was sentenced to six years in prison, but released after two because of ill health. He died in Italy in 1952 after writing his memoirs (thought to be unreliable). It was later revealed that another establishment along the lines of Salon Kitty had been run by the Gestapo in Vienna.

CHAPTER 2

HITLER'S PRINCESS SPY

Princess Stephanie Juliane von Hohenlohe was born in 1891 in Vienna, the illegitimate daughter of Ludmilla Kuranda, a Jewish woman from Prague. Her father was Max Wiener, a Jewish moneylender who was having an affair with Ludmilla while her husband, lawyer Johann Richter, was in prison for embezzlement. This, of course, was not what Princess Stephanie told Hitler – she insisted that neither of her parents were Jewish (her mother converted to Catholicism before her marriage and Richter accepted Stephanie as his own child).

Though she had no silver spoon in her mouth, Stephanie was born to high aspirations. Her first name was taken from Princess Stephanie of Belgium, consort of Crown Prince Rudolf of Austria, heir to the Habsburg throne, who had died in a murder-suicide pact with his mistress at Mayerling, his hunting lodge, in 1886.

Stephanie did poorly at school, but her parents sent her to college in Eastbourne on England's south coast to learn English, one of many languages in which she became fluent. Her mother wanted her to be a concert pianist, but her hands were too narrow to span an octave properly. She was fond of sport, particularly ice-skating – attracting boyfriends at the Vienna skating club. At the age of 14, Stephanie won a beauty competition at the lakeside resort of Gmunden in the Austrian resort area of Salzkammergut. Her reputation as a beauty grew, and

Princess Stephanie Juliane von Hohenlohe was a colourful character who charmed her way into high society, encountering members of the Nazi hierarchy along the way. She used to smoke Havana cigars, striking matches on the soles of her shoes before lighting them. Her charisma meant that nobody was ever likely to forget her.

other girls began to copy the hairstyles and clothes worn by 'Steffi of Vienna'. While studying ballet at the Vienna Court Opera, aged 16, she set herself the ambition of marrying a prince.

AIMING HIGH

One of Stephanie's father's clients, Princess Franziska von Metternich, took the girl under her wing, taught her etiquette and manners, and introduced her to high society. 'I remember her as the grande dame who used to invite me to treats as a little girl,' Stephanie recalled, 'and later to parties and balls where I flirted outrageously with eligible young men.'

Stephanie flirted with older men too, attracting a proposal of marriage from the Polish Count Josef Gizycki. A notorious playboy, the count was recently divorced from an American heiress who had returned to the US with their daughter. Stephanie rejected the proposal of this good-looking man because he was old enough to be her grandfather. Count Rudolf Colloredo-Mansfeld was also rejected because he was a skinflint. Besides, neither of the men was a prince.

Johann Richter died leaving his family in poverty. The situation was saved by Stephanie's uncle, Robert Kuranda, who had returned to Austria after making his fortune in South Africa. He made handsome provision for his sister and niece. With her money problems now behind her, Stephanie's mother started a new relationship with a wealthy businessman.

Stephanie continued to make her way in society thanks to her aunt, Clothilde, who had briefly been married to the Vienna correspondent of *The Times* and owned a house in Kensington, west London, and a mansion on the shores of Lake Wannsee, near Berlin. Clothilde was famous for her parties and she and Stephanie travelled to the fashionable resorts of Europe together.

According to Stephanie, while at a hunt dinner given by Princess Metternich in 1914, she was asked to play something on the piano. She was joined at the keyboard by Prince Friedrich Franz von Hohenlohe-Waldenburg-Schillingsfürst. The next day, he offered to drive her home, but she was chaperoned by a governess (Stephanie was pretending to be 17 but she was actually 23). Stephanie maintained that she ensnared her prince by arranging three secret trysts.

'Within two weeks he asked me to marry him,' she said.

But she was already pregnant by Archduke Franz Salvator of Austria, Prince of Tuscany, who she had known since 1911. He was the son-in-law of Emperor Franz Joseph and had ten children with the Archduchess Marie Valerie, Franz Joseph's favourite daughter. Eager to avoid a scandal, the Austro-Hungarian emperor urged Friedrich Franz and Stephanie to marry quickly.

To keep the matter out of the press, the couple travelled to London where they married in Westminster Cathedral on 12 May 1914 with only Stephanie's mother present. Although the newly-weds didn't even share the same hotel on their wedding night, Stephanie had fulfilled her youthful ambition and was now a princess, a title she would flaunt happily for the rest of her life. They honeymooned in Berlin, intending to go on to India, but the outbreak of war intervened.

MARRIAGE AND WAR

The marriage gave Stephanie her first introduction to spying. During World War I, Friedrich Franz became the chief of German propaganda and director of German espionage in Switzerland. Meanwhile Stephanie had a fling with Archduke Maximilian Eugen Ludwig, younger brother of the Emperor Karl who had succeeded Franz Joseph to the throne in 1916. Archduke Maximilian went on to marry Princess Franziska Maria Anna von Hohenlohe-Waldenburg-Schillingsfürst – keeping things in the family.

When Stephanie gave birth to a son on 5 December 1914, she named him Franz Joseph after her benefactor. She also included in his long list of forenames her real father's name, Max, and her nominal father's name, Hans.

Eager to do her bit in the war, Stephanie turned to Archduke Franz Salvator for advice. Through his position as head of the Austrian Red Cross, she went to work as a nurse on the Russian front, taking with her a butler, a chambermaid and a rubber bath. To counter the stench of the field hospitals, she started smoking Havana cigars. She later served with the same entourage on the Italian front.

Following the defeat of the Central Powers in 1918, the Austro-Hungarian empire collapsed. Like all other citizens, Princess Stephanie and her husband had to choose whether to take up Austrian or Hungarian nationality. Both opted for Hungarian and Stephanie retained her Hungarian passport for the rest of her life. The pair divorced in 1920. Friedrich Franz remarried soon after and emigrated with his new wife to Brazil in the closing days of World War II.

In Vienna, in the midst of the social unrest that followed World War I, Stephanie said she did 'nothing, except entertain the tired diplomats and ministers, in whose overburdened laps these responsibilities lie. They always like to chat with a woman after a hard day signing treaties.' She inhabited charmed circles, spending time in private dining rooms and hunting lodges with rich and aristocratic men.

When the payment of war reparations began to cause inflation in Germany and Austria, Stephanie packed her suitcases with cash and headed for Nice with her retinue, where according to her son she visited the casino 'with no brassiere under her transparent muslin dress'. She attracted wealthy admirers including Grand Duke Dmitri Pavlovich and the 2nd Duke of Westminster who she took as lovers, sharing them with Coco Chanel.

POWERFUL FRIENDS

As she travelled around Europe, her list of acquaintances became a Who's Who of the rich and famous – the Aga Khan, King Gustav of Sweden, King Manuel of Portugal, David Lloyd George, Georges Clemenceau, Margot Asquith, the Regent of Hungary Admiral Horthy, Popes Pius XI and Pius XII, the Maharaja of Baroda, Leopold Stokowski, Sir Thomas Beecham, Arturo Toscanini, Sir Malcolm Sargent, *The Times*' editor Geoffrey Dawson, Lady Cunard, Lady Londonderry, Lord Rothschild, Lord Brocket, Lord Carisbrooke, and the Duke and Duchess of Windsor.

Her wealthy gentlemen admirers were more than willing to fund her lavish lifestyle. And although she rejected the marriage proposal of Anastasios Damianos Vorres, the scion of a wealthy family who had been Greek consul general in Vienna, she was happy to spend a year travelling with him.

The wealthy American John Murton Gundy was also happy to indulge her, as was Her Bernstiehl, a married millionaire who became her 'devoted slave'. John Warden from Philadelphia introduced her to the mysteries of the stock market, where she made a killing. In 1925, she moved into a luxurious apartment on Avenue Georges V in Paris, where she was supported by neighbour Sir William Garthwaite, a British insurance tycoon. In Deauville, she met Solly Joel, the principal shareholder of the South African mining company De Beers and, in 1928, toured the continent with heiress Kathy Vanderbilt. Then there was Lord Rothermere.

THE MEDIA TYCOON

Harold Sidney Harmsworth, created Baron Rothermere in 1914, was the owner of the *Daily Mail* newspaper. He and Stephanie met in 1925 in Monte Carlo where, the story goes, he was having a run of bad luck at the tables and she helped him out with 40,000 francs. After a drink together, he invited her back to his villa. The 57-year-old peer had a weakness for younger women, particularly ballerinas provided by Russian ballet director Sergei Diaghilev. However, according to her MI5 file, a different tale describes Stephanie being introduced to Lord Rothermere by one Andre Rostin, an individual 'not of good repute and strongly suspected of being a German agent'.

Rothermere had taken control of Associated Newspapers after the death of his brother Lord Northcliffe in 1922. Until then, the papers had been fiercely anti-German, but under the influence of Stephanie this began to change. In 1927, while staying with Rothermere in Monte Carlo, she suggested he publish an article about the restoration of the monarchy in Hungary. He did so, and the piece was widely read – a group of Hungarian monarchists even offered the throne to Rothermere, who put forward his son, Esmond Harmsworth (Stephanie wanted the crown to go to her son Franz Joseph). Esmond went to Hungary where he was greeted cordially. However, the situation was complicated by the fact that the prime minister, Count Bethlen, favoured a Habsburg succession, while the regent Admiral Horthy secretly wanted the throne for himself.

Adolf Hitler receives British newspaper magnate Harold Sidney Harmsworth (Lord Rothermere) as a visitor to his retreat at Berchtesgaden.

In 1928, British intelligence reported that Stephanie was 'exercising considerable influence over Lord Rothermere'. At the time, France had an alliance with Yugoslavia, Romania and Czechoslovakia, all of whom opposed a resurgent Hungary. The French accused Stephanie of espionage and, in 1932, she quit Paris for London amid rumours that she had been expelled from France. The gossip was compounded by her regular contact with Otto Abetz, a supporter of Hitler, who was eventually expelled from France in 1939 as a Nazi agent.

Stephanie was short of money and Rothermere employed her as society columnist on a generous salary. She stayed at the Dorchester Hotel, then managed by a man she knew from Biarritz, before moving into her own apartment at 14 Bryanston Square where she was the neighbour of Wallis Simpson, the consort of Edward VIII, and the woman for whom he had renounced the throne in 1936. MI5 kept them both under surveillance there.

NAZI PROPAGANDA

The apartment at the Dorchester remained the headquarters of Nazi propaganda and possibly espionage as well, and Princess Stephanie was at the centre of it. The diplomat Sir Walford Selby, who kept a close eye on the career of the woman he called an 'international adventuress', said: 'There is no doubt that German propaganda was very active in London during those years. The Austrian government was watching these manoeuvres with the deepest disquiet, especially those of Princess Stephanie von Hohenlohe, who they knew was an agent of Hitler.'

The government in Vienna was right to be concerned. A few years later, Austria, Hitler's homeland, was annexed by Nazi Germany in the *Anschluss* of 1938 while the British stood by and did nothing. Even *The Times* demurred, arguing it could be no bad thing because England and Scotland had also been united 300 years earlier.

Still ostensibly advancing the cause of Hungary, Stephanie was sent to Belgium to interview the exiled widow of Karl, the last Austro-Hungarian emperor, and to offer her Rothermere's financial support. Next, Stephanie was despatched to Hungary where she advised prime minister General Gyula Gömbös to follow the example of Benito Mussolini, the Fascist dictator who had come to power in Italy in 1922.

Rothermere's interest then switched to Germany and Stephanie was sent to the Netherlands to visit the exiled Kaiser Wilhelm II. As Rothermere's brother, Northcliffe, had hawked the slogan 'Hang the Kaiser' during World War I, the Kaiser was sceptical. The Kaiser's son, Crown Prince Wilhelm – affectionately known as 'Little Willie' – was a member of the Nazi Party who in 1933 became a brown-shirted storm trooper. Stephanie flirted with him outrageously, visiting him regularly in Berlin and interceding between him and Rothermere. Though he welcomed Rothermere's offer of assistance, the prince insisted that Adolf Hitler had been chosen to be the saviour of Germany, not him. At the time,

Hitler was interested in the restoration of the monarchy in Germany, though his enthusiasm cooled when he gained power himself.

Hitler became chancellor of Germany in January 1933. In March, he seized dictatorial powers, and by July, Rothermere was lauding him in the *Daily Mail.* Stephanie was sent to Berlin to open a channel of communication between the press baron and the *Führer.* In pursuance of this aim she began a sexual relationship with Hitler's personal adjutant, Fritz Wiedemann, a married man with three children. He had been Hitler's immediate superior in World War I and Hitler continued to address him as '*Kapitän*'.

As a token of her affection, she persuaded Rothermere to send Wiedemann a gold Cartier cigarette case and he became a constant visitor to her suite when she stayed at the Hotel Adlon in Berlin, just a short distance from the Reich Chancellery. Wiedemann was charming and well-educated; but Martha Dodd, daughter of the American ambassador, instead gushed about his 'eroticism'. 'Tall, dark, muscular, he certainly had great physical brawn and the appearance of bravery,' she said. 'Wiedemann's heavy face, with beetling eyebrows, was rather attractive. . . . But I got the impression of an uncultivated, primitive mind, with the shrewdness and cunning of an animal and completely without delicacy or subtlety.'

THE HANDS OF AN ARTIST

In December 1933, a car was sent from the Reich Chancellery to collect Princess Stephanie from the Adlon. Hitler did not approve of women in politics, but he greeted her with a kiss on the hand. She found him ugly, though said she would have found his pale blue eyes beautiful had they not protruded. They had a 'slightly far-away expression', she said. She thought his best feature was his hands: 'truly the sensitive hands of an artist', but she disliked his low-class Austrian accent. She left with a letter from Hitler addressed to Rothermere, thanking him for his support.

When she returned to Berlin later that month she brought a photograph of Rothermere in a solid gold frame made by Cartier. On the reverse was a reprint of a *Daily Mail* article from 24 September 1930 which promoted the Nazi Party and Hitler himself and supported the removal of a clause in the Versailles Treaty restricting the size of the German army. Hitler's aide-de-camp Hans-Heinrich Lammers was shocked as Stephanie's skirt rode up when she sank back in a soft armchair to translate the article for Hitler. But Hitler was thrilled.

As the relationship between the princess and the *Führer* developed, the foreign press spokesman Ernst 'Putzi' von Hanfstaengl expressed his disapproval, warning Hitler that Princess Stephanie was a 'professional blackmailer and full-blooded Jewess'. But Hitler was so enamoured with her that he took no notice, telling Hanfstaengl he had had her family tree checked out by the Gestapo. Now when Hitler kissed her hand, he would hold on to it a long time. Stephanie said of Hitler: 'His manners are exceedingly courteous, especially to women. At least that is how he has always been towards me. Whenever I arrived or left he always kissed my hand, often taking one of mine into both of his and shaking it for a time to emphasize the sincerity of the pleasure it gave him to see one, at the same time looking deep into my eyes.' Hitler furnished Wiedemann with a budget of 20,000 Reichsmarks (around £105,000/$135,00 today) to attend to her whims.

Rothermere had been an ardent supporter of Oswald Mosley, leader of the fascist blackshirt movement in Britain. However, after a riot at a rally at London's Olympia in June 1934, and the Night of the Long Knives in Germany when Hitler ordered the murder of 77 long-term supporters he saw as a potential threat, Jewish advertisers began withdrawing their support for Rothermere's newspapers, forcing him to recant. Then, in August 1934, he received a letter from Princess Stephanie saying: 'Please let me impress upon you that you ought to see H [itler] now. I know he already has some doubts as to your sincerity. . . . He intends to discuss his present and future plans with you, and I think it is, for the first time, more in your interests than his, for you to see him.'

By this time, her mail was being intercepted, opened and read. The following year, the Foreign Office asked for her visits to Britain to be restricted, but the Home Office foresaw 'considerable difficulties with taking such a move because of the milieu in which the princess moves in this country'.

In November 1934, Ribbentrop visited London. Formerly Hitler's foreign policy adviser, at that time he was special commissioner for disarmament.

Through Princess Stephanie and Lord Rothermere he was introduced to the former foreign secretary Sir Austen Chamberlain, the playwright George Bernard Shaw and the Archbishop of Canterbury. Stephanie also had connections as a member of the influential Cliveden set.

BRITISH SUPPORT FOR THE NAZI CAUSE

Cliveden House in Berkshire has a special place in the history of espionage. It was there, in 1961, that Conservative secretary of state for war John Profumo met the call girl Christine Keeler. She was also the mistress of Soviet naval attaché Yevgeny Ivanov, a suspected spy. The ensuing scandal forced Profumo's resignation and led, ultimately, to the downfall of the Conservative government.

Back in the 1930s Cliveden was the regular meeting place for influential people who advocated the policy of appeasement towards Nazi Germany. It was there and at meetings of Rothermere's Anglo-German Fellowship that Princess Stephanie met prominent politicians who kept her informed about shifts in policy and sentiment within the British government. MI5 noted that she was particularly close to Sir Barry Domvile, founder of The Link, an openly pro-Nazi organization. In July 1940, Domvile was interned by Churchill as a threat to national security.

Cliveden was owned by the American-born Lord and Lady Astor. One of the richest men in the world, Waldorf Astor was proprietor of the *Observer* newspaper; Nancy Astor was the first female Member of Parliament to take her seat. She invited the great and the good to Cliveden, including the Queen of Romania, King Gustav of Sweden, Henry Ford, Charlie Chaplin, Irish playwrights George Bernard Shaw and Sean O'Casey, King George V and Queen Mary, and the Prince of Wales, later Edward VIII, with whom she often played golf. The political figures who gathered there included Lord Lothian, Lord Halifax, William Montagu (the 9th Duke of Manchester), Geoffrey Dawson (editor of *The Times*), and civil servant and businessman Robert Brand, who was seen as leading a 'shadow Foreign Office' advocating pro-German policies. It was at Cliveden that Princess Stephanie first met Winston Churchill.

The Conservative MP Lady Astor was an admirer of Hitler (like him, she neither drank alcohol nor smoked). The Labour Party accused her of 'fighting bravely for Hitler and Mussolini'. Naturally she welcomed Ribbentrop as a guest.

It was also through Lady Astor that Princess Stephanie met Margot Asquith, Lady Oxford, the widow of former prime minister H.H. Asquith, who spent the summer months at Schloss Fuschl, a castle near Salzburg rented by the princess. Lady Asquith was famed for her political dinner parties and through her Princess Stephanie met numerous influential people. MI5 noted: 'She has succeeded through introduction from Lady Oxford, Lady Cunard and others in working her way into certain society circles where she speaks favourably of the present regime in Germany. . . . The difficult job of selecting from British "neutrals", possible future friends of Hitler and Nazi Germany, has been given to some of Hitler's most trusted friends in this country. Hitler is counting on the help of Princess Hohenlohe, his Vienna-born friend and talent spotter. He appreciates her intelligence and advice.'

In the United States too Princess Stephanie rubbed shoulders with movers and shakers, including her old friend Kathleen Vanderbilt, automotive industry executive Walter P. Chrysler, theatrical impresario Rudolf Kommer and film director Max Reinhardt (later the ghost-writer of Stephanie's memoirs), and her cousin by marriage, Prince Alfred Konstantin Chlodwig von Hohenlohe-Waldenburg-Schillingsfürst. They gathered at her apartment at the Ambassador Hotel in New York where, despite Prohibition, alcohol flowed freely. Stephanie spent Christmas 1932 in Wedgwood, Pennsylvania with Alice and John C. Martin, owner of the *Saturday Evening Post*, *Ladies' Home Journal* and the *Public Ledger* (a Philadelphia daily newspaper); she would later write for Martin's publications.

OTHER RUMOURS

When Stephanie arrived back in Southampton on the MS *Europa* on 2 January 1933, she was met by her mother in a Rolls-Royce. Frau Richter had surprising news. On 24 December 1932, the German newspaper *Neue Freie Presse* had run a story headlined 'Princess Hohenlohe arrested in Biarritz as a spy'. It said the French newspaper *Liberté* had reported that 'a certain Princess von

H has been arrested in Biarritz by the French political police, on charges of espionage and anti-French propaganda. It was claimed that the princess had been engaged in intense correspondence with Lord Rothermere. These letters have been confiscated. Official sources in Paris, the Ministry of the Interior and the German embassy refuse to give further details. The local authorities in Biarritz immediately denied the report. However, *Liberté* claims it can confirm the mysterious arrest. The paper even claims to know that an application for bail has been turned down.'

The story was completely without foundation. In 1932, Stephanie had not spent a single day in Biarritz. On 3 January, the German press printed a correction, adding: 'The whole affair appears to be a plot engineered by the Poles against the princess. The princess is blamed for the publishing policy of Lord Rothermere, who, in a series of articles in the *Daily Mail*, has been arguing for a return of the Polish Corridor to Germany.' The Polish Corridor was a strip of land between Germany and East Prussia, taken from Germany under the terms of the Versailles Treaty and established as Poland's access to the Baltic Sea.

'Princess Hohenlohe, who is a friend of Lord Rothermere, frequently accompanied him during his stays in Berlin to meetings with German politicians,' the story went on. In December 1934, Stephanie accompanied Rothermere and his son Esmond when they had an audience with Hitler and she attended the first major dinner party given for foreign guests at his official residence since he had become chancellor. She also hosted a dinner for Hitler and other top Nazis at Rothermere's hotel. She had to translate for Hitler when he launched into a long monologue about his time in Landsberg prison after the Munich Beer Hall Putsch 11 years earlier. The dinner party was not a success. Hitler ate nothing as he would not stop talking. When Rothermere rose to propose a toast, a vase of flowers was knocked over. The crash brought SS guards bursting into the room brandishing guns. Without further ado, they whisked Hitler away.

In 1935, Hitler sent Stephanie a personal invitation to the Nuremberg Rally where he announced the infamous Nuremberg Laws, stripping German Jews of their human rights. Unity Mitford, one of the six daughters of Lord Redesdale, was obsessed with Hitler and envious of his affection for Stephanie: 'Here you are, an anti-Semite, and yet you have a Jewish woman, Princess Hohenlohe, around you all the time,' she taunted. Hitler didn't react: whatever her ethnic origins, Stephanie was useful to him. Unity referred to her rival as a *rusée* – a sly one – and was furious when she discovered that Hitler had given Stephanie a large, signed photograph, dedicated 'To my dear Princess', which she kept on her bedside table.

While Unity was described by British intelligence as 'more Nazi than the Nazis', Himmler kept her under surveillance. But the SS took no interest in Stephanie, despite her Jewish background, as she was an 'honorary Aryan'. She continued to receive invitations to the annual Nuremberg rallies, though she was annoyed to find that she had to share the dais for the Reich Party Congress for the Greater Germany in 1938 with Unity's parents, Lord and Lady Redesdale.

While the exchange of letters between Rothermere and Hitler continued through 1935, Stephanie was more than a courier, often explaining to her employer Hitler's thinking on various matters. Rothermere would then give the princess a list of questions he wanted her to put to Hitler at their next meeting.

Rothermere met Hitler again in September 1936 and at Christmas sent Stephanie to present the Führer with an expensive French tapestry. In January 1937, she accompanied Rothermere on a visit to the Berghof, Hitler's Bavarian mountain retreat at Berchtesgaden. Hitler's personal train was sent to collect them from the Austrian border and they were allowed to stay at the house, an honour never extended to any visitor previously. At meals, Stephanie would sit next to Hitler and translate for him. Though Eva Braun was in the house, she was not allowed to join the guests for meals.

Goebbels said he found Stephanie pushy. She cried when he showed the film *Stosstrupp* [Shock Troops] *1917*. During the screening, Hitler stroked her hair and later gave her an affectionate pinch on the cheek. As a memento of the visit, he sent her another signed photograph, this one showing them together at the Berghof. It was in a silver frame and the dedication read: 'In memory of a visit to Berchtesgaden.'

Before returning to London, Stephanie stayed at the Vier Jahreszeiten Hotel in Munich where Hitler sent her a large bunch of roses and a sheepdog puppy which she named Wolf after Hitler's Alsatian. On her return to London she wrote a gushing thank-you letter saying: 'You are a charming host. Your beautiful and excellently run home in that magnificent setting all leave me with a wonderful and lasting impression. It is no empty phrase when I say, Herr Reich Chancellor, that I enjoyed every minute of my stay with you.' As to the dog: 'It has given me great pleasure, not only because I love dogs – but also because, to me, dogs symbolize loyalty and friendship – which in this instance pleases me all the more.' However, she left the dog behind in Munich.

While in Munich she met an old friend from Deauville, the exiled King Alfonso XIII of Spain. Together they visited the exhibition of 'Decadent Art' that the Nazis had mounted to discredit modern artists, particularly those who were Jewish.

EDWARD VIII

On 10 December 1936, after reigning for less than a month, Edward VIII was forced to abdicate, saying famously that he could not be king without the support of the woman he loved – American divorcée Wallis Simpson. During the abdication crisis, Hitler sent Edward's cousin, Carl Eduard, Duke of Saxe-Coburg and Gotha, to England as support. An alliance between the United Kingdom and Germany was vital, Hitler said, and he wanted to speak to the former monarch personally, either in Britain or Germany.

Princess Stephanie knew Edward from her visits to Cliveden, was a neighbour of Wallis Simpson and was well-positioned to cultivate their Nazi sympathies. She was also close to Edward's brother Prince George, Duke of Kent and championed the king's cause during the abdication crisis as did Rothermere and Lord Beaverbrook, owner of the *Daily Express*, which then had the largest circulation of any newspaper in the world.

To circumvent the British establishment's objection to an American divorcée as queen, Stephanie suggested a morganatic marriage, in which the wife and her heirs are prevented from taking titles and privileges from her spouse. The marriage between Crown Prince Franz Ferdinand of Austro-Hungary and Countess Sophie Chotek, a commoner, had been morganatic. The couple were assassinated in Sarajevo in 1914, triggering the start of World War I.

Rothermere's son, Esmond, invited Wallis Simpson to dinner and suggested this, but as there was no tradition of morganatic marriage in English Common Law, a special Act of Parliament would have to be passed if it were to go ahead. Prime Minister Stanley Baldwin consulted the British cabinet and the prime ministers of the dominions, but they refused to consent to it. Nancy Astor then begged the king to give up Wallis, but he refused. Then the Archbishop of Canterbury insisted that Edward abdicate in favour of his younger brother, Bertie, who would reign as King George VI.

When the abdication statement was read out in the House of Lords, Unity Mitford was in the gallery. 'Hitler will be dreadfully upset about this,' she said. 'He wanted Edward to stay on the throne.' Speaking in the debate about the abdication, the Communist MP and fervent anti-monarchist Willie Gallacher said: 'The king and Mrs Simpson do not live in a vacuum. Sinister processes are continually at work. The prime minister told us he was approached about a morganatic marriage, but he did not tell us who approached him. It is obvious that forces were encouraging what was going on. . . . I want to draw your attention to the fact that Mrs Simpson has a social set, and every member of the cabinet knows that the social set of Mrs Simpson is closely identified with a certain foreign government and the ambassador of that foreign government.'

There were howls from the House as Gallacher was clearly referring to Ribbentrop, who had become German ambassador to the court of St James in August 1936. 'It is common knowledge,' Gallacher insisted over the tumult. He went on to say that the only answer was for the monarchy to be abolished altogether.

When Ribbentrop became German ambassador he summoned Albert Speer to London to spruce up the German embassy in time for the coronation of George VI in May 1937. Speer was Hitler's architect and later minister for armaments and war production. By this time Ribbentrop had fallen out with Princess Stephanie after he discovered that she was using her influence to try to get Fritz Wiedemann appointed as Reich foreign minister, a role Ribbentrop himself coveted. Stephanie's maid, Wally Oeler, was also privy to her plans: 'She always sleeps with Captain Wiedemann now, that's why I don't trust him,' Oeler said. 'She wants to make a minister of him, come hell or high water. . . . If he's to be a minister, he'll have to do something special. So milady is fixing it for him.'

As a result, Ribbentrop did not invite the princess to be a member of the official German delegation to the coronation party. When she discovered this, Stephanie asked Wiedemann to speak to Hitler; he ordered Ribbentrop to invite her and to apologize to Princess von Hohenlohe. Ribbentrop's excuse for not inviting her was that, as a Jewess, she would be shunned by the other guests. Instead she proved popular, even engaging the Duke of Kent in conversation. Also present were the brother of the emperor of Japan, the chief of staff of the French army, Chancellor of the Exchequer (soon to be prime minister) Neville Chamberlain, Foreign Secretary Anthony Eden (who was to resign over the appeasement issue), and that troublesome backbencher Winston Churchill. Also present were Unity Mitford's ubiquitous parents, Lord and Lady Redesdale. The music was provided by Nazi-approved musicians.

NAZI HONOURS

In May 1937, Princess Stephanie delivered a valuable jade bowl to Hitler which he displayed in pride of place at the Berghof. Hitler awarded her the Honorary Cross of the German Red Cross, which Wiedemann delivered in person to Stephanie at the Ritz in Paris. She went to Berlin in June 1938 to become 'a bride of the National Socialist Workers' Party' and the *Führer* himself pinned the Nazi Party's Gold Medal of Honour on her chest 'for services she rendered the *Führer* showing her to be a true patriot'. The medal had his signature on the back. Her audience with Hitler lasted four hours, incensing the German ambassador to the Soviet Union who was denied a personal interview. Even Göring complained that Hitler would not waste a single hour on him; nor did he know what had passed between Stephanie and Hitler when they were alone.

These private audiences became regular events. Stephanie began calling Hitler 'Adolf' and addressed him with the intimate '*du*'. Clearly, he trusted her. In January 1939, in a speech to the Reichstag he said: 'I prophesy a long peace.' This was carried in newspapers around the world. In private, he told Stephanie: 'This was the best piece of bluff I have pulled in a long time.'

Certainly by that point it was clear that she was no longer Rothermere's ambassador – her loyalty now belonged to Hitler. But Rothermere seemed oblivious to the double game Stephanie was playing; through her, Hitler and her lover Wiedemann were manipulating the newspaper baron.

After his abdication, Edward VIII became Duke of Windsor, left Britain and married Wallis Simpson in France. In October 1937 the couple visited Nazi Germany, against the advice of the British government. They met Hitler at his private residence, the Berghof, rather than at the Reich Chancellery in Berlin – again, Eva Braun was kept out of sight. Stephanie was on hand when Wiedemann made the arrangements. Wally Oeler told a friend: 'He was the one who officially invited the Duke of Windsor to Germany, as soon as they heard that he wanted to come over for a visit. . . . Anyway, express airmail letters written in pencil were going back and forth, and there were telephone conversations nearly every day.'

During the Windsors' 12-day stay in Germany, the Nazi press sang their praises and the duke and duchess dined with Nazi bigwigs including Göring and Goebbels. It was clear that the German High Command expected the former king to be returned to the throne sometime in the future – with their help.

When Princess Stephanie next met Hitler, she asked him about the impression the duchess had made on him. 'I must say she was most ladylike,' he said. The visit had gone off to his complete satisfaction.

SETTING SAIL

In the autumn of 1937, Stephanie persuaded Wiedemann to visit the United States with her. Hitler approved, though he gave Wiedemann no particular mission. However, the American ambassador in Berlin, William E. Dodd, cabled the State Department on 16 November, saying: 'Wiedemann . . . is travelling to Washington for the purpose of consultations with the German Embassy on matters concerning the Reich.'

Wiedemann brought with him his wife Anna-Luise, while Stephanie took her maid Wally Oeler, whose exit visa Wiedemann had organized. Their tickets were paid for by the fund set up by Hitler to look after the princess. On board ship, Princess Stephanie spent her time with another companion, a 41-year-old American heart-throb and baritone named Lawrence Tibbett. They had met in his dressing room after a performance at the Royal Opera House and arranged to travel to America on the same ship. They spent the whole of the five-day crossing together – the last night in Stephanie's stateroom, Oeler said.

When Stephanie's party arrived in New York, they were greeted by the German consul general, the press, a large crowd of protesters and 75 policemen, some on horseback. The crowd carried banners proclaiming: 'Out with Wiedemann, the Nazi spy' and 'I'm Wiedemann, Hitler's agent, and I've come to destroy democracy.'

The party were hustled into a taxi and taken to the Waldorf Astoria where Lawrence Tibbett was also staying. The next day they took the train to Washington DC, where they stayed at the German embassy. The Wiedemanns continued on to Chicago to monitor the activities of the German-American Bund, a pro-Nazi organization consisting of US citizens of German descent. Wiedemann told its members: 'You are citizens of the United States, which has allied itself with an enemy of the German nation. The time will come when you may have to decide which side to take. I would caution that I cannot advise you what to do, but you should be governed by your conscience. One duty lies with the Mother country, the other with the adopted country. Blood is thicker than ink . . . Germany is the land of your fathers and regardless of the consequences, you should not disregard the traditional heritage which is yours.'

Wiedemann headed on to San Francisco, while Stephanie accompanied Tibbett on a concert tour of Philadelphia and Chicago. There she contracted double pneumonia, braving the winter cold in a sheer party frock with a fur stole around her shoulders. Wally Oeler suffered too as neither Stephanie nor Wiedemann had bothered to pay her and she could not afford a coat.

Back in New York, ready to sail back to Europe, Oeler witnessed the rapprochement of her mistress and Wiedemann. She told a friend: 'One day, at three o'clock in the afternoon, we wanted to get into our room. The chambermaid, a waiter and I reached the bedroom, and the door was open. There was Captain Wiedemann having his pleasure with her, and they didn't even notice the three of us. The other Germans in the hotel were so outraged by this that they said the fellow should be reported for racial dishonour, because they knew perfectly well that the princess was born Jewish. I think one of them went and told the Frau Captain [Wiedemann's wife], but she did nothing about it. I acted as if I knew nothing. That man W behaves so badly, and yet he claims to be Hitler's right-hand man.'

In the United States, Stephanie bought a number of lavish books on American architecture, which she sent to Hitler for Christmas. His thank-you letter sent from the Berghof on 28 December read as follows:

> My dear Princess!
> I would like to thank you most warmly for the books about American skyscraper and bridge construction, which you sent me as a Christmas present. You know how interested I am in architecture and related fields, and can therefore imagine what pleasure your present has given me.
> I have been told how staunchly and warmly you have spoken up in your circles on behalf of the new Germany and its vital needs, in the past year. I am well aware that this has caused you a number of unpleasant experiences, and would therefore like to express to you, highly esteemed princess, my sincere thanks for the great understanding that you have shown for Germany as a whole and for my work in particular. I add to these thanks my warmest best wishes for the New Year and remain, with devoted greetings,
> Yours,
> Adolf Hitler

On 31 December, from Obersalzberg, Wiedemann sent a telegram to Princess Hohenlohe at the Dorchester Hotel in London, saying: 'A happy New Year and best love. Fr.' While Stephanie spent the New Year without him, he consoled himself with Eva Braun's younger sister, Gretl.

Princess Stephanie returned to the United States in February 1938, again at the expense of the Third Reich. This time she was on a mission. On board the MS *Europa* was Ralph Ingersoll, the publisher of *Time* magazine. Her task was to get Ingersoll to publish a pro-Nazi article which Wiedemann had given her, called 'Hitler the Architect', written by a member of Goebbels' staff. Stephanie failed to get the article published, but *Time* magazine did name Hitler as its man of the year in 1938.

Stephanie employed her time in the US following Lawrence Tibbett on a tour. While she was away, on 12 March 1938, the German *Wehrmacht* crossed the border into Austria and the country became part of the German Reich in an annexation known as the *Anschluss*.

OVERTURES TO BRITAIN

Soon afterwards, Hitler demanded the takeover of the western German-speaking territories of Czechoslovakia. During this, the Sudetenland crisis, the Reich chancellor gave Princess Stephanie a delicate task. She was sent as an 'intimate friend' to Britain to find out whether the government there would accept a visit from Nazi High Command.

Through her friend Ethel Snowden, with whom she had attended Nazi rallies and who had written articles for the *Daily Mail* supporting National Socialism, Stephanie approached the British foreign secretary, Lord Halifax.

Halifax recorded in his diary: 'On Wednesday, 6 July, Lady Snowden came to see me early in the morning. She informed me that, through someone on the closest terms with Hitler – I took this to mean Princess Hohenlohe – she had received a message with the following burden: Hitler wanted to find out whether H.M. Government would welcome it if he were to send one of his closest confidants, as I understood it, to England for the purpose of conducting unofficial talks.'

Hitler wanted to send Göring as his plenipotentiary. Stephanie explained: 'There is no other man of whom the *Führer* speaks with so much respect, admiration and gratitude.'

As German foreign minister, Ribbentrop was to be kept out of the loop. Halifax was suspicious of this unconventional approach and of Princess Stephanie, who was not a go-between he would have picked. Dismissing her as a 'well-known adventuress, not to say blackmailer', Halifax said that a visit from Göring would be problematic as it could not be kept secret, but he was willing to meet Wiedemann. He wrote: 'Princess H. said that

W[iedemann] would be quite happy to spend Saturday and Sunday, 16th and 17th, privately and only come to see me on Monday morning. We therefore agreed on 10 a.m. at 88 Eaton Square.'

Stephanie attended the meeting at Halifax's private residence in Belgravia and acted as interpreter. Wiedemann's aim was still to arrange a meeting between Halifax and Göring, but the British refused as the problem of the Sudetenland had not been resolved.

Worse still, the meeting did not remain secret. As Wiedemann was making his way back to Croydon Airport, the *Daily Herald* ran the headline: 'HITLER'S AIDE IN LONDON – SEES FOREIGN SECRETARY.'

The French ambassador to Berlin, André François-Poncet, said: 'The idea that Captain Wiedemann should be received by Lord Halifax was cooked up by Princess Hohenlohe, who is extremely well known to the secret services of all the Great Powers, and who at the moment seems to be serving the interests of Britain, although Captain Wiedemann, who enjoys the closest of relations with her and frequently visits her in London, is of the opinion that she chiefly feels herself committed to the interests of Germany.'

The Czech ambassador in London, Jan Masaryk, wrote to Prague saying: 'If there is any decency left in this world, then one of these days there will be a big scandal when it is revealed what part was played in Wiedmann's visit by Steffi Hohenlohe, *née* Richter. This world-renowned secret agent, spy and confidence trickster, who is wholly Jewish, today provides the focus of Hitler's propaganda in London. Wiedemann has been living with her. On her table stands a photograph of Hitler, signed "To my dear Princess Hohenlohe – Adolf Hitler" and next to it a photograph of Horthy, dedicated to "a great stateswoman".'

The new German ambassador to Britain, Herbert von Dirksen, noted what he called the 'parallel initiative of a clever woman'. In his autobiography he wrote: 'This woman, Princess Hohenlohe, a Hungarian by birth, divorced from her husband, who had lived for years in London, was able, by reason of her acquaintance with Wiedemann, to gain access to Göring and even to Hitler. The latter had received her for a conversation lasting several hours, a distinction that he notoriously denied the official representatives of the Reich abroad. But since Princess Hohenlohe was a clever woman who was working for peace, this opportunity to exercise influence on the *Führer* was only to be welcomed. Under her guidance, Wiedemann trod the polished parquet floors of London.'

Ribbentrop, who had not been informed of Wiedemann's mission, was furious when he found out; he warned Dirksen to be cautious in his dealings with Princess Stephanie. 'I replied that I had considered her above suspicion,' said Dirksen, 'since the *Führer* had granted her the honour of an audience in order to hear her views on Britain. Thus it was that this amateurish attempt to reach a compromise with Britain, made on the highest authority in Germany, ended in a tangled thicket of personal intrigue.'

Rothermere, too, was put out that the princess was now working on other people's behalf. He called her 'a very indiscreet woman' and broke off relations with her.

When Wiedemann went to the Berghof to report back to Hitler, he was kept waiting for several hours while the *Führer* entertained Unity Mitford. He had just five minutes in Hitler's presence, during which Hitler ruled out a visit by Göring and refused to speak about the matter again. Wiedemann then had to report to Ribbentrop, telling him that Halifax had said he hoped to see Hitler 'riding in triumph through the streets of London in the royal carriage along with King George VI'.

HITLER'S MYSTERIOUS COURIER

On 1 July 1938, the *Daily Herald* ran a story about Princess Stephanie von Hohenlohe-Waldenburg-Schillingsfürst and a court case about a disputed laundry bill. It also mentioned that she had a portrait of Hitler in her luxury Mayfair home, dedicated to his 'dear friend, the Princess'. The story went on: 'Described on the [court] list as "Her Serene Highness", the princess is one of the most powerful leaders of the Nazi colony here. She it is who provides the social platform for Hitler's envoys – not only in this country, but in the United States too. . . . Her wholehearted admiration of Hitler has led to a close friendship between the two, and the *Fuehrer* has given her one of the highest decorations of Nazi Germany.'

In court, the verdict went against Stephanie, and she had to pay the £46 laundry bill.

That year, the American International News Service named the princess 'Europe's Number One secret diplomat, Hitler's mysterious courier'. The story maintained that she had enormous influence over the *Führer* and that he depended on her. The *New York Mirror* concurred, saying: 'Her apartment in Mayfair has become the focus for those British aristocrats who have a friendly stance towards Nazi Germany. Her soirées are the talk of the town. Prominently displayed in her drawing-room is a huge portrait of Hitler. So it was only natural that her efforts on the *Führer*'s behalf would also bring her into contact with the "Cliveden Set", whose members include some of the most important statesmen of the British Empire.'

On 21 July 1938 the princess was in the press again. The London *Evening Standard* printed a story in its 'Londoner's Diary' column under the heading 'Friend of Hitler' which read: 'Princess Hohenlohe-Waldenburg-Schillingsfürst, who is believed to have arranged Captain Wiedemann's meeting with Lord Halifax, and who acted as Wiedemann's hostess in London, plans to acquire Schloss Leopoldskron near Salzburg, as a holiday home. The mansion was requisitioned after the annexation of Austria.'

Hitler had given her the castle to use as a salon for prominent Nazi artists and writers. It was just 10 miles (16 km) from the Berghof. British intelligence noted: 'Schloss Leopoldskron is only an hour's drive from Hitler's home and she is frequently summoned by the *Führer* who appreciates her intelligence and good advice. She is perhaps the only woman who can exercise any influence on him.'

MI5 had a warrant from the Home Office permitting them to open mail arriving at Stephanie's London home as well as mail from England addressed to the Schloss. Justifying this, her file said: 'Her connections with highly placed members of the Nazi Party and the fact that previous warrants had yielded results of considerable interest.'

The Jewish journalist and author Bella Fromm, who fled from Germany to the United States in September 1938, wrote: 'Breaking up the Wiedemann marriage was a mere bagatelle in comparison with the work of the Stephanie–Wiedemann team on behalf of the National Socialists. It was just tough on Frau Wiedemann that she was wounded and inconsolable. For these exceptional services, Stephanie was rewarded by Hitler with Schloss Leopoldskron near Salzburg, once the home of that world-famous genius of the theatre, Max Reinhardt.'

THE ARYANIZED PALACE

The theatre and film director Max Reinhardt had fled Austria after the *Anschluss*. The rococo palace he had spent twenty years restoring had been confiscated by the Gestapo as it was 'owned by a person hostile to the state' – that is, he was Jewish. One of Princess Stephanie's biographers noted with irony that 'a Jewish woman was rewarded for her services to National Socialism with the property of a Jew deprived of citizenship'.

Reinhardt's second wife, actress Helene Thimig, said: 'What a macabre joke: Reinhardt's creation – now a palace for the Nazis! And this Aryanized palace has been placed under the management of the Jewish Princess von Hohenlohe!'

Reinhardt had bought the castle in 1918 and founded the Salzburg Festival soon after. He refused the offer of 'honorary Aryanship'. When he was away in America, a bomb was thrown into the hall of the Schloss. Rudolf Kommer, who also lived there, supported Stephanie's takeover of the castle – otherwise it would have been handed over to the military and wrecked. She rescued many of Kommer's possessions, along with some of Reinhardt's.

With Hitler's approval, Stephanie made alterations to Schloss Leopoldskron and its grounds at Germany's expense. As it was state property, the argument ran that she was increasing its value. Her extravagance drew criticism, but Wiedemann defended her in a memo saying: 'Princess Stephanie von Hohenlohe is personally known to the *Führer*. She has at all times stood up for the new Germany abroad in a manner worthy of recognition. I therefore ask all German authorities concerned with domestic and foreign affairs to take every opportunity to show her the special appreciation that we owe to foreigners who speak up so emphatically for today's Germany.'

The princess invited important guests from Britain, France and the United States to stay there while attending the Salzburg Festival; she also discussed putting on open-air operas in the grounds with conductor Leopold Stokowski.

Another visitor was ambassador Herbert von Dirksen, whose stepmother Viktoria von Dirksen had been one of Hitler's earliest supporters. As the Berghof was just over the border, Stephanie was disappointed that Hitler himself did not visit.

Wiedemann attended, sometimes with his long-suffering wife and children. He was helping Stephanie's son Franzi secure a job in government service and offered to deal with the problematic papers that were needed to prove his Aryan ancestry. Franzi eventually found a job with I. G. Farben, the chemical company that used slave labour from the concentration camps and manufactured Zyklon B, the poison used in the gas chambers. Wiedemann's close relationship with the wife of one of the directors meant he could pull strings there.

Stephanie had her own connections with wealthy art lovers and suggested that art objects acquired from the annexation of Austria be sold for much needed foreign currency. She also played a part in the Sudetenland crisis. At the Nazis' request, she invited British shipowner and Liberal politician Lord Runciman, Britain's official mediator between the Czech government and the Sudeten German Party, to stay at Schloss Leopoldskron.

Time magazine noted her contribution, saying: 'Princess Hohenlohe-Waldenburg-Schillingsfürst, confidante of the *Führer* and friend of half of Europe's great is scheduled to sail from England to the US this week. Since the fall of Austria, Princess Stephanie, once the toast of Vienna, has lent her charms to advancing the Nazi cause in circles where it would do the most good. As a reward the Nazi government "permitted her to take a lease" on the sumptuous Schloss Leopoldskron near Salzburg, taken over from Jewish Max Reinhardt after *Anschluss*. During the Czecho-Slovak crisis she did yeoman service for the Nazi campaign. When Mr. Chamberlain sent Lord Runciman to gather impressions of conditions in Czechoslovakia, Princess Stephanie hurried to the Sudetenland castle of Prince Max Hohenlohe where the British mediator was entertained.'

Runciman was criticized for spending too much time with Stephanie, rather than resolving the crisis. When he was recalled to London, he reported: 'Sudetenland is longing to be taken over by Germany, and the Sudeten Germans want to return to their homeland.' Clearly, Stephanie had done a splendid job.

The result of Runciman's report was the Munich Conference, where Britain, France, Italy and Germany agreed that Czechoslovakia should hand over the Sudetenland. Wiedemann wrote to Rothermere about Princess Stephanie's role: 'It was her preparation of the ground that made the Munich Agreement possible,' he said. Later this was read out in the High Court in the suit between the princess and Rothermere.

The press, too, lauded her role. Stephanie was riding high. She wrote to Hitler saying: 'There are moments in life that are so great – I mean, where one feels so deeply that it is almost impossible to find the right words to express one's feelings. Herr Reich Chancellor, please believe me that I have shared with you the experience and emotion of every phase of the events of these last weeks. What none of your subjects in their wildest dreams dared hope for – you have made come true. That must be the finest thing a head of state can give to himself and to his people. I congratulate you with all my heart. In devoted friendship. Yours sincerely, Stephanie Hohenlohe.'

THE DREAM TURNS SOUR

The princess's MI5 file reveals that at the end of 1938, or the beginning of 1939, Stephanie was in Syria with a Wilhelm von Flügge, where both were suspected of working as German agents. There were also reports of her mixing with German and Italian intelligence contacts in Istanbul.

Then things turned sour. In January 1939 Hitler found out that Wiedemann was Stephanie's lover and sacked him as adjutant, ostensibly for his poor performance at Munich. Wiedemann was sent to San Francisco as consul general, though his salary remained the same as it was at the Reich Chancellery and much higher than that of the previous incumbent. Goebbels was quickly on the case: 'Princess Hohenlohe now turns out to be a Viennese half-Jewess,' he said. 'She has her fingers in everything. Wiedemann works with her a great deal. He may well have her to thank for his present predicament, because without her around he probably would not have made such a feeble showing in the Czech crisis.'

Secret dealings were still afoot though. Then an unnamed friend of Rothermere's former private secretary Captain Jack Kruse phoned MI5 with a tip-off. The report in the file said: 'Kruse is very friendly with the princess and had known her for a number of years. On 26 June 1939 Kruse saw the princess who showed him a letter from a contact writing from the Hotel Bieux Dolen in the Hague, that stated the *Führer* had told Ribbentrop he must make it plain to the British prime minister that a gesture from Britain must definitely be made very soon, independent of the Cabinet if necessary, and that he must permit Germany to occupy Danzig.'

Danzig, now Gdansk, had been made a free city by the Versailles Treaty. It lay at the mouth of the Polish Corridor and was under the protection of the League of Nations. As Germans made up the majority of the population, Hitler demanded its return to the Reich.

Kruse told MI5 that Princess Stephanie's contact with the Nazi regime was through Ribbentrop, rather than directly with Hitler himself. There was an ongoing power struggle between Ribbentrop and Himmler; the latter told Hitler that Princess Stephanie was a British double agent. Hitler was furious and issued a warrant for her arrest; it was never enforced, but the SS began to take an interest in her Jewish origins. In an effort to protect her, Wiedemann wrote to Göring, saying: 'I ask you to protect my honour and to intercede with the *Führer* on my behalf. When I took my leave of the *Führer*, he warned me against Princess H. in the interest of my future career. The *Führer* does not believe the princess can be relied upon and thinks that various anti-German articles in the foreign press can be traced back to her.

'I have informed the *Führer*

(1) that I vouch absolutely for the princess's integrity and loyalty to the Third Reich and its *Führer* . . .

(2) that of course I have given the princess, as a foreigner, no information that might not be in the national interest. I cannot prove these things, but on the other hand I can prove that the princess had a decisive influence on the attitude of Lord R[othermere] and thus of the *Daily Mail*.'

Time magazine reported on Wiedemann's new role: 'Adolf Hitler's Man Friday, big, burly, 47-year-old Captain Fritz Wiedemann, who has carried out many a delicate mission in Europe as the *Führer*'s personal adjutant, was last week assigned to another. He will serve as consul general at San Francisco, replacing the unpopular Baron Manfred von Killinger, recalled to the Reich to report on the bombing of a Nazi freighter in Oakland Estuary, two months ago. Capt. Wiedemann's mission: to smooth ruffled US-German relations and sell the Nazi regime to an unsympathetic US.'

Ribbentrop had also turned against Princess Stephanie.

'He began to sense angrily illegitimate outside influences,' she wrote. 'He must have traced back – rightly or wrongly – some such occasional scepticism of his leader to me and thus I became an arch-fiend in his eyes.'

Time went on to say that Princess Stephanie's Jewish origins were being investigated.

While Hitler had warned Wiedemann about seeing the princess, her MI5 file said: 'We have independent evidence, of a very delicate nature, to the effect that the affair between Wiedemann and this lady is still going on.'

As she fell out of favour, her payments for running Schloss Leopoldskron were stopped.

'We also know from a very secret and delicate source that Wiedemann has advised her to recommend her creditors to apply to Major-General Bodenschatz [adjutant to Field Marshal Göring], for settlement of her debts.'

Stephanie's son Franzi was at Schloss Leopoldskron when it was seized without warning. Forced to leave Salzburg, he was tailed by the Gestapo until he could escape to England where he managed to get word to his mother that she was in danger. Meanwhile her ex-husband tried to get her title revoked on the grounds that her reputation was besmirching the family name (he failed).

At the end of January, Princess Stephanie and her mother left for London. Unfortunately, they were unable to take her mother's younger sister Olga with them, and she died in Theresienstadt concentration camp on 27 September 1942.

THE CASE AGAINST ROTHERMERE

The British authorities were not happy about Stephanie's return. 'In view of this woman's record and known activities,' wrote one Home Office official, 'there seems no real reason why we should give ourselves the trouble of looking after her and allowing her to pay such frequent and extensive visits to this country.'

But it would have been difficult to expel her because she was at the time suing Lord Rothermere. His solicitor told MI5: 'In Lord Rothermere's view, the woman was a German agent and had probably been double-crossing him before he terminated his contract with her. He thinks it undesirable that she should be permitted either to enter or remain in the country.'

After the breakdown of their relationship, Rothermere sacked Stephanie. With no source of income, she found herself in financial difficulties. So she sued him, saying he had promised to pay her £5,000 a year for the rest of her life; she also argued that he had agreed to help restore her good name after foreign newspapers had called her 'a spy, a vamp and an immoral person'. If he did not pay up, she said, she would publish her memoirs in the United States, exposing his contacts with top Nazis and his relationships with her and other much younger women. But her position was weakened when a passport control officer stopped her Hungarian lawyer, Erno Wittman, at Victoria Station. He was carrying deeply incriminating correspondence. 'This was astonishing; it appeared to be copies of documents and letters which passed between Lord Rothermere, Lady Snowden, Princess Stephanie, Herr Hitler and others,' said the officer who confiscated the letters.

The case went to court, where the princess denied being a spy. She also denied that in the early 1930s French intelligence had discovered clandestine correspondence and blank cheques in a hidden drawer in a bureau at her Paris apartment, which had led to the continental press branding her a spy. She said that as a result 'people did not want to have anything more to do with me. They cut me off and I was excluded from functions which I was entitled to attend – it was a humiliation.'

A letter from Wiedemann to Rothermere was read out in court: 'You know that the *Führer* greatly appreciates the work the princess did to straighten relations between our countries. It was her groundwork which made the Munich agreement possible.' The letter went on to say that Hitler would do what he could to re-establish her reputation. It was also revealed that Stephanie had had Rothermere's letters copied by the Special Photographic Bureau of the Department of the German Chancellor, indicating that she was embedded within the regime.

The verdict went against her with the judge finding no evidence that Rothermere had promised her a lifetime retainer or the restitution of her reputation. The following year, when Rothermere published *My Campaign for Hungary*, with a foreword by Winston Churchill, no mention was made of Princess Stephanie; but he did pay her legal fees.

Colin Brooks, who assisted Rothermere in his publishing ventures, wrote in his diary on 3 December 1939: 'I wish I had time to log here the machinations of the princess and the full reasons for the urgent haste of this new book – begun on Monday and sent to press in seventeen days. In going over the files I found one letter which might be awkward if she published her photostats.'

Meanwhile, the surveillance of her movements was stepped up. Her MI5 file said: 'Princess Hohenlohe has given us a great deal of work owing to the fact that she is frequently the subject of denunciation to the effect that she is, or has been, a trusted political agent and personal friend of Herr Hitler; that she is a German political spy of a very high order; and that she was given the Schloss Leopoldskron by Herr Hitler for signal services rendered for him.'

WAR CHANGES EVERYTHING

On 3 September 1939, three days after the invasion of Poland, Britain declared war on Germany. The *Daily Mail* rapidly reversed its editorial line on Hitler and Stephanie's friendship with Hitler was exposed. *Time* magazine reported an incident which occurred in the dining room of the Ritz Hotel in London; when the princess walked in, someone said loudly: 'Get out, you filthy spy.' Four society lady diners informed the head waiter that they would not be returning as long as Princess Stephanie was admitted, but she continued her meal unperturbed.

Ten days after the start of war, the head porter at the Dorchester approached the police saying he had important information concerning the war effort. He was referred to MI5, where he told Stephanie's case officer that her Austrian maid, Anna Stoffl, had said her employer was operating in Britain as a Nazi agent. The princess knew many influential people in Britain and regularly reported back to Hitler's agents, he said; she had direct access to the highest authorities in Germany.

Anna Stoffl was interviewed. She was apprehensive because she still had family in Austria, but as an anti-Nazi she was willing to tell the intelligence officer all she knew. 'Miss Stoffl is in no doubt Princess Hohenlohe was acting as a German agent,' the report read. 'She had lived with her for about a year in this country and travelled with her on the continent. For a time she had lived with the princess at a castle in Salzburg, placed at her disposal by the German authorities. During that time there had been a good deal of entertaining. The princess had paid a visit to Berlin when she was at the castle and had told the maid she had had an interview with Hitler.'

Anna Stoffl was sure the princess was involved in some intrigue as she always dismissed her maid from the room when she had visitors. Despite the fact that she wasn't present, Anna was sure the information passed to Stephanie by her visitors was sent straight to Berlin. MI5 said they had been keeping tabs on Stephanie since 1928 and recommended that the Home Office curtail her stay in Britain.

Stephanie's file noted that she always stayed in expensive hotels or apartments. 'She gives extravagant presents of dresses and jewellery to her friends. Princess Hohenlohe has acted as a link between Nazi leaders in Germany and society circles in this country. At Schloss Leopoldskron she has entertained prominent Nazis and introduced them to English friends. She had also played a part in arranging meetings between Lord Runciman and the Sudeten Nazis.'

The American newspapers were calling her 'a spy, a glamorous international agent and a girlfriend of Hitler' – but Stephanie took heart that the United States was not yet at war with Germany. She decided to go there to write her memoirs, sailing on the SS *Veendam* from Southampton on 11 December 1939 under the assumed name Mrs Maria Waldenburg. By then, Bella Fromm was in exile in the United States and writing about German spies: 'One of the most fanatical exponents of National Socialist ideology . . . was Stephanie, Princess Hohenlohe-Schillingsfuerst,' she wrote, 'the "princess" in quotation-marks, because she was not born in silk and satin. She became a princess by marriage. . . . She was one of the first female agents sent abroad by the Nazis before they came to power.'

British intelligence noted that the reason Stephanie gave for going to America was to see her son who was seriously ill. But they thought the real reason was to see Wiedemann and to escape the UK before being interned as a Nazi agent. In the House of Commons, an MP asked the Home Secretary why she was being allowed to leave the country. Did he not know that 'this woman is a notorious member of the Hitler spy organization'? The Home Secretary responded that she had been granted a 'no return' permit – a one-way ticket – and would not be allowed back to the UK. Nevertheless, the MP was outraged and said she should be arrested and charged with espionage. 'She is a political intriguer and adventuress of the first water and should be treated with the utmost suspicion,' he fulminated.

ESCAPE TO NEW YORK

A journalist spotted Stephanie on the quayside when she arrived in New York 11 days later. The immigration officer spotted her too. Since Wiedemann had arrived in America, the FBI had been on the look-out for the princess. She arrived with a visitor's visa and 106 pieces of luggage. Already there was information that Princess Stephanie and Wiedemann would be working together again soon. Wiedemann had been posted to San Francisco, but the rumour ran that he was being readied to take over as German ambassador in Washington DC. This suggested to the FBI that 'Wiedemann is not *persona non grata* with Hitler'.

Press photographers descended on the Waldorf Astoria where Stephanie was staying. She contacted Wiedemann and he crossed the continent to visit her, but Princess Stephanie did not want to be seen in the company of a well-known Nazi. Instead she wanted to see the literary agents Curtis Brown about her memoirs. On their advice, she took part in press interviews to stir up interest and discussed a series of articles with *Town & Country* magazine.

On 22 January 1940, the *New York Times* published a piece under the headline 'Princess Plays Role In Nazi Diplomacy'. The story ran: 'The princess is without doubt the star among a whole group of female members of the former German aristocracy, who have been recruited by Hitler for a wide variety of operations, many of a secret nature. They have been acting as political spies, propaganda hostesses, social butterflies and ladies of mystery.' It concluded: 'On orders from

Fritz Wiedemann was Hitler's superior in World War I and later became his personal adjutant. He was exiled in 1939 to San Francisco when he became consul general to the United States.

the Nazi party, Princess Hohenlohe has placed the heads of Lords, Counts, and other highly placed personages at the feet of Hitler.'

Curtis Brown employed Rudolf Kommer to ghost-write Stephanie's memoirs. While she was busy working on publicity, Wiedemann took up with another spy, Baroness Felicitas von Reznicek; she was 14 years his junior and he had met her at a cocktail party.

In March 1940, Stephanie took the train to Los Angeles. By the time she reached California, Baroness von Reznicek had been ordered home to Germany. Wiedemann was concerned that the princess's memoirs might reveal information that could only have come from him. He met with Stephanie in Carmel, 90 miles (146 km) down the coast from San Francisco. They were, of course, under round-the-clock observation by the FBI. The pair met again in Fresno where she booked into a hotel as Mrs Moll. Soon after she checked in, she received a phone call from a public booth. While she met for lunch with Wiedemann at the Omar Khayyam restaurant, her room was searched.

That afternoon she checked out of her hotel and drove with Wiedemann to the General Grant National Park, where he signed the visitors book: 'Fritz Wiedemann, consul general in San Francisco'. Later they drove to Sequoia National Park where they rented a chalet in Kaweah Camp as Mr and Mrs Fred Winter from San Francisco.

That evening they ate in the camp coffee shop run by a Mr Kock, 'a fanatical Nazi supporter' the FBI noted. They retired to their cabin and left the following morning. Years later, when questioned about this, Stephanie insisted that she had spent the night alone in the cabin while Wiedemann slept in the car.

They drove to Santa Clara, then on to San Francisco where Stephanie moved into the consul general's residence along with her mother and son, apparently with the blessing of Frau Wiedemann. In an official memo to Berlin, Wiedemann explained that he was protecting her from the American press who were now describing her as the new Mata Hari. Wiedemann himself was now accused of heading an espionage network that operated throughout America and the Western world.

This accusation was dubious as it came from Alice Crockett, the divorced wife of an American general who was suing Wiedemann for non-payment of her services (plus expenses). She seems to have replaced the princess as Wiedemann's lover. Crockett said the German government had given Wiedemann a budget of $5 million (worth around £65m/$83m today) for his espionage operation and he had employed a number of agents. One of them was 'Princess Holenhole' [*sic*] whose job was to 'contact and pay the aforementioned employees the aforementioned sums of money for espionage activity on behalf of Government of Germany and the defendant, Fritz Wiedemann'.

WIEDEMANN'S NETWORK

Crockett had accompanied Wiedemann on one of his many trips to Mexico where he was suspected of making contact with Central American states with a view to blocking the Panama Canal to US shipping in the event of the United States being drawn into the war. While Princess Stephanie also visited Mexico, she was mainly active north of the border. J. Edgar Hoover, head of the FBI, noted: 'On September 3, 1940, Princess Hohenlohe, as Mrs. H. Warden of Philadelphia, Pennsylvania, registered at the Palace Hotel, San Francisco. She checked out the same date and an immediate inspection of the room which she had occupied reflected that intimate relations had existed during the time that the room was occupied by "Mrs. Warden".'

According to Crockett, Wiedemann's network was to promote strife in the United States, stir up class and racial hatred, and encourage strikes to undermine America's preparedness for war. Factory supervisors, foremen and workers were recruited to the task. Wiedemann directed the activities of the German-American Bund and supplied them with ammunition. He also had contacts with pioneer airman Charles Lindbergh and car manufacturer Henry Ford, who were both pro-Nazi. Crockett said that on Wiedemann's behalf she made a trip to Berlin to see Hitler and Himmler. She had run up $5,000 (£65,000/$83,400 today) in expenses and was owed $500 (£6,500/$8,340) a month for six months work – that is, $3,000 (£39,000/$50,000) or $8,000 (£104,00/$134, 86) in total.

Wiedemann also had contacts with the *Auslands-Organization*, the overseas wing of the Nazi Party under the control of Walter Schellenberg. MI5 described AO as 'a ready-made instrument for intelligence, espionage and ultimately for sabotage purposes'. Its leading lights in the Americas were Wiedemann and Princess Stephanie, and they were funded by I. G. Farben.

On 27 November 1940, Wiedemann and Stephanie had a meeting with Sir William Wiseman who had been head of British intelligence in the United States during World War I. After the end of the war, he had remained in the US as an investment banker and was on hand to advise his intelligence counterpart during World War II. Their meeting discussed the possibility of Britain and Germany making a separate peace, and it was agreed that a proposal would be conveyed to Hitler by the princess, travelling via Switzerland on her Hungarian passport.

But Suite 1024–1026 of the Mark Hopkins Hotel in San Francisco where the meeting was taking place had been bugged by the FBI. FBI director J. Edgar Hoover noted that Princess Hohenlohe dominated the conversation, though some doubts were expressed about how she might be received by the *Führer*. A summary ended up on the desk of President Franklin Delano Roosevelt. It said: 'The princess stated she would have to take that chance but that Hitler was genuinely fond of her and that he would look forward to her coming, and she thought Hitler would listen to her. . . . She stated she would make Hitler see that he was "butting against a stone wall" and make him believe that at the opportune moment he must align himself with Britain.'

One of the powerful arguments that Stephanie would advance was that the *Luftwaffe* had just been defeated in the Battle of Britain and the invasion of Britain was postponed indefinitely. She would also point out how strong America was and that 'anybody that told Hitler that the German Reich was stronger than the United States, was telling damn lies'. There was little doubt that, if the United States joined the war, it would be on Britain's side. (Roosevelt had already breached strict neutrality by sending aid to Britain in the shape of 50 destroyers.) At the end of the meeting, the group agreed that they should bypass the British ambassador in Washington, the Marquis of Lothian, and go direct to Churchill, who Stephanie knew personally.

In November 1940, Stephanie's visitor's visa expired. She wanted to remain in the United States, but her renewal application was blocked by Hoover. He wrote to subordinates: 'Stephanie von Hohenlohe-Waldenburg, who uses various aliases, is very close to Fritz Wiedemann, the German consul general in San Francisco . . . and in the past has been suspected by the French, British and American authorities of working as an international spy for the German government. . . . The princess is described as extremely intelligent, dangerous and cunning, and as a spy "worse than 10,000 men".' Hoover recommended she be deported as soon as possible.

THREAT OF DEPORTATION

After one last tryst with Wiedemann at the St Francis Hotel, Stephanie was ordered to leave the United States by 21 December. Her son gave an interview in which he protested against his mother's deportation, saying she had no connection with the Nazis – 'she is not Jewish, has not had any cosmetic facial surgery, and is certainly not 120 years old', he said.

Stephanie and her mother moved out of the residence of the Consul General and lodged with a friend in Palo Alto. She swore an affidavit, denying any sympathy for Germany and the Axis powers and insisting that all her sympathies were with Britain. Libellous statements had smeared her good name, she said, and it had been a mistake to accept the invitation of the Consul General of Germany to be his house guest. Meanwhile, she was trying to get money out of Wiedemann.

The head of the Immigration and Naturalization Service (INS), Major Lemuel Schofield, signed the warrant for Stephanie's deportation. She was spared detention until its implementation by the kindness of her friend, Mimi Smith, who posted $25,000 (£325,000/$417,000 today) bail. The Hungarian embassy in Washington DC also managed to obtain a 20-day postponement of her deportation.

On 17 January 1941, a hearing was held at the offices of the INS. Princess Stephanie arrived in an ambulance and was carried in on a stretcher. Schofield discovered there were practical problems with her deportation. She had arrived in the United States from Britain, and the British refused to take her back. To repatriate her to Hungary, the State Department would have to secure the co-operation of the Soviet Union to allow her to ride the trans-Siberian railway. These complications meant that the case was adjourned.

The situation began to irritate President Roosevelt, who had more pressing things to worry about. 'That Hohenlohe woman ought to be got out of the country as a matter of good discipline. Have her put on a boat to Japan or Vladivostok. She is a Hungarian and I do not think the British would take her,' he told his attorney general on 7 March 1941.

The following day, Stephanie was arrested. After a week, Schofield visited her at the INS detention centre in San Francisco. She turned on the charm and the 48-year-old married man was immediately smitten. While investigations were under way to find out whether she was really a Nazi spy, Stephanie was released on the strict condition that she was to have no contact with Wiedemann or any other representative of a foreign government.

On 1 June, Percy Foxworth of the FBI's New York headquarters sent a memorandum to Hoover saying: 'It appears desirable to have Princess Hohenlohe interviewed in order that complete information which she can furnish may be available for consideration in connection with our national defense investigations . . . regarding German espionage activities'. Assistant Attorney General Matthew F. McGuire was also on the case and Hoover scrawled at the bottom of the memo: 'Not until we get from McGuire a copy of what she told Schofield, then we should ask McGuire for clearance to talk to her.'

The following day, the German author Jan Valtin, who had settled in the United States in 1938, told a congressional committee hearing that Wiedemann's consulate was a clearing house for the Gestapo. Meanwhile Wiedemann was touring America, photographing bridges, roads and dams from Colorado to Florida. The report from McGuire that Hoover wanted was still not forthcoming, though its contents were leaked to the *Washington Times Herald.*

By 1 July Princess Stephanie and her mother were ensconced at the Raleigh Hotel in Washington DC. Schofield was also in residence. According to the FBI: 'When Schofield was in the hotel . . . he spent the whole time with Princess Hohenlohe, either in her room or his. On one or two occasions it was obvious that Princess Hohenlohe had spent the whole night with Major Schofield, as she was found in his room at 8.30 or 9 a.m.' The bureau also noted that they 'indulged in a great deal of drinking on these occasions'.

Stephanie's son, Franzi, was trying to get back to England. The British secret service sent a telegram from New York to MI5, saying: 'Have you any objection? One cannot, however, neglect the possibility that this may be a move by the Gestapo to kill two birds with one stone, i.e., (1) to attempt to double-cross us through Princess Hohenlohe, and (2) to place an agent in the UK.'

NUMBER ONE NAZI

As war loomed, Roosevelt ordered the closure of all German government residences in the United States. Wiedemann travelled to Los Angeles to give the records he had not burned to the German consul, Georg Gyssling, who was about to leave on the SS *West Point.* Wiedemann also met Stephanie's second cousin by marriage, Ludwig Ehrhardt, who would later become the *Abwehr*'s espionage chief in the Far East. Then he made his way back to Berlin via Lisbon, and from there went to Argentina, where the Nazis already had extensive links. Moving on to Rio de Janeiro, Wiedemann met Gottfried Sandstede, the Gestapo leader in South America and, according to the Brazilian newspaper *O Globo,* 'Number one Nazi in the Americas'. The article said that Wiedemann was answerable to

Hitler, who had given him $5 million (£65m/$83m today) to fund spy rings in America. When the Brazilian police searched Wiedemann's room, they found a list of Nazi agents in California.

Wiedemann was then posted to the Chinese port of Tientsin, travelling there via Japan. He was joined by Klaus Mehnert, who as professor of anthropology at the University of Honolulu had conducted a covert study of Pearl Harbor. Wiedemann remained in Tientsin under Japanese occupation until the end of the war, when he was captured by the US army and shipped back to Washington DC.

According to a *Time* magazine report in October 1945: 'Captain Fritz Wiedemann, Hitler's company commander in World War I, German consul general in San Francisco for two stormy years and spy extraordinary for the Third Reich, was back in the US for a brief stay. Newsmen who remembered Wiedemann as a tall, black-haired fashion plate scarcely recognized the baggy-suited, greying, unshaven man who de-planed from an Army transport at California's Hamilton Field. Hitler's onetime personal adjutant was to be a star witness at war crimes trials of top Nazis.'

Interrogated about his time as consul general in San Francisco, Wiedemann said he had received 'a great deal of information through his good friend Princess Stephanie Hohenlohe'. He also gave evidence at the Nuremberg Trials. Charges against him were dropped in 1948 after the FBI failed to hand over the huge file it had on Wiedemann and Stephanie.

In an effort to help his new lover, Major Schofield wrote to the newly appointed attorney general Francis Biddle, saying: 'Princess Hohenlohe has suggested making a public statement about the dangers threatening this country and the whole world, and at the same time demonstrating the weaknesses of Hitler and his policy, and showing how he might possibly be overthrown.'

In a long memo, he pointed out all the ways Princess Stephanie could aid America's anti-Nazi propaganda. Meanwhile, he wrote to Stephanie: 'Everything about you is new and different and gets me excited. You're the most interesting person I've ever met. You dress better than anyone else, and every time you come into a room, everyone else fades out of the picture. . . . Because of you I do so many crazy things, because I'm mad about you. Now you know.'

INTERNMENT

Although Attorney General Biddle had ordered that she be sent back to California, Hoover traced Stephanie to a small house in Alexandria, Virginia. Schofield was seen to visit often. However, on 28 November 1941, Roosevelt wrote to Hoover, saying: 'I spoke to the attorney general about the Hohenlohe case and he assures me that he has broken up the romance. Also, he thinks it best not to change the present domicile as the person in question is much easier to watch in that place. Please do a confidential recheck for me.'

When the attack on Pearl Harbor on 7 December 1941 brought the United States into the war, Princess Stephanie was arrested leaving a cinema. Although she was a Hungarian citizen, a complaints commission found against her, and Attorney General Biddle signed an order for 'the internment of Princess von Hohenlohe-Waldenburg, German citizen, resident in Alexandria, Virginia, as she is a potential danger to public security and peace in the United States'.

Searching her home, the FBI discovered her signed picture of Hitler and the Gold Medal of the Nazi Party. The name of Biddle's wife was also found in her address book. Princess Stephanie spent seven months in an internment camp in Gloucester City, New Jersey. While she was there, Lutheran pastor Reverend Schlick was prosecuted after she tried to get him to smuggle a letter out for her. He said he was unaware that she was 'a very dangerous foreign woman'. However, he also admitted he had been a member of the German-American Bund.

In her letters to her mother Stephanie described conditions in the camp as appallingly unhygienic. There were, she said, 20 women living in the filthy room and the prisoners she was interned with were prostitutes – or, as she put it, 'sluts with venereal disease'. In winter, the camp was freezing. She made an appeal to Sir William Wiseman to intercede, but he didn't reply. Her only visitor was her mother, who arrived in Schofield's official car. Roosevelt was furious, even more so when he discovered that her son Franzi, also in detention on Ellis Island, had written to his mother saying that 'Uncle Lem' – that is, Schofield – was arranging his release.

Despite orders from the highest authorities, Schofield refused to break off contact with the princess. Roosevelt wrote to Hoover, complaining: 'Once more

I have to bother you about that Hohenlohe woman. This affair verges not merely on the ridiculous, but on the disgraceful.'

He followed this with a letter to the attorney general, saying: 'If the immigration authorities do not stop once and for all showing favour to that Hohenlohe woman, I will be forced to order an inquiry. The facts will not be very palatable and will go right back to her first arrest and her intimacy with Schofield. I am aware that she is interned in the Gloucester centre, but by all accounts, she enjoys special privileges there. The same is apparently true in the case of her son, who is being held on Ellis Island. To be honest, this is all turning into a scandal that requires extremely drastic and immediate action.'

Biddle responded by transferring Stephanie to a remote camp in Texas, under close custody. She insisted that her guards carry her bags and feigned shock that she had not been provided with a private drawing room on the train and had to sit in a regular coach. But she took the opportunity to flirt outrageously with two men who bought her a glass of white wine and some peanuts.

On 15 February 1942, a report from Special Agent D.M. Ladd to Hoover made it clear the princess had 'a very influential friend in the State Department whose mistress she had been; the princess stated that this friend had the authority to permit Axis aliens to enter the country and to keep anti-Axis aliens out of the country'. Her 'friend' was thought to be Breckinridge Long, who was assistant secretary of state with responsibility for problems arising from the war and controlled immigration.

While she was interned, the princess was visited by the psychoanalyst Walter C. Langer, who was interviewing people who had known Hitler in an attempt to compile a psychological profile of the *Führer*. Stephanie refused to co-operate, saying she would only help if Langer got her released. He responded by saying that this was not in his power. Stephanie did, however, let slip one nugget of information concerning the private life of Eva Braun and Hitler. 'Eva quite often spent the whole night in Hitler's bedroom in Berlin,' she said. This was illuminating as a question mark had always hung over his sexuality.

Schofield also moved to Texas. He visited the camp and ordered the governor to extend special privileges to the princess. An FBI special agent visiting on 16 July 1942 found her on a payphone, speaking in German, unsupervised. A member of the prison staff liked to keep her company and let her help censor the mail. Thanks to Schofield, those who showed kindness to Stephanie received a raise. He also arranged for her to travel to New York to discuss the publication of her memoirs with her agent.

On 3 August 1942, Hoover sent a message to his New York office, saying: 'In view of the interest which has been shown in this matter by the President of the United States and the Attorney General, you are directed to obtain all developments concerning it immediately and submit the same to the bureau for the attention of the espionage section.'

In an effort to secure her release, the princess was willing to double-cross Schofield and offered to dish the dirt on him to Hoover, but he did not rise to the bait. She even claimed she hadn't slept with a man since 1920. 'Where some women take pleasure in giving themselves, I take pleasure in denying myself,' she said.

In 1944, she tried to convince a parole board that her friendship with Wiedemann had never been intimate, and that he and his wife were merely friends. The board was not convinced and she was not released until 9 May 1945, the day after VE Day.

BLACKLISTED

Stephanie was given notice that she would be deported on 9 April 1946. Hungary was by then under Soviet occupation and she was on a blacklist as far as Britain was concerned. Her MI5 file describes her as 'a notorious intriguer who had in the past had extremely close relations with the Nazi leaders' and said: 'She must still be regarded as a highly dangerous person.' They continued to track her movements until 1949.

Schofield remained loyal, however, and she moved to New York to be near him after he had quit the INS to work for a private law firm. After seeing her out on the town, columnist Robert Ruark noted in March 1947: 'Princess Stephanie Hohenlohe-Waldenburg-Schillingsfürst plays a not insignificant role in New York society today. This is no less interesting than if I were to report that Joachim von Ribbentrop had been seen dancing at the Stork Club, or that Eva Braun was staying as a guest at the Long Island home of Mr and Mrs Bigname. Compared to this Hohenlohe hustler, Mata Hari was definitely bottom of the range, and Edda Mussolini a raw beginner, a tool of the fascists, who couldn't say "no". . . . Before the war, la Hohenlohe was a close friend of Adolf Hitler and his most trusted female spy.'

In June 1947, she appeared at an immigration hearing with Schofield. The INS were at a loss as to what to do with her. Her Hungarian citizenship had lapsed and the British were still unwilling to take her back. She was finally allowed to retire to Schofield's farm in Pennsylvania. In 1953, she features in the New York Dress Institute's list of best-dressed women and she appeared at the Easter Parade in a Chanel dress.

She lived with Schofield until his death in 1954, then moved to another New Jersey farm that belonged to Herbert N. Straus, the owner of Macy's department store, taking as her lover his neighbour, the multi-millionaire Albert Monroe Greenfield. The following year, she returned to journalism as a special correspondent for the *Washington Diplomat*, an international society magazine. Moving back to Manhattan, she took as her lover a US air force general.

In 1959, she moved to Geneva to be near her son who was working for a Swiss bank. There she met up with Wiedemann, who was writing his memoirs which, in the end, made no mention of her. She made a living writing for the German magazine, *Quick*. She became so influential as a fixer for the magazine that she was invited to the inauguration of President Lyndon B. Johnson. Then she went on to work on a competing title, *Stern*, where she published interviews with Princess Grace of Monaco and the wife of the Shah of Iran.

Still considered a Nazi spy, she was denied a visa to visit Britain until she appealed directly to the Home Secretary. But her cosmopolitan connections attracted the German publishing giant Axel Springer, who was said to be 'the final Caesar to her Cleopatra'. She acted as his 'ambassadress' to leading political figures, including Henry Kissinger. On 13 June, she died in Geneva of a burst stomach ulcer. According to her son, 12 ambassadors attended her funeral, which was reported in 300 syndicated American newspapers.

CHAPTER 3

SECRETS OF THE RUSSIAN TEA ROOM

By the start of World War II, Anna Wolkoff had long been under investigation by Maxwell Knight, an MI5 spymaster who headed Section B5b which specialized in counter-intelligence. (Knight coincidentally signed official documents 'M' – a detail picked up by a colleague in naval intelligence named Ian Fleming.) Anna was the eldest child of Admiral Nikolai Wolkoff, the last Imperial Russian naval attaché in London. When the Bolshevik Revolution occurred in Russia 1917, he and his family remained in London and eventually naturalized as British subjects in 1935. The Wolkoffs had been stripped of their status and wealth in their homeland, so were ardently anti-communist. And as many of the leading revolutionaries such as Leon Trotsky, Gregory Zinoviev and Lev Kamenev were Jewish, they were also fervently anti-Semitic.

To make a living in London, the Wolkoffs opened the Russian Tea Room, a meeting place for White Russian émigrés, in South Kensington. They were well connected: Anna's mother Madame Vera Wolkoff, a former maid of honour to the Tsarina, was a close friend of Queen Mary, wife of George V and mother of Edward VIII and George VI. Anna designed clothes and ran a shop in the West End called Anna de Wolkoff Haute Couture Modes, which boasted among its clients Wallis Simpson. But at the beginning of 1939 it was closed down, with Anna blaming competition from Jewish rivals.

Anna Wolkoff was a Russian emigré and secretary of the anti-Semitic Right Club. Her family ran the Russian Tea Room in Kensington which was frequented by White Russian exiles. Her reactionary views drew her towards the growing fascist movement in Britain.

THE RIGHT CLUB

Anna's views naturally drew her to the growing fascist movement in Britain. She joined the Right Club, an anti-Semitic secret society which had been founded by Captain Archibald Maule 'Jock' Ramsay, MP, and funded by the Duke of Westminster. Anna made the uniforms; she also visited Nazi Germany several times in the 1930s and made contacts in the Gestapo there.

Other members of the Right Club included William Joyce, who fled to Germany and later became the radio propagandist Lord Haw-Haw, and author A. K. Chesterton, second cousin to G. K. Chesterton. The club often convened in the Russian Tea Room. Like other groups on the far right and far left, it was infiltrated by agents working for Maxwell Knight.

With the outbreak of war in September 1939, MI5 had bigger fish to fry and Knight was told to end his surveillance of Anna Wolkoff – but he persisted. At the time, she was trying to get a job in the foreign language section of the Ministry of Information's Postal and Telegraph Censorship Department. Other members of the Right Club were also attempting to find sensitive posts in government to further their political agenda and aid the anti-war cause. One of them had already penetrated the newly created Ministry of Economic Warfare, set up to undermine Germany's financial and industrial sectors.

Anna was already communicating with contacts in Germany. To avoid the wartime censors, she sent letters to the continent via Jean Nieuwenhuys, a diplomat at the Belgian embassy. She and other members of the Right Club stepped up the propaganda, venturing out of the Tea Room at night to plaster the surrounding streets with anti-Semitic slogans such as 'This is the Jews' War!', and scratch insults on the windows of Jewish-owned shops.

THE SOVIET SPY

In February 1940, Tyler Gatewood Kent, a junior diplomat at the US embassy, visited the Russian Tea Room. He was introduced to Anna by a mutual friend, Barbara Allen. There was an instant attraction. Scion of a distinguished Virginia family, Kent was an accomplished linguist. Fluent in Russian, in 1934 he secured a job as a translator in the US embassy in Moscow, when the United

Right-wing politician Captain Archibald Maule 'Jock' Ramsay with his wife in Eaton Square, London. He founded the Right Club and had contacts with German fascists.

States first recognized the Soviet Union. His pay was poor and he supplemented his salary by selling confidential information to the Soviets. His contact was Tatyana Alexandrovna Ilovaiskaya, a lover provided by the NKVD, the Soviet secret police. Kent later became privy to more sensitive material when he was promoted to a position in the code room; his continued co-operation was ensured by blackmail.

In October 1939, when he transferred to the US embassy in London, he took with him a collection of stolen documents. In London, he again worked in the code room and had access to coded telegrams between Franklin Roosevelt and Churchill, then First Lord of the Admiralty. Churchill famously signed himself 'Naval Person'.

Eager to supplement his income once more, Kent tried to find a Soviet contact to whom he could sell the telegrams, so immersed himself in London's expatriate Russian community. He met Irene Danischewsky, the wife of a Russian-Jewish businessman, and they became lovers though they could only meet up during the day, when her husband was at work. Kent therefore had the evenings to himself.

When he returned to the Russian Tea Room, Anna was delighted to see him as her Nazi contacts were keen to know what was going on at the US embassy. Kent was also happy to talk to her about Russia and life there under communism.

AN INTERVIEW WITH THE CAPTAIN

After the British security services raided the homes of two members of the Right Club, Anna's brother Alexander warned her to cut her ties with it. Through a previous lover, Lord Cottenham, Anna had met Sir Vernon Kell, director of MI5. While she admitted to being an anti-Semite, she insisted that she was a true patriot and asked Sir Vernon how she should respond to her brother's warning. He invited her to meet him at the War Office the following afternoon to discuss her concerns.

At the meeting, he introduced her to a 'Captain King' – Maxwell Knight – who asked Anna the name of the person who had passed the warning to her brother. She said she believed it had been Prince Kyril Scherbatow, formerly private secretary to Sir Henri Deterding, erstwhile chairman of Shell Oil and

Alexander Wolkoff's one-time boss. Deterding had been an admirer of the Nazi Party and was one of the financial backers of the British Union of Fascists. After he retired in 1936, he moved to Germany; on his death, in February 1939, he was given a swastika-swathed funeral with wreathes from Hitler and Göring, and a Nazi spokesman read a tribute from the *Führer*.

Wolkoff thought she had thrown her interrogators off the scent, but Kell and Knight were not deceived. They allowed her to believe she was in the clear. Wolkoff then arranged to take Tyler Kent to dinner with Jock Ramsay, telling Kent that Ramsay would be a useful contact. Over dinner they discussed politics and Kent disagreed with Ramsay about the causes of the war. The following day, Anna and Kent visited Ramsay again. This time Kent told Ramsay that he had documents detailing the run-up to the conflict – would he like to see them? Of course, Ramsay said that he would. Later Ramsay visited Kent's flat at 47 Gloucester Place and was shown some documents Kent had stolen from the American embassy. They proved that Churchill was urging Roosevelt to join Britain in the war against Germany at a time when Hitler was petitioning the Allied powers for their support. Kent made it clear that he would be happy to sell them.

The Wolkoff interview had piqued Knight's interest in the Russian Tea Room. Sometime earlier he had recruited Marjorie Amor who had been secretary to the Christian Protest Movement, a White Russian group that campaigned against the suppression of Christianity in the Soviet Union. Ramsay had also been a member of this group. One afternoon, when Marjorie was taking tea at Ramsay's house, his wife invited her to join the Right Club. 'Captain Ramsay thinks you will be most useful when the time comes,' Mrs Ramsay assured her. 'We think that there will be a Communist rising and then we shall have to take over. Mosley has tried often and hard to get Jock to join in with him and – this is for your private ear – he promised him Scotland.'

Ramsay was now calling himself 'The Leader' – a translation of Hitler's '*Führer*' and Mussolini's '*Duce*'. Members of the Right Club discussed how they could aid German troops when they arrived. One man who worked for a haulage company said he would pretend to misplace the keys to the firm's garage, then provide the invading paratroopers with transport.

Over tea at the Ramsays' house, Marjorie was introduced to Anna Wolkoff. Anna invited her to the Russian Tea Room and they became firm friends. Marjorie called Anna 'the little Storm Trooper' and Anna boasted that she would ride in Himmler's car at the Nazi victory parade in London. She also said she had given Ramsay a channel of communication to Berlin via her friend Margaret Bothamley who had moved to Berlin in July 1939. And she let slip that she knew a 'most interesting man from the US embassy'.

Another of Maxwell Knight's plants was Hélène de Munck, a Belgian-born agent who knew Anna from the Russian Tea Room. The two women shared an interest in clairvoyance, spiritualism and the occult and Hélène visited Anna's flat in Roland Gardens to give a demonstration of fortune-telling. Afterwards, Anna asked Hélène if, when she was next visiting Belgium, she could take some documents with her. Hélène reported to Knight that Anna had also said: 'Hitler is a god . . . and it would be wonderful if he could govern England.'

DINNER WITH FASCISTS

Kent was aware of Anna's interest in him. While planning to spend Easter weekend at Bexhill-on-Sea with June Huntley, the wife of a friend, Kent sent Anna a gift – some Chesterfield cigarettes which had been imported for the US embassy. In a covering letter he wrote that he would like to see Anna when he returned. To give the correspondence an intimate touch, he concluded with a few sentences in Russian and signed it Anatoly Vasilievich, a pseudonym borrowed from the prominent Russian anti-communist.

Since Anna's affair with Lord Cottenham had faltered, she encouraged Kent's interest. When he returned from Bexhill, they spoke on the phone and she invited him to her parents' flat. By then she was addressing him as Anatoly. Over dinner, they discussed communist Russia and the Wolkoffs' support for National Socialism.

Anna then invited Kent to accompany her to a private function at the Holborn Restaurant, a famous London eatery on the corner of Kingsway and Holborn. The host at the dinner was Sir Oswald Mosley. Ignoring the seating plan, Anna insisted that Kent sit next to her.

CHAPTER 3

On 9 April 1940, the day Nazi Germany invaded Denmark and Norway, Anna was introduced to James Hughes, the chief of intelligence for the British Union of Fascists, at the Russian Tea Room. He asked her to smuggle a sealed envelope to the continent. It was addressed to Herr W. B. Joyce, Rundfunkhaus, Berlin.

Anna's father had warned her not to trust Jean Nieuwenhuys, suspecting that he was Jewish. In casual conversation at the Tea Room, Nieuwenhuys mentioned that Hélène de Munck had said she had a contact at the Romanian embassy. Anna asked Hélène whether she though the contact could smuggle a letter out of the country for her, and Hélène said he probably could. Anna handed over Hughes' letter, telling Hélène it was for William Joyce, Lord Haw-Haw. Of course, it ended up in the hands of Maxwell Knight, who had it copied and deciphered.

The letter gave Joyce advice on how his talks were being received and supplied material he could incorporate. The original letter was then forwarded to Joyce by MI6. Hélène phoned Anna to tell her the shipment had been successful. Later, Anna visited Hélène's flat with a further letter for Joyce, typing another one while she was there. She signed off 'PJ' – 'Perish Judah' – a popular salute among British fascists.

Hélène delivered both letters to Knight, who now had enough evidence to prosecute Wolkoff for attempting to communicate with the enemy, in contravention of the Official Secrets Act of 1920. However, hoping to round up the entire fifth column, he stayed his hand. MI6 smuggled Anna's letters to the continent, and posted them.

Jock Ramsay wanted copies of the telegrams Kent had shown him. On 13 April 1940, Anna went to Kent's flat, taking with her a photographer friend named Nicholas Smirnoff, another White Russian with similar political views, who made copies of them.

London's émigré Russians still followed the Julian calendar, not the Gregorian calendar that the Bolsheviks had imposed on the Soviet Union. On Orthodox Easter Sunday, Kent joined Anna and her family for their traditional meal. Afterwards, Anna wrote to her Uncle Gabriel in Switzerland to suggest that Kent rent his London house which was only a short walk from the US embassy.

AMERICAN SECRETS

Kent stole further telegrams from the US embassy which detailed an arrangement known as 'Lend-Lease', that would allow Roosevelt to avoid the Neutrality Act passed by Congress which restricted the supply of armaments and food to belligerent nations. Roosevelt was running for president again in 1940 on the platform of keeping America out of the war. While claiming to be an isolationist, he was, in fact, aiming to supply Britain and France. He feared that if his plan was exposed, he could lose the election to a Republican, Lend-Lease would be scuppered, and Britain and France would be left without food and arms.

By this point, Anna and Kent had become lovers. While lunching with Admiral Wilmot Nicholson and his wife Christabel, two other leading lights in the Right Club, it became clear to their hosts that Anna and Kent were more than just good friends. Later Kent dined with Admiral Nicholson at the United Services Club and showed him stolen documents; he invited the admiral round to his flat to view the Churchill–Roosevelt correspondence.

Anna and Kent were also seen dining together at La Popote in the basement of the Ritz – which Lord Haw-Haw reported was where the rich circumvented the strictures of rationing. Anna later shared an account of the intimate evening with Marjorie.

Keeping an eye on the burgeoning affair, Marjorie reported to Knight: 'There is no doubt that Tyler Kent is a definite fifth column member. He is always reporting to Anna Wolkoff matters which he claims he obtains from confidential sources in the American embassy and which, to say the least of it, are damaging both to the Allies and America.'

Kent had mentioned to J. Edgar Hoover that he had seen a message from Guy Liddell, who had taken over from Vernon Kell as director of MI5. Upon hearing this, Maxwell Knight became concerned about other secret correspondence Kent could have obtained. Kent's home was placed under surveillance, but as he held a diplomatic passport it would be difficult for the security services to obtain a search warrant.

More damaging still, Kent passed on a report that Joseph Kennedy had sent to President Roosevelt. Kennedy was the American ambassador to the Court of

St James's and father of future US president John F. Kennedy. The report said the situation in Britain was so bad that serious internal trouble might develop at any time. Discussions in the War Cabinet were acrimonious – Churchill was under duress as he had lost his following in the country, thanks to his disastrous intervention in the defence of Norway.

After dining with Ramsay, Kent was invited to join the Right Club and entrusted with its membership list for safekeeping. Concerned that his own house might be searched, Ramsay asked Kent to keep the list safe – under lock and key at the American embassy perhaps? But Kent's position there was by no means secure. He had read a message from Joseph Kennedy to the State Department asking for specialist code clerks. Fearing that he might get re-assigned to a less sensitive area of the embassy, Kent asked Anna to get copies of the keys to the code room and the file room cut for him.

When they spoke on the phone, Kent and Anna communicated in Russian, hoping this would confound anyone listening in. Kent was now a regular companion to Anna and her fascist friends, including Pamela Jackson and her husband Derek who believed that all Jews in England should be slaughtered. Pamela was one of the Mitford sisters, a couple of whom had already established links with fascism. While Unity Mitford fawned over Hitler, the third sister, Diana, married Oswald Mosley in secret at Goebbels' Berlin home. Hitler was one of the guests.

Back in London, Anna and Kent's round of social engagements included dinner at L'Escargot in Soho with Colonel Francisco Marigliano, the Duke del Monte, assistant military attaché at the Italian embassy and a spy who already had a copious MI5 file. Italy had not yet entered the war and Marigliano insisted that his country would remain neutral. Nevertheless, he was willing to use the diplomatic bag to smuggle sensitive material out of Britain. After dinner, Anna and Kent danced cheek-to-cheek at the glamorous Embassy Club.

The couple were dining à deux at Kent's flat when Neville Chamberlain announced Hitler's invasion of the Low Countries. What was needed, Chamberlain said, was a coalition government; he announced his resignation and said that Winston Churchill was to form a new administration. While Anna was mortified, Kent continued to express pro-German sentiments, even in public. He spent as much time as he could with her, when he was not double-dealing at the US embassy.

STRICTLY PERSONAL

On the evening of 15 May 1940, Kent was on shift in the code room when a coded message was sent by 'Former Naval Person' – Winston Churchill – to President Roosevelt. It was headed: 'SECRET. STRICTLY PERSONAL AND CONFIDENTIAL FOR THE PRESIDENT. MOST SECRET AND PERSONAL.'

In it, Churchill outlined the dire situation in Europe. He begged Roosevelt for help in every way short of engaging in combat. Particularly, Churchill asked for the loan of 40 or 50 old American destroyers, along with aeroplanes, anti-aircraft guns, ammunition and steel. He added: 'I am looking to you to keep that Japanese dog quiet in the Pacific, using Singapore in any way convenient.'

This message reached Anna Wolkoff, who had copies made by Nicholas Smirnoff. These were then forwarded to the Italian government by the Duke del Monte. Kent was on hand in the code room to decode Roosevelt's reply to Churchill. As far as it was in his power, Roosevelt gave Churchill almost everything he had asked for. That evening, Kent read Roosevelt's message to Anne, who made a copy and sent it to del Monte.

Unable to obtain a warrant, Maxwell Knight decided to conduct an illegal search of Kent's apartment. He broke in one evening when Kent was working at the embassy and found hundreds of stolen documents, including the Churchill–Roosevelt correspondence. Knight reported back to Guy Liddell, who decided that Anna Wolkoff and Tyler Kent should be arrested. But first MI5 would have to get permission from the US authorities, as Kent's diplomatic passport afforded him immunity from prosecution.

As ambassador Joseph Kennedy was known to be pro-German, MI5 arranged a meeting with his deputy, Herschel V. Johnson, who was a friend of Liddell's. The British security services handed Johnson a briefing document which detailed the relationship between Anna and Kent. Johnson was furious that he had not been informed earlier. Knight told him that Scotland Yard intended to arrest

Kent the following Monday morning and simultaneously to conduct a search of his flat. Johnson promised the US embassy's full co-operation and asked Joseph Kennedy to suspend Kent's diplomatic status.

That weekend, Anna and Kent drove out to Surrey to have tea with a friend, returning in time to attend Admiral Nicholson's birthday party. Kent brought along a portfolio of stolen US documents. Then Kent worked another shift in the code room.

When he turned up a little before midnight, he discovered another message marked: 'SECRET AND PERSONAL FOR THE PRESIDENT FROM FORMER NAVAL PERSON.' When he left the embassy at the end of his shift at 8 a.m., he took a copy with him.

Kent had the day ahead of him planned. He was meeting Irene Danischewsky at his flat in the morning and they would visit Kew Gardens in the afternoon. The evening would be spent dining with Anna, the Duke of del Monte and his latest paramour, and they would then perhaps go dancing in the Embassy Club.

THE NET TIGHTENS

On the morning of 20 May 1940, a car carrying Maxwell Knight and three police officers collected second secretary Franklin Gowen from the US embassy. They drove to 47 Gloucester Place and a maid let them in. They shoulder-charged the door to Kent's flat, knocking it down and arresting him. In the bathroom they found a half-naked Irene Danischewsky. The couple were taken away for questioning.

Danischewsky was quickly freed. Kent denied having any documents belonging to the US government, or even knowing Anna Wolkoff. She, too, had been picked up by the police and MI5 who presented her with a detention order issued under the Emergency Defence Regulations. This was read to her, along with her rights.

The search of Kent's flat brought to light a hoard of documents, along with Ramsay's membership list of the Right Club which included the name of Lord Redesdale and those of a number of MPs, both Conservative and Labour. There was also a large sum of money.

Knight and Gowen took the stolen documents back to the US embassy. Kent was also taken there for an interview with Ambassador Kennedy who asked him why he had the embassy's codes and telegrams at his home. Kent insisted that he had only taken them out of interest. Kennedy pointed out that Kent had applied for a transfer to the US embassy in Berlin. 'You weren't going to take them there?' he asked. Kent didn't answer. He was taken to Canon Row police station, then remanded in Brixton. Anna was held at Rochester Row, before being taken to Strangeways prison in Manchester.

On 20 May 1940 Tyler Kent was dismissed from government service, losing his immunity. He was charged with five breaches of the Official Secrets Act and two counts of larceny. Anna Wolkoff was charged with breaching the Official Secrets Act and infringing the Defence Regulations, for attempting to communicate with William Joyce. Fortunately for them both, the death penalty for espionage offences did not come into force until a week after they were arrested.

The British government rushed through an amendment to the Emergency Defence Regulations, allowing it to detain without trial British Fascists and Communists (the Soviet Union was allied to Nazi Germany at the time). Under these special circumstances, the government won the right to intern anyone likely to endanger public safety, the defence of the realm, public order, or the prosecution of the war. Ramsay and other members of the Right Club were rounded up, along with Oswald Mosley. To maintain their cover, Marjorie Amor and Hélène de Munck were also interned and continued their undercover work in jail.

SPIES ON TRIAL

Wolkoff and Kent appeared in the dock of the Old Bailey on 23 October 1940. As the charges against them involved the Churchill–Roosevelt correspondence which could still damage Roosevelt's prospects in the presidential election the following month, the trial was held *in camera*. Both defendants pleaded not guilty.

The case against Kent was heard first. He claimed he had taken the documents to show to the US Senate, so they could see that the president was duplicitous

US embassy worker Tyler Kent (third from left in dark coat) returns home after serving five years of a seven-year sentence for spying, 1945. Kent was convicted of stealing secret documents and passing them on to Nazi sympathizers.

in his foreign policy – promising neutrality while supporting the British. The jury found him guilty on six of the indictments (one of the larceny charges was dismissed on a technicality).

Marjorie Amor and Hélène de Munck testified against Wolkoff. During three days in the witness box, Anna claimed that Kent was going to use the documents to write a book and she had made photographic copies to illustrate it. But the prints had not been found in Kent's flat and she declined to call him as a witness to explain why. She admitted sending a letter from James Hughes to William Joyce; implausibly she said she had only done so to ensnare Hughes at a future date. Calling Ramsay and Mosley as defence witnesses did not help either. The jury found her guilty on all charges.

Kent was sentenced to seven years in prison. At the end of the war he was deported to the United States where the authorities declined to press charges. His views remained rabidly right-wing and he was subjected to six FBI investigations between 1952 and 1963, all of which ended inconclusively.

Anna Wolkoff was sentenced to ten years' penal servitude. In fact, she joined others detained under the Defence Regulations at a prison in Aylesbury. There she spent her days reading, dressmaking and gardening. On her release in June 1947, she was stripped of her British citizenship. Friends of the family in Cricklewood took her in, but she maintained contact with her fascist friends and MI5 continued to keep her under surveillance. She moved to a shabby apartment in South Kensington, but her return to dressmaking was hampered by the authorities, who refused to allow her to disguise her identity. She died in a car accident in Spain in 1973.

CHAPTER 4

SOME SORT OF KINK

Dorothy Pamela 'Sweet Rosie' O'Grady worked as a prostitute before she got involved in spying. She was known for her strange sexual proclivities. When in prison for espionage, she would sleep naked under the bed and keep herself tied up in painful positions for hours on end. The prison medical officer reported that O'Grady inserted an alarming collection of objects into her vagina. A light bulb, more than 50 pieces of broken glass, 100 pins and a small pot were recovered. Dorothy herself said she 'must have been suffering from some sort of kink'.

She also claimed that her so-called spying was a joke – a joke that would nearly cost her her life. Like other spy trials held during the wartime, the proceedings were held *in camera*, so those who had not attended the hearings dismissed her as a sad fantasist.

However, when the papers concerning the case were released in 1995, it was discovered that Dorothy had drawn maps of Britain's coastal defences which proved to be 'terrifyingly accurate' and 'would be of very great importance to the enemy'.

It also seems she got a sexual thrill from her espionage activities, even getting a kick from the idea that she might be executed for her treachery.

CHAPTER 4

DIFFICULT START

Known to the secret service as 'Sweet Rosie O'Grady', Dorothy had a troubled background. Adopted as an infant in 1897 by a couple named George and Pamela Squire who lived near Clapham Common in south London, she was educated at a local convent school. Pamela died when Dorothy was ten years old and George, who was chief library attendant at the British Museum's repository at Hendon, employed a housekeeper who he then married. Dorothy's stepmother was cruel to her. She pulled her hair and told her that the Squires were not her real parents.

'It was a terrible shock,' said Dorothy.

At 13, she was sent to St John's Hostel, a live-in training school for girls entering domestic service. At 17, she went to work as a servant to the rector of Christ Church in Harrow, to the north-west of London. She never saw her adoptive father again.

She then began a career of crime. In 1918, she was convicted of forging banknotes and sent to borstal. In court, her address was given as the London Female Preventative & Reformatory Institution (Friendless and Fallen). She was returned there after serving 19 months.

In 1920, while in service in Brighton, she was convicted of stealing clothes and sentenced to two years' hard labour. On her release she turned to prostitution and, between 1923 and 1926, appeared in court four times for soliciting in Soho, an area of London thought to be a fertile recruiting ground for spies. The records of her arrest show that she sometimes used the pseudonym Pamela Arland, a name she would use again during her career in espionage.

The first time she was arrested for soliciting she pleaded not guilty, though she didn't contest the charge on subsequent occasions. Later, in letters from prison, Dorothy said she had waited years to wreak her revenge for being wrongly convicted that first time. Her bitterness was fuelled by the fact that a puppy she loved had died because there was no one to look after it while she was kept on remand. She claimed that on the night of the arrest she had only been out on the street because the puppy was sick and she was looking for a pharmacy. In a letter written from prison, dated 21 November 1940, she said: 'You may think it silly and, as you say, a hopelessly inadequate reason for what I have done, but he was all I had and I loved that dog more than anything in the world, and there was nothing I would not do at the time to obtain revenge for his death.'

In another letter she said: 'I have no wish to help this country. I hate it, or rather the authorities in it, too much to ever want to assist them. I have waited some 16 years for this.'

She never forgave the British for the death of her dog and felt that allying herself with Nazi Germany gave her the opportunity to strike back at the establishment she hated.

SPYCLISTS

In 1926, shortly after her release from jail, she married Vincent O'Grady, a fireman 20 years her senior. When he retired, they moved to the Isle of Wight where they ran Osborne Villa, a small boarding house on the Broadway in Sandown. There they catered to the large number of German tourists visiting the island under the Nazi *Kraft durch Freude* – Joy through Strength – programme. Clearly the O'Gradys would have been exposed to impromptu propaganda. Some of their guests would have been members of the Hitler Youth on cycling tours. A German cycling magazine told readers visiting Britain and other foreign countries to 'make a note of the names of places, rivers, seas and mountains. Perhaps you may be able to utilize these sometime for the benefit of the Fatherland.' The *Daily Herald* newspaper called them 'spyclists'.

The Isle of Wight was strategically important when it came to invasions. The French attacked it during the Hundred Years War (1337–1453). In 1377, French and Castilian forces besieged Carisbrooke Castle. Henry VIII further fortified the island to protect the naval base at Portsmouth, helping to defend it from the French in the Battle of the Solent in 1545, where famously the *Mary Rose* was sunk. A large garrison was stationed on the island during a threatened French invasion in 1759. There were further fears of a French invasion in the 1860s when new fortifications and gun batteries were added. Defences were again strengthened in the early years of the 20th century. These were mothballed after World War I, only to be revived in 1938 as the international situation worsened. The eight-and-a-half-mile-long beach at

Sandown Bay, running from Culver Down and Yaverland to Shanklin and Luccombe, would have been an ideal landing ground and, from her modest home in Sandown, Dorothy O'Grady was well positioned to observe the build-up of the defences there.

It seems that something went wrong with the O'Gradys' marriage. Dorothy left the Isle of Wight temporarily, later telling the *Daily Mail* that she had lived with a Dutchman before the war and a Dutch friend had been hanged during the conflict. It is true that two Dutch spies – Carl Meier and Charles van den Kieboom – were executed in Pentonville prison in December 1940, under the wartime Treachery Act. Dorothy later told MI5 that she had been recruited by her Dutch friends. 'It is unlikely that O'Grady was fantasizing as these two executions were not widely reported at the time,' the *Mail* said.

With the outbreak of war, Vincent O'Grady was recalled to duty in London and Dorothy returned to Sandown. With her husband away, she only had her black retriever Rob to keep her company. She would take him for daily walks on the beach, although under wartime regulations the beaches were largely out of bounds with only limited access for civilians.

CROSSING THE LINE

Sandown Bay was defended by the 12th Infantry Brigade. Along the beach there were anti-landing-craft defences, dragons' teeth anti-tank obstacles, mines, barbed wire, concrete pillboxes, trenches, recommissioned World War I naval guns, anti-aircraft guns and searchlights, along with an experimental Chain Home Low radar station to detect shipping and low-flying aircraft on Culver Cliff, next to the Royal Navy's shore signals and wireless station. Modern equipment had been installed under Culver Fire Command, and sections of the piers at Sandown, Ventnor and Shanklin had been removed to stop them being used by the enemy as landing stages.

On 9 August 1940, O'Grady ignored a 'No Trespassing' sign and crossed the barbed wire at Yaverland. On the beach, she was stopped by squaddies of the Royal Northumberland Fusiliers. This was the third time she had been spotted and they said they would have to report her. She offered them ten shillings (nominally 50p – perhaps worth around £26/$33 today). They refused to take it and escorted her to Bembridge police station three miles away.

After her name and address were taken, she was searched. A small swastika badge was found under her coat lapel, along with cut-out Nazi paper flags. She was carrying a torch, a pencil and a notebook containing detailed drawings of the defences and maps of Sandown Bay. Although she was considered little more than a nuisance at first, she was summoned to appear in the magistrates' court in Ryde on 27 August charged under the Defence Regulations with 'entering the foreshore, contrary to Regulation 16a and acting in a manner likely to prevent or interfere with the performance of HM Forces'. She did not turn up at court.

The police were sent to fetch her. At her home they found a note on the door saying: 'No more milk till I return.'

By absconding Dorothy had made the matter much more serious. She was now a fugitive and the police considered her to be a quisling and a fifth columnist. The resulting manhunt extended across southern England in case she had escaped from the island, though this was unlikely. A travel permit was required to travel to and from the Isle of Wight, and it had to be shown at the ferry port. MI5 obtained a warrant to open her mail.

Dorothy had taken Rob with her to stay at Latton House, a guesthouse in Totland Bay on the other side of the island. She registered under the name Pamela Arland. The Freshwater peninsula there was also heavily defended. During her three-week stay, she was again seen walking in restricted areas. She also perpetrated acts of sabotage. Using a pair of nail clippers she cut the wires connecting the searchlights to the gun emplacements. With the help of local schoolboys, whom she bribed, she made maps of the gun sites. And she tried to bribe the policeman who had attempted to arrest her at Alum Bay with chocolates and cigarettes.

At Latton House, the police caught her trying to flush papers down the toilet. She told the officers who had come to arrest her that they would be 'wiped out' when the Germans came. One of them asked: 'Did you consider you were assisting this country by committing these acts?' She replied: 'Who wants to?'

In the police car on the way to Yarmouth, she took 20 ephedrine tablets from her handbag and swallowed them. A search of her room found more notebooks containing annotated maps showing the gun emplacements, radar stations and military barracks. The question was: had she been acting alone? In a letter to her husband, she asked if anyone else had been caught. Elsewhere she had claimed to be a member of a four-man spy ring, although she did not know the names of the other three spies.

But how had she been communicating with them or her handlers? She had no wireless and there was no evidence that she had been sending coded messages through the post. She told MI5 she had given drawings and maps to a German agent who paddled ashore in the middle of the night. This was unlikely as the Isle of Wight was heavily guarded. However, MI5 conceded that the information she had gathered was very accurate and would be of great use to the enemy in the event of an invasion. She was charged with nine breaches of the 1911 Official Secrets Act, the 1939 Defence Regulation Act and the 1940 Treachery Act. These included 'conspiracy with intent to help the enemy; making a plan likely to assist the enemy's operations; intent to impede the British Armed Forces by cutting a military telephone wire; forcing a military safeguard; approaching a prohibited place for purposes prejudicial to the state; making a plan of potential use to the enemy; acts which might prove prejudicial to the nation's defence; sabotage and possession of a document with information purporting to relate to the nation's defence measures'. Four of the charges carried the death penalty.

SENTENCED TO DEATH

She stood trial in Winchester on 16 December 1940. The following day, the Dutch spy Charles van den Kieboom was hanged. Dorothy's trial was held *in camera*. As no evidence could be found that she had passed on the intelligence she had gathered, she was tried as a saboteur rather than a spy. She pleaded not guilty and the trial went on for two days. She was found guilty of cutting military telephone lines and drawing maps that would be of use to the enemy in the event of an invasion. The judge donned his black cap and sentenced her to be hanged on 7 January 1941. Eighteen spies were given the death sentence by the British courts during the course of the war. Dorothy was the only woman to be sentenced to death. Awaiting execution, she was sent to Holloway women's prison in London where she was accused of signalling to German planes then bombing the capital.

Later, Dorothy said: 'The excitement of being tried for my life was intense. The supreme moment came when an official stood behind the judge and put on his black cap for him before he pronounced the death sentence. The man didn't put it on straight. It went over one of the judge's eyes and looked so funny that I was giggling inside and had a job not to laugh. It was hard to keep a straight face and look serious and solemn as I knew a spy should. I found it disappointing that I was going to be hanged instead of shot. My next disappointment was to learn they would put a hood over my head and tie my hands behind my back before taking me to the scaffold. This upset me. I protested, "What is the good of being hanged if I can't see what is happening?"'

Dorothy's barrister appealed the sentence, arguing that the judge had misdirected the jury, while the prosecution wrote to the Home Office saying that if she was reprieved it would encourage the Germans to use more female spies. But the appeal was successful and her sentence was commuted to 14 years, which she was to serve in Aylesbury prison in Buckinghamshire. A prison psychologist's report said she was 'a deeply troubled woman who regularly self-harmed, and had attacks in which she has to "obey people" inside her who encourage her to do harmful acts to herself'.

While she was detained, Dorothy wrote to her husband saying that she was 'explaining everything for the first time'. This amounted to a full confession. She sent another confession to the Home Secretary which concluded with the words: 'I know I acted foolishly but I did not realize the gravity of my acts at the time.'

She served just nine years and retired to Osborne Villa on the Isle of Wight where she was shunned by other residents who were convinced she was a traitor. She gave a series of newspaper interviews, trying to convince the public that she was just pretending to be a spy because it made her feel important. After her death in 1985, Barry Field, the MP for the Isle of Wight, sought to prove her innocence. But when he had her file opened, he said he was shocked at the depth of her treachery.

Author Adrian Searle, who also examined the file, said: 'I have always had an open mind about her, but with this evidence, particularly the detailed maps which were clearly made by somebody trained in intelligence-gathering, the finger firmly points to the conclusion that she was a spy.'

After the war, she had deliberately given the impression of being a harmless eccentric with a dangerous wartime fantasy – a convenient cover story for her sinister pro-Nazi activity. In his book *The Spy Beside the Sea*, Searle catalogued the evidence against her: 'A raft of witness statements showed that her attempt at bribery on Yaverland beach was not an isolated incident. She had several times tried to gain access to areas within military zones by offering soldiers chocolates or cigarettes in her endeavours to garner the highly sensitive information she needed for her maps and pencil sketches. Her degree of success was amply demonstrated by the depth of detail she was able to include on her map of the particularly sensitive coastal area around Sandown Bay, a key piece of evidence in the prosecution's case. While clarity was in places sacrificed for the sheer amount of information she chose to include, the map was, on the face of it, a comprehensive guide to the geography and the military installations in place at that vital period – from the position of gun emplacements and searchlights to the location of barbed wire obstacles; from the presence of troops to the number of soldiers sleeping at a given time; from lorries apparently camouflaged by trees to the steepness of cliffs.'

CHAPTER 5

A MARRIAGE OF CONVENIENCE

Marie Louise Augusta Ingram was one of many young women who emigrated from Germany after World War I in the hope of finding a better life in Britain. To get their stay, they married a British subject. Marie took her chance when she met her future husband, an RAF sergeant, in 1922 while he was serving in Cologne.

Marie was well-educated and when she was arrested she said that her father was a director of the Reich Railways and her brother-in-law was on the German general staff. However, in Britain she was employed as a domestic servant to people working in public service, especially those in the more sensitive departments. In 1940 she was living in Southsea, near the naval base at Portsmouth, and working as a general maid to a prominent naval officer who was involved in important work for the Admiralty. She was also close to William Swift, who worked as a storekeeper at the naval dockyard and Archibald Watts, the district secretary of the British Union of Fascists.

Marie tried to obtain information about tanks from a Corporal Baron in the Royal Tank Corps and said she knew how to get the information across to Germany. She had been introduced to Baron by a man named Cecil Rashleigh,

Marie Ingram joined the British Union of Fascists. She worked as a general maid to a prominent naval officer who was involved in important work for the Admiralty.

who she urged to join the BUF. Rashleigh went to the home of Watts and enrolled, though Marie had told him: 'Watts has no guts. The man of action for this district is Swift.'

At Watts' house, Rashleigh heard him in conversation with four soldiers who were 'disrespectful to the King and the Army'. Watts gave them copies of the BUF's newspaper *Action*.

On 18 May 1940, Marie told Rashleigh that in three weeks' time England would be invaded by Germany. According to Swift: 'This government has played right into the hands of our party; by enrolling in the Local Defence Volunteers [LDV] you can obtain arms and ammunition.'

The LDV or Home Guard was commonly referred to as 'Dad's Army'. Swift said that the arms and ammunition could be used to protect German parachute troops when they landed. Rashleigh duly joined the LDV, hiding his BUF membership card behind a picture in his house on Swift's advice.

'Mrs Ingram told me that at the present time Mosley and Hitler were more like brothers,' Rashleigh said. Swift had told him that high officials at the Portsmouth Guildhall were members of the BUF, but he kept nothing on paper in case his house was raided. Swift said: 'Hitler would not negotiate with anyone in this country except Sir Oswald Mosley, the Leader.'

Swift denied sending soldiers to see Marie Ingram and she denied ever having spoken to a soldier about obtaining blueprints. However, it is clear that she was one of the many spies employed in harbour surveillance. In the run-up to the intended invasion it was vital to be aware of troop deployment around the ports and the defensive facilities there.

Marie was apprehended after speaking to a man painting the block of flats where she was employed. The man later told the police that Mrs Ingram had said she was a German and loyal to the current regime, and that the war had been brought about by Jews, Communists and Freemasons.

In her opinion, Churchill was 'a disaster to the real 100 per cent British people' and Britain would be better off under a fascist regime. 'The Germans will be in England within three weeks,' she said. 'The Royal Family and the Cabinet will be publicly executed and Oswald Mosley will become ruler of Britain under German control.'

Sir Oswald Mosley, founder of the British Union of Fascists, with four bodyguards. Ingram believed Mosley would become ruler of Britain under German control.

Marie extolled the virtues of the BUF, invited the painter and decorator to join, and gave him Watts' address. He went straight to the police station. Then, under the auspices of Special Branch, he attended BUF meetings where he was told: 'Inform us what boats are leaving, what cargoes they carry, how many men are in the troopships.' This information, he was told, was transmitted to other agents, by coded cable or telephone.

Marie also boasted that she was getting hold of good information which she sent out of the country. She asked the painter to look out for disenchanted men who would be ready to join the LDV, as it was important to have as many armed conspirators as possible to help the German forces when the invasion began.

Corporal Baron also provided valuable information. After infiltrating the local BUF, he was told by Swift that their main job was to assist the German paratroopers who would land in July or August. The exact date was to be transmitted to him by radio. Baron contacted Whitehall and the authorities pounced.

In Marie Ingram's house, a photograph of Hitler and two swastika flags were found, along with a translation of a speech by Hitler and a book containing elementary exercises in German. At her trial at the Old Bailey in June 1940, Marie admitted spying and tried to use the court as a rostrum for her Nazi views. She boasted about German victories and said the court could convict her and give her whatever sentence they liked – she would be free within a month 'when the swastika will fly over London'.

The naval officer who employed her was working on the design of mines, and his house overlooked the Solent, so she had a clear view of the ships coming and going. It was evident that she was also the brains behind recruiting fresh members of the BUF (the organization was outlawed in May 1940).

Marie was sentenced to ten years' penal servitude. Swift got 14 years, while Watts was discharged due to lack of evidence.

When Marie was taken down, she said: 'Ten years! . . . I shall be free in a few weeks, when the *Führer* gets here.' She left the court with a defiant 'Heil Hitler!' Needless to say, she was not free in a few weeks and her appeal, heard on 27 August 1940, was dismissed.

CHAPTER 6

THE BEAUTIFUL SPY

While Dorothy O'Grady and Marie Ingram had used marriage to put themselves in a position to spy, Vera von Schalburg was a true siren who used her sex appeal to forward her career in espionage. Like O'Grady and Anna Wolkoff, she ended up in Aylesbury prison.

Vera was known by various aliases – Vera Eriksen (sometimes spelt Erichsen or Eriksson), Vera von Stein, Vera de Cottani de Chalbur, Vera Staritzky and Vera von Wedel, née Schalburg. Her birth name von Schalburg was also rendered variously as Shalburg or Schalbourg. But the one thing everyone who met her agreed on was that she was beautiful. In 1972, *Abwehr* spymaster Nikolaus Ritter, aka Dr Rantzau, wrote in his memoir *Deckname Dr Rantzau* that she was 'one of our most remarkable and beautiful female agents. There was hardly a man who was not entranced by her'. Her Slavic good looks gave her an air of mystery that sent men's pulses racing. Former OSS (Office of Strategic Services) officer Tom Moon called her a 'beautiful Nordic blonde'. But whether she was blond or not is a matter of some contention.

MYSTERIOUS ORIGINS

Like many spies, Vera had an appropriately murky background. It is generally thought that she was born in Siberia, although some maintain her birthplace

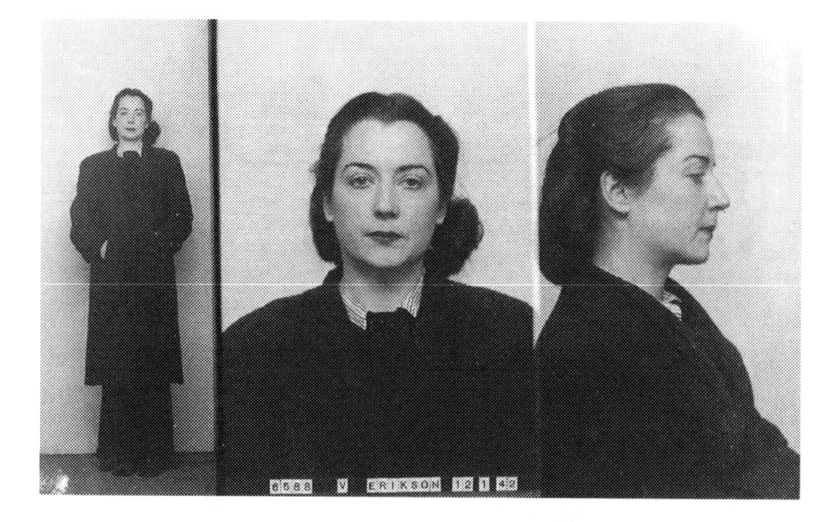

Vera von Schalburg (in this mugshot she is identified as V Erikson) was a true femme fatale – it was said that 'there was hardly a man who was not entranced by her'.

was Kiev in Ukraine, as her mother was a member of the Polish-Ukrainian aristocracy. Her father was, perhaps, an expatriate Danish industrialist. Her MI5 file does little to clear the matter up, saying: 'Her origin is something of a mystery, and her parentage doubtful. It is evident that she is partly non-Aryan. She claims that her parents' name was STARITZKY, and that she was adopted in Russia by Russians of German origin called von Schalbourg, who left that country at the time of the Revolution in 1918 and settled in Denmark where they assumed Danish nationality.'

Moon said Vera was the 'daughter of a Russian naval officer who died fighting the Bolsheviks'. There are also tales that she was born illegitimately and adopted at an early age, and that both her real parents were Jewish.

One source said she was born on 23 November 1907, though when she was captured Vera told MI5 that she was born in December 1912. The truth may remain a mystery, as beautiful women tend to be mendacious about their age – and spies lie. Hungarian military historian Ladislas Farago said she was 'the daughter of a Baltic aristocrat and Tsarist naval officer' and her real name was Vera or Viola de Witte.

According to one account she grew up in great luxury at the Tsar's court in St Petersburg. After her father was murdered by the Bolsheviks during the revolution, her mother appealed to an old boyfriend who had become a Communist official. He provided money, tickets and the appropriate paperwork for the family to flee to Paris. Somehow, in the early 1920s, they had ended up in Denmark where they bought a farm on the Jutland peninsula.

It was clear that Vera was well-educated and cultured. She had a wide knowledge of music, literature and history, speaking Russian as a mother tongue, as well as German, French, English and Danish and she was conversant with Latin.

By 1924, Vera was in Paris. Her brother Christian von Schalburg remained in Denmark, where he became a soldier attached to the Royal Life Guards, an infantry regiment of the Danish army; he went on to become a leading Nazi. It has been suggested that he joined the *Waffen-SS* to avenge the gang rape of his sister Vera by the Bolsheviks when she was six years old, which he had been forced to watch while tied to a chair. Fighting with the 5th SS Panzer Division

Wiking as an *SS-Hauptsturmführer* (captain), he was killed in action in Russia in June 1942. At Himmler's instigation the name of the *Germanische SS* was changed to *Schalburgkorps* in his honour.

A SEDUCTIVE AIR

After training at a ballet school in Paris, Vera became a professional ballerina under Anna Pavlova. She toured England in 1927 with the Trefilova ballet company, then appeared with the Ballets Russes in Paris. To make money on the side, she appeared at the Folies Bergère and the Moulin Rouge, as well as in cabaret.

Her sister-in-law later said that, on a visit to Germany, Vera fell pregnant by a submarine captain. Ladislas Farago had a different account: 'While she was still in finishing school,' he said, 'she became infatuated with a much older Frenchman, and when her mother refused to permit her to marry him, they eloped . . . Abandoned by her French lover, she was left to the not inconsiderable resources of a beautiful and charming young woman with a seductive air. But somehow Vera felt more comfortable in the gutter than in the drawing rooms. She drifted from bed to bed, danced in shabby cabarets, and lived with a succession of squalid swains in the wretched poverty of the Montparnasse slums.'

Along the way, she attracted the attention of Count Sergei Ignatieff, a professional spy working for the White Russians and, probably, a double agent also working for the Reds. As a sideline, he used and trafficked cocaine. Vera worked as a drug mule for him, carrying the dope to various European cities and possibly became an addict too. There is also the suggestion that she spied on the Communists in France for him.

In 1937, they were living together in Brussels and may have even married. The relationship was short-lived, however. When she broke it off, she claimed that he had tried to stab her. According to Vera, Sergei returned to Russia where he was executed as a spy by the Soviets. Meanwhile she went to work for the *Abwehr*. She said she was recruited by a Danish engineer called Captain Winding Christensen, aka Dr Kaiser and also thought to use the alias Jørgen Børresen. He introduced her to Dr Rantzau – that is, Nikolaus Ritter of the German military intelligence. A committed Nazi, Christensen went on to experiment on the hormone treatment of homosexuals in concentration camps.

SPYING ON COMMUNISTS

Vera told MI5 she had discovered she was on a Nazi blacklist, suspected of spying for the Soviet Union. So she contacted her brother who arranged a meeting with Major Hilmar Dierks, a senior intelligence officer at the *Abwehr*'s Hamburg office. Dierks took her on as an agent to spy on the Communists in Belgium. Vera became his mistress; again, they may possibly have married and there was an unsubstantiated claim that she had a daughter by him, but details of her love life remain unclear. She told MI5 that she was married to a Zum Stuhrig (an alias used by Hilmar Dierks), but she could not recall the location of the register office, nor the age of the groom, and finally admitted that perhaps they had not been married after all.

In another version of events, the *Abwehr* officer concerned was Hans Friedrich von Wedel, who Vera married in 1937 when she was 24 and he was 60. She was widowed after a car accident in 1940. But Wedel was another alias used by Dierks. The conflicting accounts of Vera's activities in the murky world of continental espionage were dogged by multiple aliases, but it was clear that she was more than she seemed.

Yet another tale describes her mother taking her to Brussels where she worked in a Russian restaurant. Striking out on her own, she moved to London where she worked in nightclubs and brushed up her English, only to be drawn back to Paris by a love affair with a Frenchman. They became a double act on the cabaret circuit, while Russian friends persuaded or blackmailed her into working for the secret police.

Again, her stage performances attracted admirers. A Herr Mueller plied her with champagne. He purported to be a wealthy German businessman, exporting batteries to France and the Low Countries. In a fit of jealousy, the lover who had been accompanying her attacked Vera with a knife. Mueller overpowered him and he was arrested. Back at his hotel, Mueller revealed that his real name was

Hilmar Dierks and he was with the naval section of the *Abwehr*. He introduced her to Karl Drücke – sometime spelt Druegge – and Robert Petter. With Dierks, they were running a spy network in the Low Countries and France that would help to secure German victory there in 1940.

Vera moved into Dierks' flat and they travelled around Europe together. In 1938 or 1939, she travelled to London again to make contact with German spies already in place and with other Nazi sympathizers. It seems she was also doing some work for Dierks' colleague Nikolaus Ritter, who was engaged in gathering intelligence for the *Luftwaffe*. She stayed with the Duchess of Château-Thierry, one of Ritter's contacts in London, who knew a number of RAF officers. The plan was for the duchess to open a tea room and invite officers so that Vera could exercise her charms on them. There are suggestions that Vera photographed sensitive documents she obtained there. She was also to keep note of the officers' comings and goings, and try to recruit them for the *Abwehr*.

LIAISONS

One of Vera's contacts was Major William Herbert Mackenzie, who retained an army rank because he had served in the RAF's precursor, the Royal Flying Corps. They met at a party at the duchess's in the summer of 1939. Mackenzie told MI5 that he had slept with Vera at least six times and described her as a 'very beautiful girl, who was also clever, but did not say very much'. There were other male visitors in uniform, according to the duchess. Also on hand to entertain young gentlemen from the forces was the young and pretty Countess Costenza, who was seen out with officers at expense bars and clubs. The duchess said she was a 'decent girl' but 'not the style of girl I would take about', while MI5 described her as 'another international hanger-on to London Society . . . [who] appeared to have a certain personal attraction, but . . . was no Mata Hari'. Nevertheless, intelligence expert Nigel West insists she was an *Abwehr* agent who, according to the security files, had a great many aliases.

Another member of the team was Lady Mayo, who was engaged to a French soldier. According to MI5, Lady Mayo 'appears to be consorting with officers in Scotland and encouraging some shady young women who are with her to relieve these officers of all their worldly wealth. She is a drunken and dissolute woman.'

Some seem to have been agents ostensibly working for Ritter. Sensitive material was discussed and, when war came, the Duchess of Château-Thierry and Countess Costenza were interned.

It appears that during her stay with the duchess, Vera gave birth to a son who she sent to an orphanage in Essex. There has been considerable speculation about who the father was.

Vera returned to the continent on the outbreak of war. The duchess said that Vera was in love with a Belgian and urged her to return to her mother in Brussels. The Belgian in question was thought to be Drücke. Vera was later thought to have been pregnant by him.

Back in Brussels in August 1940, Dierks told Vera that he had to leave her to go on a secret mission. She accused him of making up a story in order to run off with another woman. But he said he was going to England with Drücke and Petter: 'You know that I'm an expert on naval matters, and I have been ordered to sabotage naval installations in England.' It appears she did not believe him. When he came home from work the next day, he had to break down the door and found her unconscious. She had swallowed half a bottle of sleeping tablets. He rushed her to hospital, where she recovered.

OPERATION HUMMER NORD

The *Abwehr* rethought its plans. *Generalleutnant* Erwin von Lahousen suggested that Dierks take Vera with him on his assignment. The *Abwehr* had contacted an Italian countess in London. Before the war, she had inherited a small property in the Bavarian Alps, but German currency restrictions meant she had difficulty selling it and transferring the money out of the country. The *Abwehr* facilitated this on the understanding that the countess would transfer her allegiance from Mussolini to Hitler. Vera would play the part of the countess's long-lost niece and provide a base for Dierks' sabotage activities.

The operation had to be put on hold briefly while Vera attended the *Abwehr*'s training school in Hamburg to learn Morse code, radio transmission, microphotography and simple sabotage. On 2 September 1940, the night before the operation designated Operation Hummer Nord was to go into action, the *Abwehr* gave the participants – Vera, Dierks, Drücke and Petter – a farewell party at the Lowenbrau Restaurant. It seems they drank too much Bavarian beer laced with schnapps. Driving home, their vehicle overturned and Dierks was killed. The other three escaped with minor injuries.

The following morning, when he learned what had happened, Lahousen was tempted to call off the mission. But Operation Sea Lion – the invasion of Britain – was now overdue and Hitler was desperate for an accurate picture of what was going on across the Channel. The *Abwehr* still had three trained agents and a viable plan. That night, they were flown to Stavanger in Norway to make passage for Scotland.

Schalburg would travel as Vera Erikson, a Danish national. Drücke would assume the identity of François de Deeker, a French refugee who had arrived in Britain from Belgium, while Petter would be Swiss national Werner Heinrich Walti. All three were given addresses in Sussex Gardens in the London district of Paddington. They were issued with false papers and rations books; British clothes found in the UK embassy in Oslo after the rapid departure of the British legation the previous April; wirelesses, maps, and lists of people they should contact in Britain together with potential sabotage targets.

On the night of 29 September, they boarded a flying boat bound for the Moray Firth in north-east Scotland. The plan was to paddle ashore in a rubber dinghy, carrying with them three bicycles taken from the cellar of the British consulate in Bergen. Then they were to cycle 600 miles (966 km) southwards to London.

The flying boat landed off the coast at Port Gordon, but the sea was rough, the bicycles were ditched along the way, and the three agents landed their dinghy on the Scottish shore more than a little wet. Without their bicycles they would have to take the train to London. They decided to split up. Petter, who spoke good English, headed east towards Buckie, while Schalburg and Drücke stayed together and travelled west towards Port Gordon, carrying a large suitcase and two smaller bags.

Both stations were on the main line from Inverness to Aberdeen. From Aberdeen, Petter could catch a connection to Edinburgh, then on to England, while Schalburg and Drücke would take a westbound train to Forres. From there, they believed they could board a train through the central Highlands to Perth, then on to London.

Under wartime regulations, station names and road signs had been removed in the hope of confusing an invading force. So when Schalburg and Drücke arrived at Port Gordon at around 7.30 a.m., they had to ask where they were. The presence of two strangers at that time in the morning was already suspicious. Asked where they were going, Drücke pointed to a timetable on the wall showing the train times to Forres – which he pronounced 'forest'. He then opened his wallet and pulled out banknotes, far too many for a standard third-class ticket for a 25-mile (40 km) journey. The station master John Donald then noticed that the cuffs of Drücke's trousers were wet, as were Schalburg's shoes and stockings, and it had not rained in Port Gordon that morning.

While the porter, John Geddes, kept the two strangers talking, Donald called the village policeman PC Bob Grieve. When he arrived, Grieve asked to see the pair's identity cards – the National Registration card which UK residents were obliged to carry during wartime. The cards that the *Abwehr* had provided were poor imitations of the real thing – the handwritten details were in a distinctly Germanic script, and they didn't carry the immigration stamp seen on the cards issued to refugees.

Grieve escorted the strangers to the police cottage in Stewart Street, where he called Inspector John Simpson to report the incident, while his wife made them a cup of tea. When Simpson arrived he began questioning Drücke – to no avail. Schalburg pointed out that Drücke could not speak English. Simpson searched him and found he was carrying a box containing 19 rounds of ammunition. He then turned his attention to Schalburg who said she was a widow from Denmark. Simpson examined their ID cards again and explained their shortcomings. The couple were taken to the police station in Buckie where the questioning continued. Vera said that they had arrived in a small boat from Bergen and had stayed the previous night in a hotel in Banff, 20 miles (32 km) further along the coast. Then they had taken a taxi which had dropped them a mile from Port Gordon, leaving them to continue on foot. Her story made no sense: Banff was on the same train line as Port Gordon and

Buckie; and why had they chosen to walk a mile with a heavy suitcase when they could have taken the taxi all the way?

INCRIMINATING EVIDENCE

When Major Peter Perfect, the Scottish regional security officer, arrived, their bags were searched. They were carrying a radio transmitter, batteries, a loaded Mauser revolver, graph paper, code sheets, a list of RAF bases, a half-eaten German sausage of a type unobtainable in the UK, and a knife and torch stamped '*Hergestellt in Böhmen*' – 'Made in Bohemia'. Drücke was carrying £327, the equivalent of £18,000/$23,000 today, and Vera had £72 (£4,000/$5,100) in her purse.

Later that morning, the coastguard spotted something floating 400 yards offshore. It proved to be the pump used to inflate the rubber dinghy. The punctured dinghy was found partially submerged nearby, along with an aluminium oar identified by an RAF officer as belonging to a German seaplane. It was clear how the two spies had arrived; the question for the authorities was, were there any more of them?

Petter had made it to Buckie at 7.45 a.m., bought a ticket for Edinburgh and caught the 9.58 a.m. train to Aberdeen. No one had tried to stop him, but the presence of a stranger on board the train was noted. The police in Aberdeen confirmed that the stranger had caught a connection to Edinburgh at 1 p.m.

Arriving at Edinburgh Waverley station at 4.30 p.m., Petter was told that the next train to London was not until 10 p.m. So he checked his bag into the left-luggage office and went to have a shave and something to eat, then decided to spend the rest of the afternoon watching a film.

Having missed the suspect when he arrived at Waverley station, Scottish Special Branch located his suitcase in the left-luggage office and noticed a white tidemark, indicating it had recently been dipped in seawater. Inside was a radio transmitter of German manufacture and a codebook, along with a Swiss passport with no UK entry stamp, some food, a revolver loaded with six rounds, a box containing another 20 rounds, £190 (£10,000/$12,800) in cash and maps showing the locations of airfields. The maps were supposedly on loan to

Captain M. Holroyd of MI14, a branch of Military Intelligence specializing in Germany. When Petter turned up to reclaim his suitcase, the police were waiting. Confronted, Petter pulled a flick knife, something not seen in the UK before. When he was disarmed, a Mauser was found in his pocket.

Two pieces of paper were found. One had the name of Major Harlinghausen on it; he was the officer commanding the German air force in Norway. The other carried the name of another officer, Felf, in the 10th Air Force Corps and that of 'Andersen, Bergen, Hotel Nord' – presumably a contact in Norway.

The three spies were taken to Camp O2O, the interrogation centre at Latchmere House in south London where they were questioned by Lieutenant Colonel William Hinchley-Cooke. After lengthy interrogation, they finally admitted that their reason for coming to Britain was to report on shipping and to sabotage air bases prior to the invasion (although by that stage Operation Sea Lion had been called off). In March 1941, all three spies signed confessions.

While Drücke maintained his cover story that he was a French refugee named François de Deeker, he admitted he had been promised passage to England provided he carried a radio which he was to hand to a man outside an ABC Cinema in London. Petter continued to claim that he was a Swiss citizen named Werner Walti, but said he had been coerced into working for the Nazis. After he helped a Jewish diamond merchant escape, he had been arrested by the Gestapo and beaten up. They would have sent him to a concentration camp, he said, unless he delivered a suitcase to someone in England.

VERA'S STORY

Vera kept up the pretence that she was the niece of an Italian countess who lived in Kensington, though eventually she admitted to having been sent as a spy. She said she had taken the assignment to escape from the Germans. When she reached London, she had intended to contact her friend Major Mackenzie, who had told her he knew someone in the secret service, so she could give herself up.

Vera said her orders had been to take a room in the Dorchester and 'hand over the wireless set to a man called Wilkinson, who was tall and thin with fair hair, who would call on her at the Dorchester Hotel within the next five days'. Then she was to find a room in Soho and stay there until the invasion, which was only weeks away. The MI5 interrogators did not fully believe her story as they discovered that she and Drücke had known each other for two years.

Although Drücke had two-timed her with the proprietress of a boarding house where they met in The Hague, Vera had fallen in love with him because 'he was nice to me'. During her interrogation, the mention of his name brought tears to her eyes and she said he was 'the only man I have ever loved, and shall ever love'.

Refusing to be turned, Drücke and Petter were charged under the 1940 Treachery Act. They stood trial in the Old Bailey that June, and the jury took just a few minutes to return a guilty verdict. They were hanged on 6 August in Wandsworth prison.

Vera Schalburg did not appear in the dock. This led to speculation that her son's father was an important figure in the British establishment. Following her arrest, she had asked to see the boy and he was brought from Essex. She was plainly distressed and there were fears she would go on a hunger strike. She was transferred to Holloway women's prison, where Dorothy O'Grady was on remand. Vera had a miscarriage while she was there; the child was thought to have been Drücke's.

Later, Vera dropped her cover story and in October admitted to spying for the GRU, Soviet military intelligence. Six months after her colleagues were hanged, she admitted that she was also working for the *Abwehr*. She said that Petter was going to set up his own espionage ring and a Norwegian sabotage expert named Gunnar Edvardson was to have joined them with a trunk-load of equipment. When Edvardson arrived in England on 25 October 1940 with two others, he walked to the nearest police station and handed himself in.

STOOL PIGEON

Vera was treated so extraordinarily leniently that it was thought she must have known a lot about the inner workings of the *Abwehr*. She was sent to stay with the family of well-known actor Peter Ustinov whose father, 'Klop', worked for MI5 during the war. Agreeing to co-operate, she was interned for the rest of the war and thought to have been used as a stool pigeon, reporting on other prisoners at Aylesbury, on the Isle of Man, and at other internment camps in the UK.

Back in Berlin *Generalleutnant* Lahousen had little idea about what had become of the agents sent on Operation Hummer Nord. Months later, a Swiss paper reported that a Swiss national had been arrested in Scotland, so Lahousen knew the operation had been a failure. Five years later, when Lahousen and other *Abwehr* chiefs were themselves interned at Bad Nenndorf camp near Hanover, he learned more.

During Lahousen's interrogation, a British colonel told him that Petter had been hanged because he had tried to shoot a British police officer when he was captured. He did not know what had happened to Drücke.

Lahousen then asked what had happened to Vera – or the 'Beautiful Spy' as the British called her.

'She came over to us,' said the colonel. 'If you ever want to see her again, well, I would have a look around the Isle of Wight. I think you might find her there – with another name, of course, and nobody has the slightest idea of her background.'

Sometime later, Vera's elderly mother received a phone call in Copenhagen from a woman with a husky voice, who said: 'Frau von Schalburg? I just want you to know that Vera is still alive, and maybe you will see her one day.'

And the Countess Costenza? It turned out that she had been a British agent all along.

CHAPTER 7

THE EXOTIC DANCER

Known simply as Adrienne, she was said to be the cleverest spy in the Balkans during World War II.

Adrienne began her career in espionage as a dancer in the Budapest cabaret, also known as the Papagello. There in 1940 she met the new US ambassador to Bulgaria, 49-year-old George Howard Earle. As US minister to Austria in 1933, he had been one of the first to warn the Roosevelt administration of the dangers of the Nazi regime.

A black-eyed beauty, Adrienne was quick-witted and intelligent with an amazing facility for languages. She was comfortable with all levels of society. Her father was highly regarded and lived variously in Monte Carlo, Bucharest and Budapest, but largely in the Latin quarter of Paris. Her aunt was Magda Lupescu, whose affair with King Carol of Romania led to his abdication. They later married.

THE DOUBLE AGENT

Adrienne knew most of the fascists in the Balkans and Earle, whose mission was to keep Bulgaria out of the war, realized that she would make a useful spy. He also found her beautiful, amusing and fascinating. He took her with him to

Sofia, where he put her up in the Hotel Bulgarie, before renting a house for her near one of the city's famous parks. A man named Diello, who claimed to be an Albanian journalist, visited her there. Diello had been recruited by the German intelligence service, run by SS chief Ernst Kaltenbrunner. He turned Adrienne and she became a double agent, spying on Earle for the Nazis.

In March 1941, Bulgaria signed the Tripartite Pact and joined the Axis bloc. Earle was not a great success as an ambassador in Sofia and, in the same year, after getting into a brawl with a group of German businessmen in a nightclub, he was recalled. However, in January 1943, he returned to Europe as naval attaché in Istanbul, where his brief was to keep an eye on the situation in Bulgaria, hoping to play a role if it broke away from the Axis.

In this, Earle believed Adrienne would be an invaluable aid. He tried to get her into Turkey but she was stopped at the border, so she returned to the Papagallo in Budapest. One night, her cabaret act over, she was visited in her dressing room by a man who brought greetings from Diello, who was then in Ankara. The stranger was one of Kaltenbrunner's agents in Budapest.

Adrienne was eager to get back together with Diello, but the Germans wanted her to resume her relationship with Earle. They used their influence with the Turkish government who, this time, admitted her to the country.

UNDERCOVER IN TURKEY

On her arrival in Ankara, Adrienne was surprised to find her 'Albanian' lover working as a valet to the chief councillor of the German embassy. In fact, he was now German Intelligence's chief agent in Turkey. Adrienne did not understand that various intelligence agencies in Germany were as keen to spy on one another as on the enemy. The German legation in Ankara was particularly sensitive. The ambassador was former chancellor Franz von Papen. Kaltenbrunner did not trust von Papen and suspected that he was holding secret negotiations with the Allies.

Adrienne went on to Istanbul to monitor Earle's movements. Fortunately, Earle also made frequent trips to Ankara to see the American ambassador there so Adrienne would accompany him and seize the opportunity to have secret trysts with Diello. During these she would impart all the information she had gathered through her association with Earle, which Diello transmitted to Berlin.

THE GO-BETWEEN

Diello then started working as valet to the British ambassador, Sir Hughe Knatchbull-Hugessen. The results were initially disappointing. The ambassador was highly security conscious, tight-lipped and left no papers lying around. Then one day Diello reported that there was to be a meeting of the Big Three – Churchill, Roosevelt and Stalin – at which the final defeat of Hitler would be planned.

In Berlin, the news was a bombshell. If the story was confirmed, Diello would need to discover where the meeting was being held. The spy asked the Germans for $30,000 in US currency. For several days, German Intelligence trawled through the foreign newspapers for confirmation. When none was found, Kaltenbrunner sent a handful of his best men to Turkey to contact Diello, but as he could not be seen talking to Germans, Adrienne was employed as a go-between.

She passed on the message that the Germans were willing to pay Diello if the story was confirmed and he could keep them informed of the progress of the meeting. She reported back that Diello had made a copy of the key to the ambassador's safe. He could gain access to it at night, photograph any significant documents and return them without being detected.

Confirmation that there was to be a meeting of the Big Three came from a German agent in the United States who reported that Roosevelt and his aides had left the country on the USS *Iowa*. The $30,000 was sent to Diello via Adrienne, who was also paid for her part in what was now being called Operation Cicero.

The meeting of the Big Three was to be in Tehran. On the way, Churchill and Roosevelt met up in Cairo where they fell out over the conduct of the war. Diello informed his paymasters that Roosevelt wanted to invade north-west Europe with an amphibious assault from the Channel (in what would eventually become the Normandy landings), known as Operation Overlord. Churchill vehemently opposed this. The Western Allies had already taken Sicily and landed in mainland Italy. Churchill wanted to continue the attack on what he called the 'soft underbelly' of Europe with landings in Greece. That way the Allies could sweep up through the Balkans and cut off the Red Army before it reached Germany. Otherwise, he argued, Eastern and Central Europe would fall to the Soviets. The Nazis were delighted with the news that there was a deep disagreement between the Western Allies.

Further news came via Adrienne that Stalin had agreed with Roosevelt that the Western Allies should open a second front in France. Stalin argued that operations in the Mediterranean were a mere sideshow. Adrienne told the Germans that Diello would deliver full details of all the meetings at Tehran for a further $100,000, which was forthcoming.

When the funds arrived by plane, Adrienne handed over a full report on the negotiations at Tehran. There are indications that the information finding its way into Diello's hands had been planted by the Allies. As no invasion of France was possible without using Britain as a base, the report gave the impression that Churchill would veto the French landings and insist on an attack through the Balkans. Instead of sending them to France, the Germans left some reserves in the Balkans in case of an Allied assault.

This did not matter to Adrienne and Diello. They made off with the money and disappeared to South America. But they may not have been quite as clever as they thought as it seems that at least some of the cash they were paid was counterfeit. The other protagonist in this story, George Howard Earle, went on to serve as assistant governor of American Samoa.

CHAPTER 8

IL DUCE'S DARLING

The French actress, journalist and spy Madeleine Coraboeuf (later Magda de Fontanges) was born in 1905, the daughter of French painter Jean Coraboeuf. Her mother died when she was just seven. After a short-lived marriage to a policeman named Laferrière, she moved from her home in western France to Paris where she took the surname Fontanges after one of Louis XIV's mistresses and became an artist's model.

She embarked on a stage career, playing minor roles at the Odéon and then at a well-known music hall. This gave her an entrée into society. She moved in political circles and, using her connections, became a journalist for a Parisian evening newspaper. When Mussolini had proclaimed the new Italian empire, following the invasion of Abyssinia (Ethiopia) in 1936, she went to Rome as a special correspondent and secured an interview with him. She also became his lover.

'One hour with you and Ethiopia means nothing to me,' he declared.

MUSSOLINI THE RAT

Mussolini was promiscuous and fickle. After the affair was over, Magda was found in her room, suffering from an overdose of Veronal (a barbiturate). The Italian police searched the room and seized a diary and a number of photographs.

Madeleine Coraboeuf (later Magda de Fontanges) leaving her Paris flat after police seized her memoirs in 1937.

Magda was penniless at the time and was given £150 (£10,000/$12,800 today) to cover her hotel bill and a ticket back to Paris. One of her friends told *Paris Soir*: 'Her passion is intrigue. Her adventures in political circles were numberless.'

In 1937, she shot and wounded the French ambassador to Rome, Comte Charles de Chambrun, at the Gare du Nord. She accused him of thwarting her love affair with *Il Duce*. The police arrested her and, in her apartment, found a large framed photograph of Mussolini, inscribed 'To Mme Magda Fontanges' and signed 'Mussolini', along with a diary containing the names of various celebrities she had met in Rome.

While on remand in La Petite Roquette women's prison, she fretted about her pet poodle who had been left at the flat. 'My poor dog has had nothing to eat for 24 hours,' she said. 'I must have him with me or he will die of hunger.' She was so insistent that the dog was brought to her and she was allowed to keep it with her. The poodle dined on her prison food, while she survived on biscuits and a glass of champagne. When bailed, she was arrested while attempting to flee over the border into Spain.

Magda was found guilty of the shooting, but as the comte had suffered only minor injuries, she was fined 100 francs (less than £1). She was then barred from entry into the United States where she was under contract to appear at a New York nightclub. Mussolini laughed, but he did not find it so funny when the impecunious Magda sold her kiss-and-tell story 'I Was Mussolini's Mistress' to the American press.

AGENT NO. 8006

To ensure that he would have no further trouble from her, Mussolini arranged for Magda to work as an agent for the Gestapo. As Agent No. 8006, she was paid $42.50 (around £600/$770 today) a month plus expenses to act as a German spy in Brussels and Marseille. The arrangement was terminated in 1943 when she refused to return to Italy to discover whether Mussolini and Italian Foreign Minister Ciano were trying to make a secret peace deal with the Allies.

In 1947, she appeared in front of a military tribunal in Bordeaux, charged with supplying intelligence to the enemy. She looked haggard and shabby, wearing an old tweed jacket and a divided shirt, her hair unwashed and uncombed. Endeavouring to impress the court, she recounted the names of the French ministers she had slept with. She admitted selling information about them to the Italians, just as she had sold information about Mussolini and other Italians to the French, and information about the Italians and the French to the Germans.

Magda Fontanges was sentenced to 15 years' hard labour, had her property confiscated, was to suffer 'national indignity' for the rest of her life and was barred from Paris and other large cities in France for 20 years. As she left the court, she said: 'My only regret is that I wasn't hanged with the *Duce* instead of his last mistress, Clara Petacci.'

She was released from prison for health reasons in 1952, to remain under house arrest in the town of Melun. But, flouting the conditions of her sentence, she moved to Paris where she planned to manage a bar. She was arrested and sent back to prison. Freed again in 1955, she was then accused of stealing a valuable painting by Maurice Utrillo from her lawyer and suspected lover. The press said she had a grudge against lawyers.

Magda was found dead in her apartment in Geneva in 1960 after swallowing an overdose of sleeping tablets.

CHAPTER 9

THE PEACH OF PEARL HARBOR

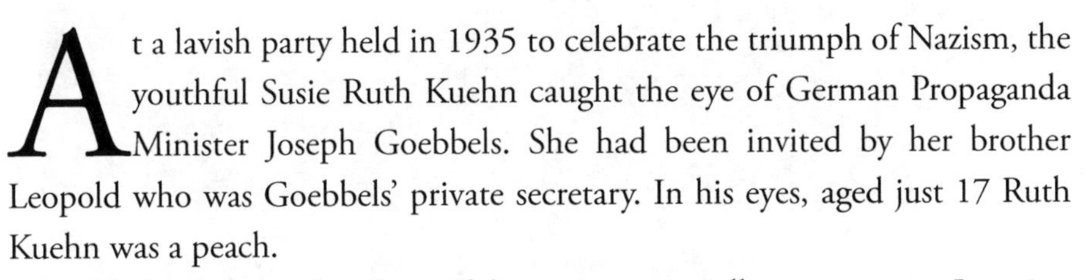

At a lavish party held in 1935 to celebrate the triumph of Nazism, the youthful Susie Ruth Kuehn caught the eye of German Propaganda Minister Joseph Goebbels. She had been invited by her brother Leopold who was Goebbels' private secretary. In his eyes, aged just 17 Ruth Kuehn was a peach.

Goebbels was partial to beautiful women, especially young ones. Ignoring his long-suffering wife Magda, Goebbels zeroed in on Ruth. He danced with her the whole evening and they got a little drunk together. In Nazi Germany it was considered an accolade to sleep with the propaganda minister and Ruth joined his stable of mistresses. This undoubtedly provoked a certain amount of jealousy among the other women, and Magda, of course, and Ruth became an inconvenience.

MOVE TO HAWAII

Karl Haushofer had served as a general on the Western Front in World War I and was a close friend of Hitler's deputy Rudolf Hess. He took it upon himself to forge closer relations between Germany and Japan. At the time, the

Joseph Goebbels (pictured here with his wife Magda) danced all night with Susie Ruth Kuehn and they got a little drunk together. Goebbels was an incorrigible womanizer.

Japanese said they needed European recruits to carry out espionage work for the *Kenpeitai*, Japan's equivalent of the SS. All of a sudden, Goebbels saw a convenient way of getting Ruth out of the country.

Ruth's stepfather, Dr Bernard Julius Otto Kuehn, had served in the Imperial German Navy during World War I as a midshipman on board a cruiser. His ship had been sunk by a British battleship in 1915. Taken prisoner, he learned English in a prisoner-of-war camp.

After the scuttling of the German fleet in 1919 and the signing of the Versailles Treaty that restricted its reconstruction, there was essentially no German navy to which he could return. Instead, Kuehn studied medicine. As a student, he joined various nationalist organizations and became an early Nazi convert. Heinrich Himmler was a personal friend and, when the Nazis came to power, Kuehn joined the Gestapo. He claimed that he was promised the position of chief of police in one of Germany's major cities. Instead, Goebbels decided that Ruth together with Bernard Kuehn, his wife Friedel and their six-year-old son Hans be posted to Hawaii.

Bernard's cover story was that he was a linguist with an interest in Hawaii, even though he spent his time learning Japanese. He and Ruth travelled around the islands, ostensibly studying the topography and the old stone houses of the early settlers. Bernard wrote a number of articles on early German settlers on the islands, which were published in Germany.

As Hawaii was home to the US Pacific Fleet, the Kuehn family also took to the water, swimming, sailing and motor-boating. Being young and attractive, Ruth was bombarded with invitations to parties. She dated servicemen and wheedled information out of them. She ran a beauty parlour and gleaned information from the casual talk of her clients, the wives and girlfriends of US military personnel. Asked what she thought of the Nazis, Ruth claimed she knew nothing about them, saying: 'I was too young when we left Germany.'

Bernard sent the information they collected to the Japanese consulate. Dr Haushofer also wanted copies of his reports. As the Kuehns were working for Berlin and Tokyo, they insisted on being paid by both employers. During their first three years on the islands, around $70,000 was transmitted to their bank in Honolulu by the Rotterdam Bank Association; Friedel and Ruth also made trips to Japan as couriers and returned with cash. Neither the FBI nor naval intelligence took any notice, although the Kuehns had an expensive home hung with beautiful art and adorned with exquisite silver, with no obvious means of paying for it. Neighbours assumed that they had large investments in Germany and the Netherlands. Eventually, the FBI became suspicious of their dubious contacts among the German and Japanese communities, but no real evidence of their spying came to light.

MOVEMENTS OF THE PACIFIC FLEET

At first, the intelligence Ruth provided was little more than tittle-tattle, but as she grew more glamorous and desirable, her stepfather encouraged her to raise her game and she began dating officers. At home, the Kuehns entertained American military personnel lavishly and expressed an interest in their work. Ruth, particularly, knew how to handle men and get what she wanted out of them.

After they had been spying for some time, Ruth and her stepfather were invited to a meeting with the Japanese vice-consul, Otojiro Okuda. The information they had been providing was good, he said, but now Japan needed detailed information on the deployment of the Pacific Fleet. They would be paid well for it. Ruth asked for $40,000 (about £600,000/$770,000 today). They negotiated a down payment of $14,000 with the balance to be paid on delivery.

Supposedly to find a quiet place for his studies, Bernard took a second home overlooking Pearl Harbor. An elaborate signalling system had been worked out. A light shining in the dormer window of their house at Oahu, from 9 p.m. to 10 p.m., meant that the aircraft carriers had sailed. A linen sheet hanging on a clothes line at their home on Lanikai Beach between 10 and 11 a.m. meant the battle force had left the harbour. There were eight such codes which could be used in various combinations.

To gather further information, Ruth became engaged to a high-ranking officer stationed at Pearl Harbor. The couple would take daily strolls through the fortified parts of the harbour that were normally off limits. Ruth's brother Hans, then aged ten, accompanied them dressed in a sailor suit. He was invited on board ships or into the gun emplacements round the harbour where soldiers and sailors would explain how their equipment worked. He would be debriefed by their father when he got home. Ruth also bought a pair of powerful binoculars so she could keep an eye on the fleet's comings and goings.

Thanks to the Kuehns, the Japanese now had a detailed chart of the anchorage and details of the ships moored there. On 1 December 1941, Ruth completed the picture by spending the night with her fiancé. When the Japanese attacked Pearl Harbor on the morning of 7 December, they knew what their main objectives were; Ruth guided them to their targets using a torch flashed from the dormer window. The devastating results are a matter of history.

The Japanese consul had arranged for a submarine to come and pick the Kuehns up, but he fled without even a toothbrush. Two US intelligence officers had spotted the light flashing from the window and the Kuehns were arrested before the submarine could rescue them. Searching the house, the officers found the binoculars and a large amount of cash, some of it in Japanese currency.

FBI Special Agent Robert Shivers and the local police went to the Japanese consulate, where they found the staff burning reams of paper. Some documents rescued from the flames showed the signals that the Kuehns had used to convey the movements of the fleet.

At first the Kuehns denied everything. But the evidence against them was overwhelming and Bernard confessed. In an effort to protect his wife and stepdaughter, he claimed he was solely responsible. But Ruth said she was in charge and her father had merely followed her orders, while Friedel insisted that she had bought the binoculars and was the leader of the gang.

On 21 February 1942, just 76 days after the attack on Pearl Harbor, Bernard Otto Julius Kuehn was found guilty of espionage and sentenced to death 'by musketry' in Honolulu. Ruth's trial was imminent and he was determined to save her. He promised to tell US naval intelligence everything he knew about Axis operations in the Pacific. His sentence was commuted to 50 years' hard labour on Alcatraz. He served just four years before being deported.

Ruth and Friedel were interned and deported back to Germany at the end of the war. Ruth was not present when her beauty parlour in Hawaii was sold off. Her elder brother Leopold, who had stayed behind in Germany with Goebbels, died on the Russian front.

CHAPTER 10

THE AMBASSADOR'S DAUGHTER

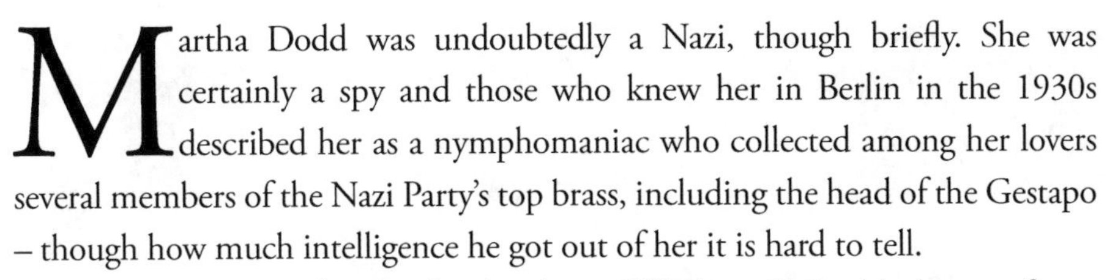

Martha Dodd was undoubtedly a Nazi, though briefly. She was certainly a spy and those who knew her in Berlin in the 1930s described her as a nymphomaniac who collected among her lovers several members of the Nazi Party's top brass, including the head of the Gestapo – though how much intelligence he got out of her it is hard to tell.

Born in 1908, Martha was the daughter of William E. Dodd, then professor of history at Chicago University. In the late 1920s, she toured Europe with her mother. Back in Chicago, as an assistant literary editor on the *Chicago Tribune*, she wrote short stories and had a busy social life. An attractive woman, she was reputed to have had many lovers, including the writers Carl Sandburg and Thomas Wolfe who, on a visit to Berlin, told a friend that Martha was 'like a butterfly hovering around my penis'.

Her biographer John Lewis Carver said: 'Martha was a vivacious, flirtatious, fair-skinned sexy girl, far more interested in amorous escapades than in those serious matters. But she, too, had her serious side. She wrote short stories and poetry, and made up her mind to become a writer.' She had a short, unhappy marriage to a wealthy banker. 'I had to choose between him and "adventure",' she said. 'I couldn't help making the choice I did.'

NYMPHOMANIAC AND NAZI SYMPATHIZER

In 1933, President Roosevelt appointed her father ambassador to Berlin where Hitler had just come to power. Martha went to Germany with her father. She was immediately captivated by the new regime. Carver said: 'Nazism meant good-looking, tall, blond men to her and she liked what she saw. She was painting the Nazi capital red, but in a social way. She went out on the town every night, flirting, drinking and dancing, mostly with young men who happened to be Nazis. She gained a dual reputation. Insiders described her as a nymphomaniac in her sex life and a Nazi sympathizer in her politics.'

She became an ardent supporter of the transformation of German society that was going on at the time, and admired Hitler for what he was doing for the unemployed. Through journalist friends, Dodd met her first senior Nazi, foreign press chief Ernst 'Putzi' Hanfstaengl, whose son was Hitler's godson. Hanfstaengl and Martha had an affair. Impressed, he wanted to introduce her to the *Führer*.

Martha Dodd with her parents – her father became US ambassador to Germany in 1933.

'Hitler needs a woman,' he told her, according to her memoir *My Years in Germany*. 'Hitler should have an American woman – a lovely woman could change the whole destiny of Europe. Martha, you are the woman!'

Dodd arranged to meet Hanfstaengl for tea at the Kaiserhof. As soon Hitler and his entourage came in, Hanfstaengl took Dodd to his table, where Hitler kissed her hand and murmured a few words. His face was weak and soft, Dodd said, but his eyes were 'intense, unwavering, hypnotic'. She did not remain at his table for long as she had only been in Berlin for a few months and spoke little German. However, she said she was struck by his 'quiet charm, almost a tenderness of speech and glance', and his 'appealing helplessness'.

Dodd never spoke with Hitler again, though she saw him regularly at social events and the opera, and sat near him in the diplomatic box at the 1936 Olympics. Though she liked him, he was not her type. 'I believe that Hitler is completely asexual,' she wrote in her memoir.

That certainly wouldn't have worked for Martha. She counted among her lovers the American journalist Louis Fischer, the French diplomat Armand Bérard, and the scientist Max Delbrück. There was also Prince Louis Ferdinand Hohenzollern, grandson of the deposed Kaiser, with whom she attended family celebrations and formal balls at the palace in Potsdam. She dated Jewish men, noting that when they went out, she felt 'the sneers of the crowds, the mutterings and under-the-breath insults'.

Among the top Nazis she bedded were senior *Luftwaffe* officer Ernst Udet, a flying ace from World War I who she later immortalized in her novel *Sowing the Wind*. Then there was Fritz Wiedemann, who she shared with Princess Stephanie von Hohenlohe. She found the intrigue exciting.

'Certainly Wiedemann was a dangerous man to cross, for despite his social naivety and beguiling clumsiness, he was as ruthless a fighter and schemer as some of his compatriots,' she said.

A HOUSE OF ILL REPUTE

While ambassador Dodd and his wife were happy to let Martha come and go as she pleased, the US Consul General George Messersmith grew concerned

Harvard graduate Ernst Hanfstaengl was Hitler's foreign press chief. In the early days, he had introduced Hitler to Munich's high society, but he was later destined to fall out with the Führer *and move back to the US.*

and wrote to the State Department about her conduct. While he judged the affair with Udet harmless, he feared that information mentioned casually in the embassy was making its way back to Hanfstaengl.

'I often felt like saying something to the Ambassador about it,' Messersmith wrote, 'but as it was a rather delicate matter, I confined myself to making it clear as to what kind of a person Hanfstaengl really is.' Later in an unpublished memoir, he wrote that 'she [Martha] had behaved so badly in so many ways, especially in view of the position held by her father'. The Dodds' butler put it more succinctly: 'That was not a house, but a house of ill repute.'

'This reputation gained confirmation when she started an affair with a sinisterly handsome Nazi official, Rudolf Diels by name,' said Carver. 'He was then chief of the Nazi secret service. His curriculum included spying on Martha's own father and the American embassy in Berlin.'

She knew she was dealing with a dangerous man, noting that when he arrived at a party he 'created a nervousness and tension that no other man possibly could, even when people did not know his identity'. He was the head of the Gestapo, but simply the look of him was terrifying. He had 'the most sinister, scar-torn face I have ever seen'. But his eyes were penetrating, his lips 'lovely' and he had 'jet-black luxuriant hair'. She loved the fact that everyone else was afraid of him and called him the 'Prince of Darkness'. He gloried in the epithet.

'He took a vicious joy in his Mephistophelian manners and always wanted to create a hush by his melodramatic entrance,' she said. He was also a vicious sadist.

It was from Diels, head of the Gestapo, that Martha first learned the art of espionage. She said: 'I was intrigued and fascinated by this human monster of sensitive face and cruel, broken beauty. We went out quite a lot, dancing and driving. I went to his office once and saw dictaphones on the desk in an unpretentious, large and somewhat bare room. He gave me the first indication of how spying was done.'

She was captivated by this sinister world.

'There began to appear before my romantic eyes a vast and complicated network of espionage, terror, sadism and hate, from which no one, official or private, could escape,' she said.

Martha completely overlooked any ulterior motive for Diels' courting her. The American embassy was a high priority target on the Nazi espionage list and she had direct access. Diels was making love to the ambassador's pretty, petite, vivacious daughter in the hope that he could gain inside information. His aim was to turn Martha Dodd into a Nazi spy.

FLAUNTING THE AFFAIR

It was hardly a secret. A Jewish friend told her at a cocktail party: 'Martha, you are very silly, and you are playing with fire . . . you are being used by Diels. . . . There is some sort of trouble ahead and you may get yourself unwittingly involved.'

But Martha was adamant.

'I saw no reason whatever not to see a lot of Diels if I could,' she said. 'He gave me, consciously and unconsciously, a picture of the backstage workings of espionage that I could not have got anywhere else.'

She flaunted their affair.

'So I went out with Diels for drives in the country and to nightclubs where we knew we would be seen,' she said.

How much he succeeded in converting her to spying for the Nazis was not recorded as their relationship was summarily curtailed. The Gestapo was taken over by the SS in 1934 and Diels was fired. He narrowly escaped being killed in the Night of the Long Knives, disappearing for five weeks while the purge was going on. When he reappeared, he was demoted and became security chief in Cologne. He was probably saved from execution by his marriage to Ilse Göring, cousin to Hermann Göring.

PERSECUTION

Martha became disillusioned with Nazism after the Night of the Long Knives, the disgrace of her lover and the growing mistreatment of Jews. In *My Years in Germany*, she recalled an incident that was, perhaps, a little close to home: 'There was a street-car in the centre of the road from which a young girl was being brutally pushed and shoved. We moved closer and saw the tragic and tortured

Rudolf Diels was a protégé of Hermann Göring. In 1944, he was arrested by the Gestapo after the 20 July plot to assassinate Hitler and imprisoned, but he somehow survived.

face. She looked ghastly. Her head had been shaved clean of hair and she was wearing a placard across her breast. We followed her for a moment, watching the crowd insult and jibe and drive her. Quentin and my brother asked several people around us, what was the matter. We understood from their German that she was a Gentile who had been consorting with a Jew.'

The woman had been forced to wear a placard that said: 'I have offered myself to a Jew.'

But Martha did not give up sex or spying. In September 1933, she had met Boris Vinogradov, who was first secretary at the Soviet embassy. For once, she had to be discreet. The United States did not recognize the Soviet Union until November 1933 and such a liaison would have put her father in a difficult position.

But Vinogradov was not just a diplomat. He was also a Soviet intelligence agent with the NKVD. In March 1934, he was ordered to recruit Martha Dodd. A message was sent to the Berlin station chief, saying: 'Let Boris Vinogradov know that we want to use him for the realization of an affair we are interested in. . . . According to our data, the mood of his acquaintance is quite ripe for finally drawing her into our work. Therefore we ask Vinogradov to write her a warm friendly letter and to invite her to a meeting in Paris where . . . they will carry out necessary measures to draw Martha into our work.'

The lovers went to Paris and travelled back to Berlin via Moscow. On 5 June 1935, Vinogradov wrote to his spymaster: 'Currently the case with the American is proceeding in the following way. Now she is in Berlin, and I received a letter from her in which she writes that she still loves me and dreams of marrying me.'

That October, Vinogradov was recalled to Moscow and another agent, Emir Bukhartsev, took over Martha's case. He reported: 'Martha argues that she is a convinced partisan of the Communist party and the USSR. With the State Department's knowledge, Martha helps her father in his diplomatic work and is aware of all his ambassadorial affairs. The entire Dodd family hates National Socialists. Martha has interesting connections that she uses in getting information for her father. She has intimate relations with some of her acquaintances. . . . Martha claims that the main interest of her life is to assist secretly the revolutionary cause. She is prepared to use her position for work in this direction, provided that the possibility of failure and of discrediting her father can be eliminated. She claimed that a former official of the Soviet embassy in Berlin – Boris Vinogradov – has had intimate relations with her.'

SOVIET SPY

Codenamed Liza, Martha passed on information from her father's private conversations. One NKVD directive requested that she send them summaries of her father's reports to Roosevelt – in particular they desired intelligence on Germany, Poland and Japan.

She continued spying on her father for the Soviet Union until he was recalled in 1937. Bukhartsev was executed as a 'Gestapo agent' during one of Stalin's periodic purges. In March 1937, Martha went to Moscow to ask permission to marry Vinogradov, telling the authorities: 'It goes without saying that my services of any kind and at any time are proposed to the party for use at its discretion. Currently, I have access mainly to the personal, confidential correspondence of my father with the US State Department and the US President. My source of information on military and naval issues, as well as on aviation, is exclusively personal contact with our embassy's staff.'

In December, she travelled back to the United States with her father. The following June she married Jewish millionaire Alfred Stern who was a backer of the American Communist Party. She wrote to Vinogradov a month later, telling him of her marriage and saying: 'You know, honey, that for me, you meant more in my life than anybody else. You also know that, if I am needed, I will be ready to come when called. . . . I look into the future and seeing you in Russia again.'

By the time the letter reached Russia, Vinogradov had been executed in another of Stalin's purges. Nevertheless, Martha's enthusiasm for communism never waned and she continued working as a Soviet spy, though she lived in her husband's luxurious apartment in midtown Manhattan with two servants, a driver and a personal secretary.

'She considers herself a Communist and claims to accept the party's program,' read one NKVD dispatch. 'In reality, 'Liza' is a typical representative of American bohemia, a sexually decayed woman ready to sleep with any handsome man.'

In 1939, she published her best-selling memoir known as *Through Embassy Eyes* in the United States, which included devastating descriptions of high-ranking Nazis. Of propaganda minister Joseph Goebbels, who stood five feet tall and had a deformed foot, she said: 'If there were any logic or objectivity in Nazi sterilization laws Dr Goebbels would have been sterilized quite some time ago.' The book was promptly banned in Germany.

In 1953 the House Committee on Un-American Activities subpoenaed Martha and her husband. They fled to Mexico but were indicted for espionage, and feared extradition. Paying $10,000 (about £75,000/$96,000 today) for Paraguayan passports, they escaped behind the Iron Curtain, settling in Prague. But they were lonely and unhappy in Czechoslovakia, struggling with the language and growing disillusioned with communism. When their son Robert was diagnosed with schizophrenia, his parents blamed the stresses of exile for his illness. After spending most of the 1960s in Cuba, they returned to Prague.

In 1979 a federal court cleared the couple of all charges, citing lack of evidence due to the deaths of crucial witnesses. But the Sterns still could not return to the United States. They hadn't paid taxes during their exile and the accumulated debt was enormous.

After her husband's death in 1986, Martha wrote to a friend: 'Nowhere could be as lonely for me as it is here.' Martha Dodd Stern, who had described herself in her 1939 memoir as 'young and reckless', died in Prague in 1990, aged 82.

CHAPTER 11

THE DANISH COLUMNIST

In the autumn of 1941, the future US president, John F. Kennedy, joined the US navy and was posted to the Office of Naval Intelligence (ONI) in Washington DC, where he gained a reputation as a playboy. It was there that he met the former Miss Denmark and newspaper columnist Inga Arvad.

AN ENGLISH EDUCATION

Inga was born in Denmark in 1913, and educated in England, Paris and Brussels. She married at 17, but divorced two years later and moved to Copenhagen. By 1935 she was married again, to the Hungarian movie director Paul Fejos, who had cast her as the lead in his 1934 feature film *Flugten fra millionerne* (*Flight From the Millions*). When Fejos' move flopped, Inga decided to abandon acting and moved to New York to pursue a career in journalism. She enrolled at the Columbia School of Journalism, and after graduating began to report from Berlin, writing feature profiles of newsmakers in general, including top Nazi officials.

She interviewed Hitler several times and genuinely admired him – Inga had visited Germany before he came to power and had witnessed the chaos and misery that followed the end of World War I. Hitler was much taken by her and

Inga Arvad was elected Miss Denmark in 1931 and, in 1936, she was invited to be Adolf Hitler's guest at the Berlin Olympics. She went on to become a scriptwriter with Metro-Goldwyn-Mayer as well as a Hollywood gossip columnist.

called her 'the perfect Nordic beauty'. She socialized with him and accompanied him to the 1936 Olympic Games in Berlin. They had private dinners together and he presented her with an inscribed photograph in a silver frame. Perhaps it escaped his notice that Arvad is a Jewish name, appearing in Ezekiel 27:8, meaning 'in exile' or 'wanderer'.

Inga attended Göring's wedding, where Hitler was to be best man, and she described Goebbels and Rudolf Hess in glowing profiles. Goebbels noted in his diary that he had been interviewed by 'a beautiful Dane . . . enthusiastic about the new Germany'. Inga also wrote about Leni Riefenstahl's 1935 propaganda film *Triumph of the Will* which, she said, left her 'captured, captivated and . . . convinced'.

MEETINGS AND MIGRATION

The FBI believed that Inga was the niece of the chief of police in Berlin, former admiral Magnus von Levetzow, whose father had been Danish and who organized a meeting with Goebbels for her. But it turned out that they were not related by blood. She was close to the Swedish businessman Axel Wenner-Gren, owner of arms manufacturer Bofors, a major shareholder in Krupp, and a friend of Hermann Göring. While resident in the Bahamas during World War II, Wenner-Gren was the Duke of Windsor's personal banker. He also funded Fejos' filming of the lost Inca cities in southern Peru. These expeditions were thought to be a cover for Nazi incursions into South America. US naval intelligence believed that Wenner-Gren's yacht, the largest in the world and purchased from Howard Hughes, was being used to refuel German U-boats. He was blacklisted by the US as a suspected Nazi agent. However, he sent Inga a monthly remittance in lieu of the maintenance cheques that her husband was supposed to provide.

In 1940, Inga and Fejos immigrated to New York and she used her interviews and photos with Hitler to find newspaper work. Because of her close acquaintance with Hitler, she was suspected of being a German spy and the FBI began tracking her movements. She separated from her husband and moved to Washington DC, where she contacted the *New York Times'*

Washington correspondent Arthur Krock who was 'stupefied' by her beauty. They had an affair and he recommended her to Frank Waldrop, editor of the isolationist *Washington Times-Herald*. Waldrop was also an FBI informant who said he was 'never sure about Inga'. But he asked her to write a human interest column on new arrivals to wartime Washington, called 'Did You Happen to See?'

The 24-year-old John Kennedy was one of those she interviewed. He fell in love with the 28-year-old Dane who, he said, 'exuded sexuality'. She said she found him 'refreshing' because 'he knows what he wants'.

A PASSING AFFAIR

Inga was separated but still married at the time and she gave Kennedy to understand that theirs would be a passing affair. 'I wouldn't trust him as a long-term companion, obviously,' she said. 'And he's very honest about it. He doesn't pretend this is forever. So, he's got a lot to learn and I'll be happy to teach him.' Early on in their relationship, Kennedy had told her that one day he would run for the presidency – so he was obviously a catch. But generally she found sex with him unsatisfactory. She complained to Arthur Krock: 'He was awkward and groping. A boy, not a man. Intent upon ejaculation and not a woman's pleasure.'

On searching the newspaper's archives, another reporter on the *Times-Herald*, Page Huidekoper, found a picture of Inga in Berlin. The caption read: 'Meet Miss Inga Arvad, Danish beauty, who so captivated Chancellor Adolf Hitler during a visit to Berlin that he made her Head of Nazi Publicity in Denmark. Miss Arvad had a colorful career as a dancer, movie actress and newspaper woman before Herr Hitler honored her for her "perfect Nordic beauty."'

Huidekoper, who had worked for Joseph Kennedy at the US embassy in London when Tyler Kent was arrested, contacted the FBI. She mentioned this to Kennedy's sister Kathleen, who also worked at the *Times-Herald*. Kathleen – nicknamed 'Kick' – told Inga.

Others had their suspicions too. 'Her English was not perfect,' said Kathleen's boyfriend John White, another employee of the *Times-Herald*, 'it was better than

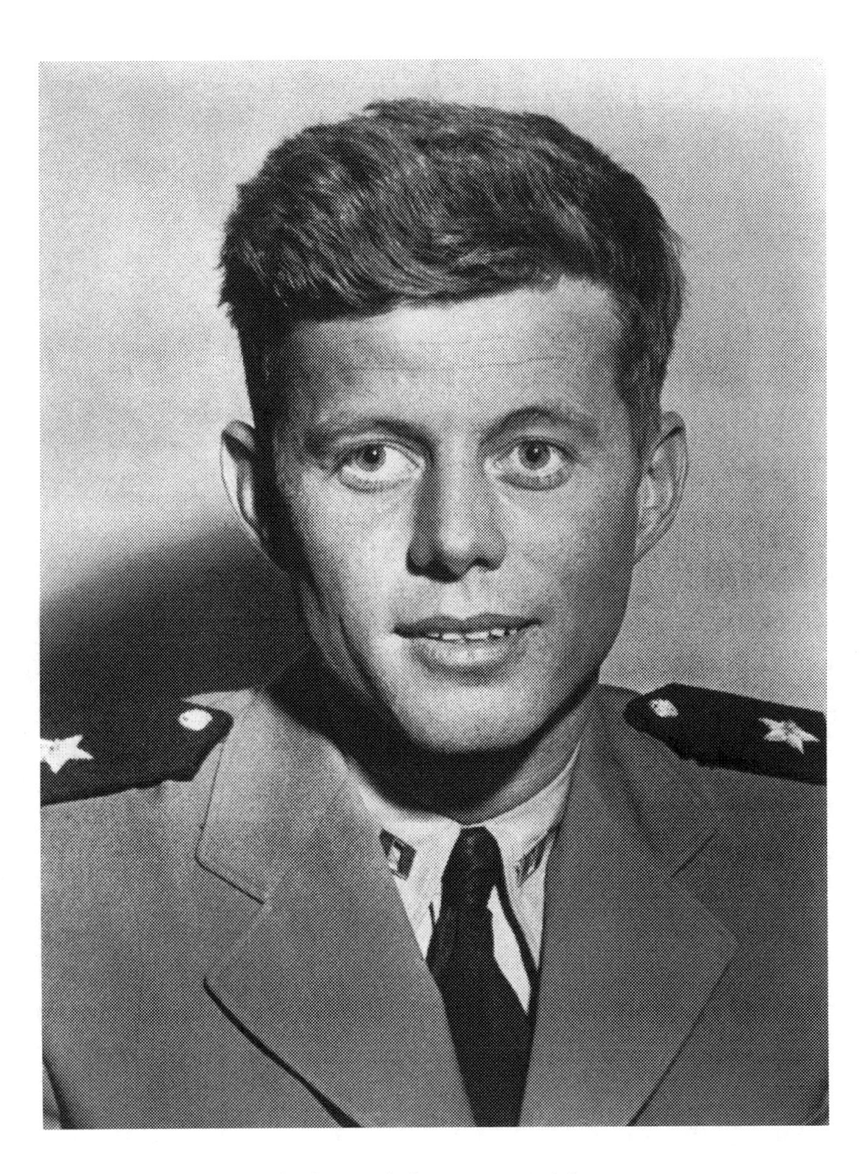

John Kennedy photographed as a junior grade lieutenant in the American navy.

perfect. "I have gooey eyes for you", she'd say. Gooey eyes . . . She was very smart – certainly smart enough to be a spy – but also extremely loving. What was it that enchanted Jack? Oh, sex. She was adorable. She looked adorable and was. She was totally woman. She wasn't handsome, she was gorgeous. Luscious, luscious is the word. Like of icing on the cake.'

Of her relationship with Kennedy, White remarked: 'Inga lets him walk all over her like linoleum.'

Waldrop was also keeping an eye on the situation. 'We all sort of knew that he was really smitten with her beyond the ordinary,' he said.

Beyond the suspicions of her co-workers at the *Times-Herald*, cosmetics magnate Elizabeth Arden, another of Inga's interviewees, called the FBI and told them that Arvad was a Nazi sympathizer. She also supplied copies of their correspondence.

A GERMAN SPY?

The FBI called Inga in for an interview. She explained that she had interviewed Hitler twice, along with Goebbels and Göring, as a journalist. However, it was noted that she had quit her job on *Berlingske Tidene*, Copenhagen's largest newspaper, in January 1936, long before the Olympic Games in Berlin that summer where she had been seen sitting in Hitler's box ostensibly as a member of the foreign press. Hitler was there, but she said she did not remember being photographed with him, nor did she pose with him. She also played down her contacts with other top Nazis. However, a search of her office belied this.

'In her desk,' the FBI report said, 'were located numerous articles which had been prepared by her. . . . Most of these articles concerned her contacts with high officials in the German government. . . . The following are excerpts of articles which were written by her, one concerning Dr Paul Joseph Goebbels, another concerning Emmy Sonneman and her husband, Hermann Göring. This article set out the information that Arvad was fortunate enough to obtain in an interview with Miss Sonneman prior to her marriage and that Miss Sonneman had been so impressed by the many kind enthusiastic words of Arvad that she wired an invitation for Arvad to be a private guest at her wedding. She spoke of having attended his wedding and described the actual wedding and the dress of Adolf Hitler. She stated that while in Berlin she stayed with her uncle, a chief of police in Berlin, and his former Admiral who used to be aide-de-camp of the Old Kaiser, through whom she met Dr Goebbels. Through Goebbels she arranged an interview with Hitler.'

Of her first meeting with Hitler in the Reich Chancellery, Inga had noted that the SS guards were the 'tallest and prettiest' in Germany. She then recalled being rushed through a long maze of corridors to a huge room where Hitler was seated at one end.

The report continued: 'She stated, concerning this, "I raised my arm and said, 'Heil Hitler.' He looked baffled, but I repeated it over again when I got no answer. Hitler was obviously embarrassed. He offered me a chair and sat down on the edge of another one himself. His first question was, 'What happened to Dr Goebbels?' but as I did not carry the *Mefisto* about in my pocket, I looked rather blank. Later, I was told that Hitler never received anyone alone and the person by whom one has been introduced always accompanies the guest."'

Inga gave an account of the meeting with Hitler, concluding: 'He is not as evil as he is depicted by the enemies of Germany. He is without doubt an idealist; he believes that he is doing the right thing by Germany and his interests do not go any further.'

Inga was plainly won over by Hitler and he was entranced by the 22-year-old Danish beauty.

'I tried to get away a few times when it seemed that the interview had lasted long enough,' she said, 'but Hitler kept me back and a little later Dr Goebbels, who had attended an important conference, joined us. It was about two hours later when I left and Hitler said, "I have enjoyed myself so much that I beg you to visit me every time you return to Berlin."'

The resulting article, which appeared in *Berlingske Tidende* on 1 November 1935, was headlined 'An Hour with Adolf Hitler'. In it, Inga wrote: 'One likes him immediately. He seems lonely. His eyes, which are tender hearted, look directly at you. They radiate power.' Rumours soon abounded that Inga was Hitler's mistress. These, of course, were noted in her FBI file.

The Danish press attaché Per Faber said that the Nazis must have 'certain hopes with regards to Miss Arvad's usefulness'. They certainly tried to recruit her as a spy. After her second interview with Hitler, she had attended a party at the home of a German prince when a top man in the Nazi Party said: 'We will pay you, furnish you with a large expense account, and all we would ask is that you go to all the parties and report to us what the conversations there are about.'

Not wishing to cause any offence, Inga said she had replied: 'Let me think about it.'

German foreign minister Konstantin von Neurath had seen the encounter and offered to walk her home. On the way, he advised her to turn the offer down, but warned: 'But this man cannot be refused without recrimination.' News of her refusal was almost certain to reach the ears of Himmler, and he would arrange a visit from the Gestapo. Inga left Berlin the following morning, although she returned to Germany the following year to board a ship in Hamburg to sail to Southeast Asia with Fejos.

FOREIGN ADVENTURE

For the trip, Inga learned Morse code and how to use a shortwave radio. Fejos had taught her how to fire a rifle. In the harbour at Penang they saw the *Southern Cross*, Wenner-Gren's lavish yacht. They were invited on board for dinner. Inga claimed that Fejos saved Wenner-Gren's life twice when they went on a tiger hunt. Another eyewitness denied this, and Wenner-Gren made no mention of it in his diary.

After that, the couple split. Inga went to New York, and Fejos to Peru, pursued by the FBI who Roosevelt had put in charge of monitoring Axis incursions into Latin America that could threaten the Panama Canal and American airbases in the Caribbean.

In late summer 1941, the government of Argentina announced that 500,000 Nazi troops were already in South America. Fejos' expedition, financed by Wenner-Gren, was headed towards the remote area in which they were stationed. Wenner-Gren was then blacklisted, his assets frozen and he was denied any business dealing with the United States or Britain. Inga also alleged that Wenner-Gren had offered her $1 million to be the mother of his child. She later told

Kennedy that the only reason she was being harassed by the FBI was because of her association with Wenner-Gren.

When the FBI questioned Inga about her photograph with Hitler in his private box at the 1936 Berlin Olympics, she said she did not recall such a picture. After the interview, Inga asked for a letter from the FBI saying she was not a spy. It was not forthcoming.

AMERICA AT WAR

There was soon another reason for the FBI's interest. On 4 December 1941, three days before the Japanese attack on Pearl Harbor, the *Times-Herald* published excerpts from secret US war plans allegedly approved by President Roosevelt under the headline 'F.D.'s Secret War Plans Revealed'. The plan outlined five hypothetical war scenarios, each designated with a different colour. The fifth plan envisaged America joining Britain in offences against the Germans in North Africa and on the continent.

On 8 December 1941, the United States declared war on Japan. This was rapidly followed by a declaration of war on the United States by Hitler and Mussolini. Hitler made reference to the *Times-Herald* story, saying: 'President Roosevelt's plan to attack Germany and Italy with military forces in Europe by 1943 at the latest was made public in the United States, and the American government made no effort to deny it.'

There was talk of prosecuting the owner of the *Times-Herald*, Cissy Patterson, for treason, along with some of her staff. President Roosevelt was not interested in pursuing the matter, but the public were not so forgiving. Until then, Hitler had made no plans to attack the United States; it was widely believed that he had been emboldened by 'the dirty fascists at the *Times-Herald*', who had also revealed that it would take 18 months before the United States was ready to send an expeditionary force to Europe.

With America now at war with Germany, President Roosevelt insisted that FBI boss J. Edgar Hoover become personally involved in the investigation of Inga Arvad. As a journalist, she had written flattering portraits of Hoover's deputy – and reputed lover – Clyde Tolson and Hoover's long-serving secretary Helen

Gandy. It was suspected that these were designed to throw counter-espionage agents off the scent. Tolson reported rumours that Inga was seen being driven around Berlin in 'a huge state car in which the curtains were tightly drawn', implying that something illicit was happening in the back of the limousine. What's more, with her sycophantic articles about senior staff, it appeared she was toying with the Bureau.

An agent watching her apartment reported a naval ensign staying the night. The man wore 'a gray overcoat with raglan sleeves and gray tweed trousers. He does not wear a hat and has blonde curly hair which is always tousled . . . known only as Jack.' It took Hoover just a couple of phone calls to establish that this was John F. Kennedy.

INGA BINGA

Hoover had Inga's phone tapped, her mail intercepted, and her apartment broken into and bugged illegally. Soon he had tapes of Kennedy making love to his 'Inga Binga'. She called him 'Honeysuckle' or 'Honey Child Wilder'.

Kennedy knew the risks he was running with Inga. 'I'm afraid she's dangerous,' he told his friend Henry James. 'She certainly has connections with the Fascists in Europe, Germany especially. But as to being a spy, it's hard to believe she's doing that, because she's not only beautiful, but she's warm, she's affectionate, she's wonderful in bed. But you know, godammit, Henry, I found out that son-of-a-bitch Hoover had put a microphone under the mattress!'

It was, however, Inga who spotted that her phone was being tapped. James warned Kennedy to break off the relationship or risk going to jail for consorting with the enemy.

Early in his political career, Kennedy had boasted that when he got to Washington he would get the tapes back. He never managed it. Hoover's file on Inga swelled to over 1,200 pages. When Kennedy became president, Hoover let it be known that details of his affair with a suspected Nazi spy were being 'safeguarded' by the FBI.

'He'd always be walking around with a towel around his waist,' Inga's son Ronald said his mother told him. 'That's all he ever wore in the apartment – a towel. The minute he arrived, he'd take off all his clothes and take a shower. . . . If he wanted to make love, you'd make love – now. They'd have 15 minutes to get to a party and she'd say she didn't want to. He'd look at his watch and say we've got ten minutes, let's go.'

Inga also told her son that she was pregnant when she married again and didn't know whether his father was her husband or Kennedy. Hoover leaked his suspicions to his friend, the nationally syndicated columnist and influential radio news commentator Walter Winchell.

On 12 January 1942, Winchell reported: 'One of Ex-Ambassador Kennedy's eligible sons is the target of a Washington gal's affections. So much so that she has consulted her barrister about divorcing her exploring groom. Pa Kennedy no like.' Inga had interviewed Winchell two months earlier.

A few days after the Winchell snippet appeared, Hoover warned Joseph Kennedy: 'Jack is in big trouble and he should get out of Washington immediately.'

After just 90 days with the ONI, Kennedy was on the verge of being cashiered, if not court-martialled as a security risk. Captain Howard Kingman, assistant director of the ONI, wanted Kennedy thrown out of the navy as quickly as possible. But political influence exerted by his father Joseph kept him in uniform, though he was quickly posted to Charleston Naval Yard in South Carolina.

Kennedy later told a reporter: 'They shagged my ass down to South Carolina because I was going around with a Scandinavian blonde, and they thought she was a spy.' After taking a trip on ONI business, he wrote to Inga, saying: 'I've returned from an interesting trip, about which I won't bore you with the details as if you are a spy I shouldn't tell you and if your [sic] not you won't be interested.'

His move to South Carolina didn't put an end to the affair. With little to occupy his mind, he became even more besotted with Inga. They exchanged love letters, spoke on the phone and spent long weekends together in Charleston. Inga checked into Room 132 of the Fort Sumter hotel under a false name. During two weekend visits, the FBI field agent reported they 'engaged in sexual intercourse on a number of occasions'. When the couple realized that their room was bugged, they moved to the Marion Hotel, using a different name. But the

FBI soon caught on. Once Kennedy even went absent without leave to visit Inga in Washington, but there was no escaping surveillance there.

During their conversations, Inga remarked that a speech by Churchill was 'defeatist' and said that British soldiers were 'no damned good'. She and Kennedy condemned Churchill for manoeuvring America into the war; they also said he had forecast, wrongly, that 'the Japs would fold up like the Italians'.

Agents noted that Inga had also renewed her affair with Danish writer Nils Blok who she knew from Columbia. After he spent the night with her in Washington, Blok wrote to her saying: 'How round and luxurious, warm and lovely your breasts are; how I have even felt that I was kissing your soul when your breasts heaved.' Her breasts, he said, 'have told me much more than you have ever expressed with words . . . and taught me more about you, about life, and why one should get up in the morning . . . why a man can be glad to be alive.'

She read his letter twice the day it arrived and twice more the following morning before putting it in the trash. FBI agents recovered it and filed it in a plain brown envelope marked 'OBSCENE'.

THE OLD GOAT

At Hoover's direction, the FBI maintained round-the-clock surveillance and J. Edgar Hoover accumulated more tapes of the future president's activities. In one memorable recording, Inga told Kennedy she was pregnant and accused him of enjoying the pleasures of youth without the responsibility. At the same time Inga was spending nights with financier Bernard Baruch, one of President Roosevelt's closest advisers on economic matters. She called him 'the old goat'. He was an important contact as he was in charge of putting together the workforce needed to build the atomic bomb.

Baruch had been a presidential adviser and chairman of the War Industries Board in World War I. Inga told him: 'You played the leading role in the last war and I am playing it in this one apparently.'

Through her job as a reporter, Inga had other sources of intelligence. She interviewed Admiral Henry A. Wiley, chairman of the Navy Board Production

Awards. When Kennedy complimented her on the article she said: 'I do the most terrible work – I don't know why.'

'You don't know what is good and what is bad,' he replied.

'I know that you are good – and damned bad,' was her response.

Hoover sent a report on his 'current investigation of this woman as an espionage suspect' to the US attorney general, warning that Inga might be 'engaged in a most subtle type of espionage activities against the United States'. The special agent running the investigation was Sam McKee, one of the men who gunned down bank robber Pretty Boy Floyd in 1934. He said the case had 'more possibilities than anything I have seen in a long time'. In February 1942, the director of the Alien Enemy Control Unit of the Department of Justice wrote to Hoover asking for a 'report of all the information you have in your files in respect of . . . Mrs Inga Fejos, 1600–16th Street, NW, Washington, D.C. which I desire in considering whether a Presidential Warrant of apprehension should be issued'. A similar request came from William 'Wild Bill' Donovan, director of OSS, forerunner of the CIA.

In Charleston, Kennedy was still working in naval intelligence, but at a lower level. There it became clear to him that he was also under surveillance by Naval Security. They, too, bugged Inga's apartment and kept her under surveillance.

Kennedy wanted to marry Inga and took her to the family home at Hyannis Port, Massachusetts, but his father opposed the match. Ingrid was not a Catholic, though that did not stop Joseph Kennedy from trying to seduce her himself. The FBI subsequently extended their investigation to include Kennedy Senior.

However, after some time John Kennedy's ardour cooled. When Inga spoke of getting her marriage annulled, he had little to say on the matter. It was clear they would never wed.

'We are so well matched,' she told him. 'Only because I have done some foolish things must I say to myself "no". At last I realize that it is true. We pay for everything in life.'

Without the backing of his father, Kennedy knew the affair must end. Continuing it would endanger his career and damage the family.

'There is one thing I don't want to do,' Inga told him, 'and that is to harm you. You belong so wholeheartedly to the Kennedy clan, and I don't want you ever to get into an argument with your father on account of me. . . . If I were but eighteen summers, I would fight like a tigress for her young, in order to get you and keep you. Today I am wiser.'

Her divorce was finalized in June 1942. She tried for a job at the Office of War Information in New York, but was barred by Roosevelt. So she moved out to California to work as a Hollywood gossip columnist, where she was still watched by the FBI.

THE AFFAIR WITH BOOTHBY

Inga went on to have an affair with British member of parliament Robert Boothby, the long-term lover of the wife of Prime Minister Harold Macmillan. Boothby's colourful private life led to rumours about his sexuality and participation in homosexual orgies laid on by East End gangster Ronnie Kray. Apparently, he begged Inga to marry him, but she broke off the engagement after her closeness to Hitler risked losing Boothby his seat in the 1945 election. The following year, Inga married Tim McCoy, a star of cowboy movies.

As Kennedy was a security risk, he could no longer remain in intelligence. His commanding officer Captain Samuel A. D. Hunter said: 'It seemed the best thing to do was to transfer him to a seagoing unit.'

When Kennedy was finally posted to active duty, commanding a patrol torpedo (PT) boat in the Pacific, fellow officers nicknamed him 'Shafty' and complained that he spent more time chasing models than pursuing enemy submarines. But he continued to write to Inga, talking of having 'dinner and breakfast' when he got back. He took the precaution of having his letters hand-delivered by a trusted friend.

In 1943, Kennedy's PT boat was cut in half by a Japanese destroyer. Two men were killed, and another two badly wounded. Kennedy led the remaining men to safety. He figured that the loss of his ship would be a blow to his career, but when he returned to the United States, Inga was on hand as the first journalist to interview him. Her account of his heroism brought him to public attention and was a stepping stone in his meteoric political career.

BEDTIME READING

Kennedy's affair with Inga had another unexpected outcome. In Washington, DC, Lyndon B. Johnson lived next door to J. Edgar Hoover and used to borrow FBI files as bedtime reading. It was one of the reasons why he was able to control the Senate when he was majority leader from 1955 to 1961. Naturally, Johnson read Kennedy's file with interest. It proved useful when he ran for the Democratic nomination for president in 1960. An alternative meaning of LBJ, it was said, was 'Let's Block Jack' – the coalition to prevent JFK securing the nomination. But Kennedy had more money than Johnson and ran a superbly organized campaign.

At the Democratic convention in Los Angeles in 1960, Kennedy won the nomination on the first ballot. Johnson was furious. Early editions of the newspapers gave the names of three men who Kennedy was considering as his running mate – Johnson's was not among them. LBJ went to Kennedy and told him that he would use the FBI file to blow Kennedy's 'family man' image out of the water if he did not put him on the ticket. Particularly damaging would be details of Kennedy's wartime affair with Danish beauty queen Inga Arvad. According to an FBI file, the *Führer* had actually been to bed with his perfect Nordic beauty. A pro-Nazi Swedish journalist had also taken her as his mistress. With the war still lurking in recent memory, the revelation that Kennedy had slept with a woman who had also had a relationship with Hitler would, at the very least, have lost him the Jewish vote.

Kennedy and his brother Bobby agonized over the decision, but could see no way out. Johnson had boxed them into a corner and, finally, Kennedy conceded. 'I'm 43 years old,' he told Johnson. 'I'm not going to die in office. So the vice presidency doesn't mean a thing.'

Johnson saw it differently. 'I looked it up,' he said. 'One of every four presidents has died in office. I'm a gamblin' man, and this is the only chance I got.' The next day Johnson was named as vice-presidential nominee. Three years later, history proved that his gamble had been right.

The question remained: was Inga a spy? Reviewing the files in 1960, FBI deputy director Cartha Deloach said: 'The investigation on Inga Arvad never conclusively proved that she was a German espionage agent. She had an amorous relationship with John F. Kennedy. And basically that's what the files contained. She was never indicted, never brought into court, never convicted.'

Inga Arvad died of cancer on a ranch in Arizona in 1973. She was survived by her husband Tim McCoy and their two sons.

CHAPTER 12

THE GERMAN MATA HARI

John F. Kennedy was not the only man who went on to have a political career after being involved with a suspected Nazi sex spy in his youth. As British secretary of state for war, John Profumo was force to resign in 1963 after admitting an affair with 19-year-old call girl Christine Keeler, who was simultaneously sleeping with Soviet naval attaché Yevgeny Ivanov. But he also had an intimate brush with a Nazi Mata Hari while at Oxford in the 1930s and continued writing to her while he was an army officer and member of the House of Commons during the war.

At the height of the Profumo scandal in 1963, the British security services unearthed letters and files concerning his relationship with Gisela Klein. A 1940 MI5 memorandum revealed that Profumo had met Klein in Oxford in the early 1930s. She 'was ostensibly studying English, and [he] got to know her well. She was always hard up. Later she became a mannequin and made a large number of useful contacts. Lady Astor is alleged to have expressed the opinion that she was a spy.' Klein was also described as 'exceedingly clever, witty and companionable'. Gisela Klein met John Profumo in the early 1930s.

The security services were already monitoring her. Earlier reports describe her as being 'of striking appearance' and using 'invitations and help from male friends to make ends meet'.

Gisela Klein

'She came to England, professed to be anti-Nazi, went to Oxford soi-disant to learn English [and] made great friends with lots of well-known young men,' MI5 noted. 'Known to be associated with a certain Jack Profumo, a wealthy British subject of foreign origin . . . she should be carefully watched and investigated.'

NUMEROUS AFFAIRS

The MI5 file indicates that Gisela was believed to have had affairs with a number of men, including 'two French military officers and a French prince'. MI5 noted disapprovingly: 'She appears to move in fashionable society and it is considered likely that she depends to a large extent on invitations and help from male friends.'

The first tip-off that German-born Gisela Klein was a spy came in 1938 from the Paris correspondent for *The Times*, Thomas Tucker-Edwardes Cadett. He wrote to the paper's assistant manager reporting that a young English aristocrat, Lord Erleigh, had 'picked up a pro-Nazi mannequin called Klein who is the mistress of the German military attaché here . . . your friends in MI5 might like to know this'. The information was passed on to MI6 who later concluded that Gisela was travelling across Europe, including to Italy and Greece, providing secret information to the Nazis in Paris during World War II.

A later report noted that, in 1942, she was living in Nazi-occupied Paris as the mistress of an officer in German intelligence with whom she had a child. General Stülpnagel, the German military commander of occupied France, even 'offered her a job of running a secret information service. She accepted and operated under cover of a commercial information bureau.'

Profumo had become a Conservative MP in 1940, while serving in the army, but he remained in contact with Klein and was probably unaware of her Nazi espionage activities. Her letters to him were innocent enough. For example, in 1942, she wrote saying: 'I'm with sixteen other girls, all mannequins, showing our new fashions in Zurich . . . I love it.' She added: 'Though I'm not nearly as happy as I used to be at 88 Seymour Street [the address of her digs in Oxford].'

She went on to say: 'Jack darling, I find it very difficult to write this letter as I cannot get used to the idea that I'm free to write to you without a censor.'

Switzerland remained neutral throughout the war and the mail was uncensored; but the letter did not escape the attention of the British authorities. MI5 intercepted it and noted that the German spy who wrote it 'appears to be trying to seek information'. When questioned about his relationship with her during the war, Profumo admitted to having met Gisela in 1936, and said that he 'got to know her well'.

Major Astor, Lady Astor's son, said in 1945 that Gisela had spent some time in Cairo and Alexandria where she was 'said to have known every officer in both places'.

After the liberation of Paris in 1944, she was imprisoned for espionage in Fresnes prison. Later she was transferred to a jail on Rue Suchet, where Edward Winegard, an American of German origin serving with the US forces, was in command. On her release, Gisela married Winegard in Hamburg. They moved to Tangier in Morocco, where they worked for the radio station Voice of America. But in April 1950, Gisela was dismissed from her job as a filing clerk there 'when it was discovered that she had worked for the Germans during the war and was 100 per cent pro-German'.

INTIMATE LETTERS

Profumo was Conservative MP for Kettering between 1940 and 1945, and for Stratford-upon-Avon from 1950 until his resignation in 1963. Winegard briefly separated from his wife when he discovered intimate letters from Profumo, written on House of Commons notepaper. Later Profumo wrote to Christine Keeler on War Ministry notepaper, fuelling the concern that he might have opened himself to blackmail there too.

In 1963, MI6 officer Cyril Mackay wrote to Arthur Martin who was heading the investigation into the Profumo affair at MI5, saying: 'Although it is not particularly relevant to the current notorious case, Geoffrey thought you might like to have for your files the attached copy of a report from our representative [redacted], dated 2nd October 1950, which makes mention of an association between Gisela Klein and Profumo which began ca 1933 and had apparently not ceased at the time of this report.'

The MI6 documents also reveal that Gisela Winegard had an application for a UK visa rejected in 1951. The head of British intelligence in Tangier added: 'We have good reason to believe Mr and Mrs Winegard have recently engaged in blackmailing activities and now think it is possible their intended visit to the UK may be connected with this affair.'

Gisela's application for a six-week visa named Jack Profumo, 'MP for South Kettering' as a reference. She was banned from entering Britain, with MI5 noting that 'her activities for the last ten years are certainly consistent with a high degree of espionage'. It was noted that she and her husband had been in trouble with the American authorities in 1947–8 for 'having harboured one of the chiefs of a German spy ring'.

Gisela died in Florida in 1991, aged 77.

CHAPTER 13

THE SPANISH AFFAIR

Mussolini and his Fascists took over Italy in 1922; Hitler and the Nazis came to power in Germany in 1933; and Francisco Franco's nationalists, the Falangists, seized power in Spain during the Spanish Civil War of 1936–9. As commander of the Army of Africa in Spanish Morocco, Franco was already planning his takeover in 1935, and he asked Italy and Germany for assistance. The Nazis were eager to help and decided to send Angelica Dubrow, a special agent with the newly established Spanish Section of the Gestapo. The mission was top secret.

BLONDE AND ALOOF

A svelte blonde, Angelica had movie star looks and dressed elegantly. On 10 June 1935, she boarded the Munich Express at the Anhalter Bahnhof in Berlin. From Munich she took a first-class wagon-lit to Rome. At the border, she presented customs officers with a British passport in the name of Miss Helen Holborn.

She was, of course, German and had served the Nazis in a counterfeiting operation during hyperinflation under the Weimar Republic. The forged passport had a stamp showing she had entered Germany from the Netherlands. This, too, was bogus but had been added to help explain why she was leaving Germany with a large sum in foreign currency despite the tight monetary restrictions.

On the journey Angelica remained aloof and read the magazines she had brought with her. Occasionally a man would try to talk to her but was quickly rebuffed. It seemed she had no interest in male companionship. However, there was one man on the train she was interested in, even though she paid him no special attention. He was a Spaniard named Fernando Queseda and he was also seated in first class.

Born in Barcelona, Quesada had olive skin and jet-black hair. When the customs officials checked his luggage they found silk shirts and a collection of perfumes, along with other trappings of a well-off gentleman. His case was trimmed with silver. He only had ten marks in his pocket, but his air of self-assurance invited no further questions.

From Rome, the two passengers travelled on to Naples, where Angelica checked into the Parkers Hotel. That night she dressed in a pale blue suit, selected a bouquet of white carnations and asked the doorman to call a cab. The driver dropped her at the port. From there she walked to a restaurant called the Zi' Teresa. It was full so she waited near the entrance for a table. A waiter saw the carnations and approached her. He explained that he had no spare tables, but if she did not mind sharing, he could find her a seat.

He led her to a table in the corner where a man was sitting – he rose and introduced himself. He was Italian, and his name was Gaston d'Ette. Ostensibly a representative of an Italian car company, he had been an agent for the Fascist government since Mussolini's rise to power.

A few minutes later, Fernando Queseda entered the restaurant. He, too, was led to their table. The three had not met before but they knew each other by name. Queseda was a crook who dabbled in espionage. He had been implicated in a racket smuggling American cigarettes into Spain and, unfortunately, his photo had been in the papers following a scandal about bribery and gambling. Queseda had come to the meeting at Zi' Teresa to represent General Franco, while Dubrow and d'Ette each represented their respective governments.

Clearly it was in the interests of Italy and Germany to see another Fascist government in Europe. Franco wanted 80 planes to help consolidate his grip on

Spain, and the Axis powers agreed to send the planes to North Africa secretly. Germany would supply the airframes and Italy the engines; Spanish industrialists would guarantee payment.

The problem was how to get them there. The British and French were hostile to Franco, and both had fleets patrolling the Mediterranean. The plan was to crate up the airframes in the factory at Nuremberg and mark them as 'toys' for customs purposes. Others airframes from Solingen would be marked 'small assorted ironware'. They would be shipped to Naples where the engines would be waiting, and then they would be carried as regular cargo on small freighters to Morocco, where they would be assembled.

LE CAPITAINE SOLITAIRE

At dinner, Quesada announced that these plans would have to be ditched. A mystery ship had appeared off Morocco. The captain was always seen alone and was known as *Le Capitaine Solitaire*. There had been increased radio traffic in the area and the suspicion was that the *Capitain*e was working for the British secret service. His boat had a shallow draught and operated in waters barely navigable by other vessels. This made it difficult to catch him. It was feared that it would be impossible to land the plane parts secretly in Morocco as a number of the freighters in the area had been sunk.

Quesada suggested assembling the planes in Italy, then flying them to Morocco. Gaston d'Ette protested that this would be impossible without inviting international condemnation of Italy, which was at that point planning the invasion of Abyssinia.

Dubrow suggested instead that they ship the crates to Libya, which had been under Italian control since 1911. A temporary factory could be erected in the desert where the planes could be assembled, then they could be flown by night to Morocco secretly along a southerly route.

Consulting a map, Dubrow suggested that they ship the crates to the small port of Zuara, 50 miles (80 km) west of Tripoli. The plan was agreed, but Angelica was keen to know more about the *Capitaine* as she thought he might still pose a threat.

The information on him was skimpy at best. His vessel was a typical smuggler's boat, 75 ft long (23 m)and diesel powered, with a funnel, a low bridge and no mast. The *Capitaine* was often seen wearing a bright red beard.

MAN IN A RAINCOAT

The three agents waited in Naples while the airframes were shipped from the German port of Emden and the engines arrived from Italian factories. While the crates were being loaded on to a freighter, another truck drove up. A man in a light raincoat got out. He was wearing a pair of gold-rimmed glasses and a hard hat. From a gap where an upper tooth was missing a long cigar protruded. He had the paperwork to load another crate. The first mate argued, but the paperwork was in order and an additional crate marked 'Handle with care' in German and Italian was eventually stowed in the hold.

The port of Zuara was ringed with barbed wire. Troops and additional policemen had been brought in to guard it. Some distance from the town, an Italian airbase had been prepared. Security was stepped up there too. A makeshift factory had been set up, along with a barracks to house the pilots.

The three agents arrived at Zuara with the crates, which were loaded on to trucks and then driven to the airbase where mechanics awaited. Assembly was under way when, on the evening of 16 August 1935, the local chief of police arrived with a bottle of wine. He and the three agents drank toasts to the success of their mission, which now seemed assured.

Angelica asked casually whether anything was going on at the port. The police chief said nothing except that a British fishing boat had come in for repairs. She immediately asked the size of the boat. It was a 75-footer. And the captain? He had a red beard.

The police chief reassured them that the boat really was damaged – he had seen it with his own eyes. But the agents insisted on seeing for themselves. When they arrived back at the port the fishing boat was, seemingly, deserted.

Suddenly there was a thunderous explosion and the sky lit up. The agents rushed back to the airbase – the factory where the planes were being assembled was in flames. Figuring that *Le Capitaine* must be involved, the police chief stationed two officers on board the fishing boat to guard it.

Two weeks later, the two officers reported to their consul in the French port of Oran in Algeria. They said that while they were guarding the fishing boat, it had suddenly put out to sea. The rough conditions meant they were seasick and easily disarmed. They expected to be dumped overboard, but instead were put ashore on a lonely beach near Oran. From there they had been able to walk into town.

It is not known what happened to Fernando Quesada. He was probably consumed in the bloodbath of the Spanish Civil War. The Italian agent, Gaston d'Ette, found himself exiled to the island of Lipari where he committed suicide six months later. Angelica Dubrow was seen in Rio de Janeiro in 1938; she never returned to Germany.

The actions of the red-bearded sailor had hampered Franco's plans and the military coup which triggered the Spanish Civil War was postponed until July 1936. In October, Franco proclaimed himself head of state and head of government under the title *Caudillo*, and his forces finally took Madrid in March 1939.

CHAPTER 14

THE VIENNESE PROSTITUTE

Lilly Barbara Carola Stein was known as the femme fatale of the Ritter Ring, whose offshoot in the United States was the Duquesne Spy Ring. Nikolaus Ritter had become chief of air intelligence in the *Abwehr* in the late 1930s. His first wife, Mary Aurora Evans, was an Irish-American teacher from Alabama, and together they had two children. Ritter visited New York on a brief tour of duty without his family in 1935. In 1937, Mary filed for divorce on grounds of abandonment, but when she tried to move back to the United States, he abducted their children.

The head of the *Abwehr* Admiral Wilhelm Canaris told Ritter to contact the former German spymaster Fritz Joubert Duquesne who was living in New York. Ritter had already met him there in 1931. A South African Boer, Duquesne had fought in the Second Anglo-Boer War. Captured during a daring attempt to assassinate the British commander-in-chief Lord Kitchener, he was sent to a penal colony on Bermuda, but escaped to the United States where he became a journalist on the *New York Herald.*

THE MAN WHO KILLED KITCHENER

During World War I, Duquesne spied for Germany and went to Brazil where he sabotaged British ships. He succeeded in killing Kitchener, joining him on the HMS *Hampshire* disguised as a Russian duke, then signalling to a German

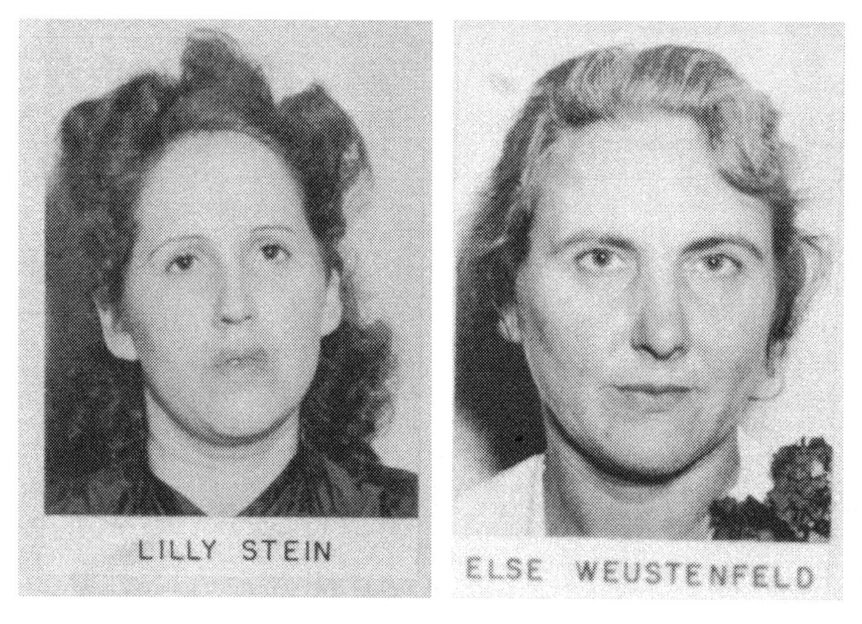

Lilly Stein and Else Weustenfeld were both convicted of being members of the Duquesne Spy Ring.

U-boat to torpedo the cruiser. Posing as British war hero Captain Claude Stoughton, he made money giving talks in New York before being arrested for fraud in 1917. The British demanded his extradition for murder on the high seas, but he escaped from jail and fled to Mexico, returning to the United States as Major Frederick Craven.

In 1932, he was arrested again for murder on the high seas, but the statute of limitations had run out before he could be extradited. Two years later he became an intelligence officer for the Order of 76, an American pro-Nazi organization. Then when Ritter contacted him again in 1937, Duquesne set up a spy ring. The *Abwehr* sent William Sebold to join it.

FBI DOUBLE AGENT

Born in the Ruhr, Sebold had served in the German army during World War I. Hoping for a better life, he emigrated to the United States in 1922 and became a naturalized citizen in 1936. Returning to Germany to visit his mother in

1939, Sebold was approached by Ritter and coerced into becoming a spy. After seven weeks' training in Hamburg, he was sent back to the United States with instructions to contact Duquesne. But even before he left Germany, Sebold contacted the US consul general, declaring himself to be a loyal American citizen and offering to work as a double agent.

Back in the States, he passed information on the members of the Duquesne Spy Ring to the FBI. Agents were particular interested in one of their number – a glamorous bleached-blonde named Lilly Stein. J. Edgar Hoover, in his usual haughty, puritanical fashion, called her a 'Viennese prostitute'.

Lilly had been born into a wealthy Austrian family. They were strict; she was rebellious. From the age of 14, she was a dedicated party girl and grew estranged from her relatives. She made money posing as a nude model.

Figure skating was one of her passions and she followed the international circuit, travelling with Heinrich Sorau, whose real name was Captain Hermann Sandel. Codenamed Uncle Hugo, he was the head of the espionage school in Hamburg and had trained William Sebold. With Lilly, Sorau masqueraded as an international businessman who had widespread interests and considerable influence within the government. These assets proved vital to Lilly, who now found her livelihood – and her life – in danger.

Following *Anschluss*, Lilly's parents died and she was denied her inheritance by prolonged legal proceedings. Most of her friends now shunned her because of her Jewish ancestry. She found herself in need of financial help: clearly, an attractive young woman could be of use to the spymaster. Sorau enrolled her in his spy school and she joined the *Abwehr*. After finishing her training, she was furnished with a German passport which classified her as 'Jewish first-degree mixture' – a so-called *Mischling* or half-Jew (in fact, she was fully Jewish). As a *Mischling*, she was initially spared the worst of the anti-Semitic persecution and allowed to travel widely throughout Europe.

In October 1939, Lilly arrived in New York on a visa supplied by Ogden Hammond Jr, the 27-year-old US vice-consul in Vienna. To avoid the British naval blockade, she had travelled on the Swedish American Lines' *Drottningholm*. After disembarking, she checked into the fashionable Windsor Hotel and sent a letter to the lynchpin of the Duquesne Spy Ring Else Weustenfeld. A German-born naturalized US citizen, Weustenfeld worked as a secretary at a law firm employed by the German consulate in New York and she lived with Hans W. Ritter, brother of Nikolaus Ritter. She was later described by the newspapers as the 'Blond Spy Mistress of Nazi Chief's Brother'. With her letter, Lilly enclosed a note from Uncle Hugo, signed 'Sorau', which read: 'I am sending this woman to you. Will you please help her?'

When Else arrived at the Windsor to meet Lilly, she was greeted with the password: 'I bring regards from your friends from Verden an der Aller.'

'What else did you bring?' asked Else.

Lilly said she had $500 (£7,000/$9,000 today) and a microphotograph of instructions for Fritz Duquesne hidden at the bottom of a box of face powder.

'The money is for Jimmy Dunn,' said Lilly, unaware that Jimmy Dunn was one of Duquesne's many aliases. She also didn't know that, after seeing nude photographs of Lilly, Duquesne was eager to meet her. He visited her as soon as she had found an apartment on West 81st Street, and she gave him the microphotograph and the money. Other agents would use her apartment as a return address when mailing information to Germany.

AN EXCLUSIVE NETWORK

Lilly set up an exclusive shop selling expensive beachwear to ladies vacationing in Florida. As well as supplementing her income as a spy, this attracted a wealthy clientele, the wives of industrialists and financiers.

To gather intelligence, she frequented the best hotels and nightclubs in Manhattan and attended the opera in search of men who might whisper in her ear 'about all sorts of developments and deals in industry and finance'. She found that high rollers could easily be persuaded to give up their secrets via pillow talk or blackmail. She was a 'well-built good-looking nymphomaniac with a sense of humour' said one FBI agent who had her under surveillance.

Agents vied for the assignment to tail Lilly because she boasted several glamorous friends, including the French actress Simone Simon and Olympic skater and movie star Sonja Henie. And in the evenings they would hang out at the fashionable 21 Club on expenses.

As well as channelling cash to support her extravagant lifestyle, Lilly was the conduit for the funds needed to run the spy ring. She would put in a request and the money would be sent via Amsterdam or banks in Latin America. She was one of the agents to whom Sebold delivered microphotographic equipment when he returned to the United States. He called her from a phone booth on West 86th Street and Columbus, then took a cab to the building she had moved to in the East 50s. Answering the door was a 24-year-old woman of a seductive manner and 'better than average looks'. Sebold could barely believe his eyes and asked twice whether she was Miss Stein. After using a magnifying glass to examine a microphotograph he had hidden in his hat, she offered him a drink. He declined; apparently that was not all that was on offer. When he said he was leaving, Lilly pouted and said: 'Now you are going and leave me all alone.'

Lilly and Sebold met in a restaurant a few days later where she told him she was in the midst of a dalliance with Ogden Hammond Jr, who had been recalled from Austria. While Hammond appeared to be a patriotic American, a left-wing magazine said he was a member of 'Washington's first Fascist family'. His father was a former ambassador to Spain and an unswerving supporter of Franco, while his brother-in-law was an attaché at the Italian embassy.

Lilly frequently met Sebold to give him information to transmit to Germany and continued to try to seduce him. An FBI report said that she got him at close quarters, 'then tried to make some subtle advances toward him and among other things said: "Why is it you American men are always afraid of women?"'

She constantly pressured Sebold for money. When he gave her $100, she used it for an abortion. In return, she passed on information passed to her by Ogden Hammond asserting that there was 'no chance of America getting into the war'.

Not all the intelligence she supplied was without foundation. On 3 September 1940, at the height of the Battle of Britain, she informed Sebold that British factories were producing 1,000 planes a month. The source was Captain Hubert Martineau, a cricketer and military officer with whom she was involved. In fact, this was an underestimate: British factories had turned out 1,601 planes in August and were set to produce 1,341 in September, far exceeding the output of the German aircraft industry. This was a considerable headache for Martha

Dodd's lover, Ernst Udet, who was director of the *Luftwaffe*'s technical office. But none of this information got back to Germany because Lilly had turned it over to Sebold for transmission.

DUMPED

As far as the *Abwehr* were concerned, Lilly's contact with Hammond was unproductive. As first they issued instructions, saying: 'Lilly should be careful and report in writing.' Then Sebold was told to dump her. 'You personally will please sever connections as instructed,' he was told. 'As reasons, say that you don't work for us anymore.'

Lilly couldn't believe that Sebold no longer required her services.

'What? Have you dropped me?' she asked.

'No, they had dropped me,' Sebold replied.

Soon after, Hammond was called in by Assistant Secretary of State Adolf Berle who told him he knew all about his affair with Lilly Stein. Hammond was asked to resign. The official reason given for his dismissal was that he had mimicked President Roosevelt 'in a reprehensible manner' at a summer party in Newport, and J. Edgar Hoover had reported it. Hammond refused to resign, swearing that 'at no time did I live with . . . or have intimate relations with' Lilly Stein. He took out an injunction against the State Department to prevent his dismissal. It was then circulated in the press that he had been involved in 'disloyal dealings' with an unnamed 'female agent of a foreign power'. He eventually lost the suit and was refused permission to appeal to the Supreme Court.

Even without the Sebold connection, Lilly continued spying for Nazi Germany. She picked up a new source – an English gentleman she met at the Hotel Pierre – and she had a new address in Cologne for Uncle Hugo.

The FBI recorded that she continued to contact Else Weustenfeld. Meanwhile Sebold, a married man, complained of Lilly's 'immoral conduct'. Weustenfeld said she knew that Lilly was 'not clean, but that Harry' – Harry Sawyer, one of Sebold's pseudonyms – 'had no reason for making such a great point' about it. Nevertheless, the FBI took great pleasure in recording every detail of Lilly's love life.

LILLY'S PECCADILLOES

Lilly was said to have a penchant for European sportsmen. There was the athlete Rudolph C. 'Rudy' Schifter, and the Austrian heavyweight boxer Romuald J. Wernikowski, who fought under the name Rex Romus, and who was seen visiting her at an apartment on East 79th Street. She dated the Swiss skating champion Georg von Birgelen and racing driver Hans Ruesch, who was thought to have posted letters on her behalf in Europe.

Lilly was casual about these affairs.

'I just look at them and they fall in love with me,' she said.

Neither Lilly nor Weustenfeld trusted Sebold, and suspected that he was embezzling money. Lilly even thought he might be a double agent, but Weustenfeld dismissed the idea, saying he didn't have 'enough courage to do that'.

On 27 June 1941, the FBI decided to round up the Duquesne Spy Ring. Some 250 special agents pounced. That evening, Lilly was entertaining a gentleman caller – a person of 'considerable importance', the FBI noted – who was generously allowed to conclude their encounter before the raid. Realizing that her apartment had been bugged, Lilly remarked: 'Well, I'll say one thing. You sure got an earful.'

She was sanguine. 'I've been expecting this for a long time,' she said.

She then propositioned the special agents who had come to arrest her. Special Agent William Friedemann described her as 'a real Aryan type', while 6 ft 3 in former Kansas typing champion Special Agent Wayne Kemp turned her down.

'It was the great incident of the night,' Friedemann said.

Raymond Newkirk, who was assigned to interrogate her, told author Art Ronnie: 'Lilly thought it a big joke. She knew she was going to jail but was satisfied that she had made enough money to make it worthwhile. She figured she had taken the Germans for a ride because she was always hollering for money for information she knew wasn't worth a damn.'

Her main concern was that she would be sent to a women's prison, but was reassured when told that there would be male guards.

'Don't you worry,' she said. 'Lil's gonna do a little business behind bars.'

J. Edgar Hoover described the investigation as 'the greatest of its kind in the nation's history' and the largest since the enactment of the 1917 Espionage Act. He told a press conference that the 'artists' model' Lilly Stein was the unnamed agent mentioned in press accounts of the Ogden Hammond Jr case.

During the trial, Duquesne alleged that Sebold had flashed 'French pornographic pictures' of Lilly at a clandestine meeting in City Hall Park and made 'laudatory remarks about her capacity as a sweetheart'. Another of the conspirators, Herman W. Lang, claimed that Sebold had offered him Lilly's services when trying to recruit him.

'He said, "Are you interested? I could make an appointment for you. If you are interested and want to have a nice time, why, I could fix it up,"' Lang testified. 'So I looked at him and said, "What ideas have you got? You know I am married."'

Pleading guilty, Lilly was sentenced to ten years for espionage with another two years for failing to register under the Foreign Agents Registration Act. She could not resist flashing a smile at the press photographers. During her stay in the United States, she had applied for naturalization, potentially raising her offence from spying to treason. She was eventually deported back to Austria, one of the few Austrian Jews to survive the Holocaust.

CHAPTER 15

THE HIGH SCHOOL SPY

According to FBI boss J. Edgar Hoover writing in *American* magazine in 1944: 'Of all the women spies we have apprehended, the one who most nearly approached the beauty of Mata Hari was little Lucy Boehmler, a schoolgirl in her teens. If we had not interrupted her career very early, she might have gone far under the Nazi standard of success.'

When she first came to the attention of the FBI, Lucy was living with her parents at Maspeth, Long Island. A doll-like girl with blue eyes, light hair, an oval face and an attractive figure, 'her principal asset, aside from an astute intelligence, was her innocent expression,' said Hoover. 'But while Lucy appeared at a glance to be a fine, healthy American high school girl, she was consorting secretly with two master spies, who were training her, while she posed as their secretary, in the arts of espionage.'

THE 'JOE K' SPY RING

Born in Stuttgart in 1923, Lucy emigrated to the United States with her parents in 1928 and went on to attend Grover Cleveland High School in Ridgewood. While her parents became naturalized US citizens, Lucy got involved with the pro-Nazi German American Bund in Queens. There she met Ulrich von der

Daily Express

No. 12,890 Wednesday, September 17, 1941 One Penny

"HE WAS RIGHT"

LENINGRAD GOES OUT TO FIGHT

Bombers smash Nazi pontoons and airfields

Express Staff Reporter E. D. MASTERMAN

STOCKHOLM, Wednesday morning.

LENINGRAD'S shock troops went into battle yesterday and hurled the enemy back as the German High Command warned the city that no humane consideration could count any more since the entire population was fighting against the invader.

TURKEY

The Express reporter who told you this—

STALIN GIVEN A WEEK

To choose—surrender or fight

Now tells you this—

NEW QUEEN OF IRAN?

Frau Buggins speaks her mind

And all Germany listens

THE FACE OF A SPY

ALL SILENT ON THE LIBYA FRONT

3 A.M. LATEST

HUNGARY TRIES TO GET OUT OF WAR

Savage blows

ON, ON, ON

De Gaulle back

Urgent need

10 panzer divisions

on Turk frontier

Bombs for Rome?

Axis planes raid Cairo, defy British warning

SIX GERMANS SHOT DOWN

—WINS— WINNERS ON SATURDAY

15 die in Eireann army explosion

Nazis report first U.S. flier captured

ITALIAN PLOT

Duke of Kent on air

THE BATTLE OF NOEL

For lead in Lord Louis film

24 airfields

We enter Teheran today

Shots at two more Paris Nazis

Swedish vice-consul detained by Nazis

He can sign for Roosevelt

Wants the Straits

Windsors to lunch with U.S. President

Fine in Straits

EXPERIENCE

Mr. Deeds meets Joe London—Page 2

Front page of the UK's Daily Express *newspaper featuring Lucy Boehmler – 'The Face of a Spy'.*

Osten (an officer in the *Abwehr*) and Kurt Frederick Ludwig – leaders of the 'Joe K' Spy Ring.

'Ludwig's eyes lighted up when he first met her at a party,' Hoover said. 'Here was not only a potentially able spy, but a delightful playmate.'

Lucy learned a lot from these men, including the details of contacts in Germany and Portugal, how to write letters in invisible ink, and how to collect the sort of information the Nazis were interested in. But soon after they employed her, von der Osten was hit by a cab in Times Square and killed. His companion – Ludwig – grabbed his attaché case and made off. Von der Osten was then identified as Senor Don Julio Lido, ostensibly a courier for the Spanish consul. The suspicions of the New York police had already been aroused by his companion's behaviour; then they found papers on the dead man's body which were largely in German, not Spanish. His clothes had no labels and he was carrying notebooks that contained the names of US servicemen and their assignments. The NYPD handed these over to the FBI.

Meanwhile, the British censor in Bermuda had intercepted messages from the mysterious 'Joe K'; as they contained vital details of US defences, the British forwarded them to the FBI. The author of the letters, which were addressed to contacts in Argentina and China, complained of the food in America and asked to be recalled to Germany.

Then the FBI intercepted a message from Joe K to his superiors, which described the death of 'Senor Lido'. Joe K turned out to be Kurt Frederick Ludwig. Born in Ohio, an American of German heritage, he returned to his parents' homeland when he was two. German intelligence was delighted to recruit him as an agent in the war effort and sent him back to the United States in March 1940 to help set up a spy ring of agents who could gather information about US troops, the order of battle and American manufacturing.

A few months before the attack on Pearl Harbor, Ludwig and Lucy toured the coast between New York and Florida, visiting every city with a large army camp or naval base nearby. Masquerading as a salesman, Ludwig used Lucy to model for photographs he took of installations, tanks, planes or marching soldiers. The pair also gave lifts to servicemen who were hitchhiking (they kept a powerful shortwave radio in their car so that conversations could be monitored). They were so devoted to their work that they spent even their leisure hours visiting aeroplane factories and flying fields on Long Island.

If they were challenged, Lucy would open her blue eyes wide and ask where the soldiers were stationed. If they were on manoeuvres, she would say she wanted to see where. Otherwise she would charm her way into getting a tour of the camp. Young soldiers fell for this sweet and innocent act. On her arrest, it was found that she was keeping a card index of all the military installations she had visited, describing their strength, the units quartered there, their armaments and other equipment.

When she appeared in court in February 1942 alongside Ludwig and six other defendants, Lucy, aged just 18, pleaded guilty. She said that although she had met Ludwig in 1940, she had not discovered until he introduced her to von der Osten in early 1941 that the men were German agents.

INCRIMINATING EVIDENCE

Ludwig was arrested on the West Coast of the USA on 30 December 1941, following the tightening of security after Pearl Harbor. Although he had made off with von der Osten's leather attaché case, he had failed to collect other incriminating evidence from his colleague's room at the Hotel Taft. There the FBI found a copy of *Fortune* magazine giving a detailed report on aviation in the USA and UK; a book entitled *Winged Warfare* by Major General H. H. Arnold and Colonel Ira C. Eaker; and an edition of *Harper's* magazine containing an article by a pilot who ferried bombers to Britain – the details of routes, altitudes and flying times had been underlined in pencil.

There was also a book of matches from Mueller's Water Mill Inn in Centerport, Long Island, where Lucy had dined with von der Osten. When asked what she had eaten there, Lucy said: 'If you must know, it was sauerbraten.'

The G-men also found two maps in von der Osten's room. One was a small tourist map of Oahu island in Hawaii (Pearl Harbor is on Oahu) and the other was a map of the United States which Lucy had studied with Ludwig and von der Osten over dinner. A letter from von der Osten, intercepted by British intelligence, revealed information that he had learned about Pearl Harbor during a brief stop at Honolulu en route from China to San Francisco. It also contained details of the US defence facilities in Puerto Rico, gleaned from a talkative naval officer he had met on board ship.

Lucy confessed she thought working for von der Osten sounded like 'a lot of fun', and it was established in court that her motivation had not been money.

'I was supposed to get $25 (about £340/$435 now) a week,' she said. 'But I never got it. All I got were excuses.'

She only received some money for expenses and had still been hoping that Ludwig would pay her. The court heard that the information she provided, some of it containing details about shipping, had been seen by Heinrich Himmler. The clear implication was that it had contributed to the destruction of ships sailing from New York.

According to *The New York Times*: 'Miss Boehmler, who had admitted she was one of Ludwig's aides, spent the entire court day on the witness stand, testifying in a soft, girlish voice about trips to airports, Army and Navy installations and power facilities along the East Coast down to Key West, Fla.'

Under the questioning of US attorney Mathias F. Correa, Lucy had something to say about each of the other seven defendants. She described the 'stoop-shouldered, small-eyed, sharp-nosed' Ludwig as the 'brains of the ring'. He kept the book of information on the identities, cargoes, origins and likely sailing plans of ships that put in at New York harbour. In the back of the book, she said, he listed the ships that were destroyed.

Ludwig had given her sheets of paper upon which she typed innocuous letters to imaginary people in Europe. One – apparently destined for Himmler – was addressed to 'Manuel Alonzo, Madrid, Spain'. On the reverse side, marked with an X in pencil, was a secret message in invisible writing. Examples of intercepts by the British were produced in court, along with charred fragments of papers burnt by Ludwig when he knew the FBI were on his heels.

INVISIBLE INK

Lucy testified that Ludwig had given her headache pills which, when dissolved in water, made invisible ink with which she had written out messages. Before doing so she had practised with ammonium chloride – Correa placed a sample of her practice work, developed by heat into brown writing, in evidence. Lucy said that Ludwig had once sent her to deliver some of the pills to Paul T. Borchardt, another defendant.

Fifty-five-year-old Borchardt was a major in the *Wehrmacht*. A professor of military geography, he had been an associate of Professor Karl Haushofer who, through his student Rudolph Hess, influenced Hitler's expansionist policies. But Borchardt had been ousted from Germany as a non-Aryan and found himself working alongside Ludwig, who he scorned as 'a blown-up turkey'.

Lucy said she had heard of Lopez's – von der Osten's – death by phone. Ludwig had instructed her to send coded messages with the news to Buenos Aires, Shanghai, Germany and to a Mr Schultz in the German consulate in Boston. She said she did not like Ludwig and that he had written to his superiors saying she was not much help to him. Nevertheless, she had travelled with him to airports and other defence facilities in Maryland, Washington DC, Virginia, North and South Carolina, Alabama, Tennessee and Georgia. Along the way she had taken notes from Ludwig's dictation. She said the two of them had collected information on forts, as well as the number of their occupants and their equipment.

They had a code which included pet names for aircraft plants in the New York area. The Grumman plant was referred to as Grace, Brewster as Bessie, and Sperry as Sarah. Incidentally, she said, Ludwig had told her that he had received a pencilled discussion of the monthly output of Sperry bombsights from a friend of Helen Paulina Mayer, another defendant. Mrs Mayer was a 26-year-old housewife whose husband Walter had gone back to Germany by the time she was arrested. She had introduced Lucy to Ludwig.

'It was remarked that the bombsights going to Great Britain were not quite as accurate as those kept here,' Lucy said.

Helen Mayer didn't trust Ludwig, but she and her husband helped him a great deal. Once Ludwig, on a tour of aeroplane factories, fortifications and naval bases in the South, wrote asking for $80 (over £1,000/$1,200 today) which he said he needed for repairs to his car. On his return, Helen and Walter had checked the car for signs of the repairs, and could find none. Nevertheless, Helen kept on trying to obtain information to send through Ludwig back to Germany.

Of the other defendants, Lucy said: 'Rene Froehlich provided information on the identities and ailments of inmates at the military hospital on Governor's Island, where he was stationed as a selectee.'

Froehlich was a 31-year-old German-born US army private who was stationed in Fort Jay, Governor's Island in New York harbour. A naturalized citizen, he had arranged mail drops for Ludwig and picked up Ludwig's mail when he was out of town. He had also supplied defence magazines and gathered information on shipping. On the stand, Froehlich assumed the role of a dim-wit who had sold Ludwig a magazine or a book, when he could. He said he was heartbroken when pretty Lucy Boehmler had stood him up twice. But during the course of the trial it was revealed that Froehlich had continued to give information to Ludwig as an army recruit, after being drafted in 1941, including information about the camp in which he'd been trained.

Twenty-year-old Hans Helmut Pagel had made trips to see Ludwig at a resort in the Poconos, where he fled after the FBI arrested 33 members of the Duquesne Spy Ring. Ludwig knew several of the culprits, Lucy said, and 'blamed Axel Wheeler-Hill's loquacity for the ring's downfall'. Carbon paper found in his car showed references to B-17 Flying Fortresses, used by the US air force for strategic bombing; they had been typed on Ludwig's typewriter.

Nineteen-year-old Frederick Edward Schlosser, also of German extraction, had helped Ludwig to make observations of various docks and army posts in the New York area and deliver the reports to various mail drops. Lucy had no specific accusations against him, but said she had seen him at meetings of the Bund, along with the others.

The court was told that Schlosser had ridden up and down the West Side Highway, noting down information on ships docked on the Hudson. He admitted to the FBI that he had given the information to Ludwig, who transmitted it to Germany. Also presented in evidence was a letter in 'secret writing' from Ludwig which read: 'The SS *Ville de Liège* was sunk off Iceland, April 13 – many thanks.'

Lucy said that another defendant, Karl Victor Mueller, had wanted to return to Germany. He had warned her to use gloves when handling the letters she mailed to avoid leaving fingerprints. Thirty-six-year-old Mueller was a machinist and

Kurt Frederick Ludwig aka Joe K blamed Alex Wheeler-Hill for the downfall of the Duquesne Spy Ring. He had a tendency to shoot his mouth off.

naturalized US citizen who had helped gather production figures. In court, he played the clown. Testifying in his own defence, his accent was so thick and his answers wandered so far from the questions put to him by his defence counsel that the *New York Times* said Ludwig 'nearly fell off his chair' with laughter. Even so, Mueller had been a diligent worker for the Nazi cause.

Lucy also admitted that at Ludwig's behest she had written a secret letter to 'Marion Pon' – their codename for Himmler – telling him that 'competition' was very bad. In other words, the FBI were closing in.

Cross-examined by the attorney for the defence, Lucy was asked: 'Do you consider Germany your fatherland?'

'I was born there,' she replied.

'Do you prefer Germany to the United States?'

'I do not.'

'Is your allegiance or loyalty as an individual to Germany or the United States?'

'To the United States.'

Lucy had taken some part-time jobs after leaving high school and beginning at business school, but she had never earned as much as the $25 – the equivalent of £340/$435 today – a week Ludwig offered her. The money had not influenced her, though.

'You knew when you accepted this position, did you not, that you were aiding Germany and injuring the United States?' asked the defence attorney.

'I never thought about it,' she replied.

Asked what her thoughts had been when she was sending information about American defence to a hostile power in Europe, she said demurely: 'I never thought about it – just did what I was told.'

So if the money had not induced her to help Ludwig, what had?

'It sounded like a lot of fun,' she replied.

After her arrest on 26 August, Lucy was taken to FBI headquarters, where she began almost at once to make and sign statements admitting her guilt. Soon she was transferred from an FBI cell to a room at the Hotel Commodore, and from there to an undisclosed place. She was taken to the movies once or twice a week and permitted to walk in a park (she said window shopping was one of her diversions).

Twice the defence attorney asked whether she hoped for or expected lenient treatment in return for serving as a witness against her former conspirators. Each time she said simply: 'I don't expect anything.'

Further testimony revealed that Lucy had been involved in the ring's attempt to send details of the US army's new 80-ton experimental bomber, the B-19, to Germany. She added that in July and August Ludwig and Helen Mayer had realized the G-men were on their trail. Mayer wanted to go to Germany, Lucy said. Ludwig asked Mayer to memorize the information they had collected on the B-19 so that she could pass it on.

In the end, Mayer had been unable to make the trip. But when she told Lucy that she had a large quantity of information to send abroad, she obtained some of the pills used to make invisible ink from her.

Lucy Boehmler was sentenced to five years. The other members of the spy ring were found guilty and sentenced to between 14 and the maximum 20 years, served by Kurt Frederick Ludwig. US attorney Mathias F. Correa said he would have recommended a much heavier penalty for the girl, but for her unstinting aid to the prosecution.

'It is desirable and necessary for you to be confined at least for the duration of this war, for reasons that you can appreciate,' Judge Goddard told Lucy. He specified that she be sent to the federal reformatory at Alderson, West Virginia, a facility which held those convicted of spying or supporting the enemy during wartime.

CHAPTER 16

SWASTIKA SWISHERY

In 1942, 55-year-old Swedish-born Gustave Beekman was living in a redbrick town house he owned at 329 Pacific Street. This run-down block near the border between Brooklyn Heights and downtown Brooklyn would become the most famous 'house of assignation' in the entire country. Beekman described himself as a professional gardener and florist. In fact, he was the keeper of a gay bordello. Prior to this he had run a similar house a few blocks closer to the water at 235 Warren Street, but had relocated after being busted in a police raid in November 1940. He had been charged with running a disorderly house, then fined and quickly released.

The house in Pacific Street attracted professional men – Wall Street investors, warehouse managers and city employees. It was within walking distance of Brooklyn Navy Yard, so attracted young military men – mostly sailors, but also marines, soldiers and merchant seamen. These men possessed information that would be of interest to the enemies of the United States, which then included Germany and the other Axis powers.

ENTRANCE FEE

There was no evidence that Beekman was paid to arrange sexual encounters, but there was an entrance fee – the bedrooms upstairs could be rented by the hour. There were sofas and comfy chairs on the lower floors. Coffee and snacks, buffet suppers and liquor were served. An avuncular figure, Beekman greeted the servicemen attracted to his establishment with a kiss or a pat on the bottom. Sometimes he had sex with them. They appeared to be willing participants.

The comings and goings did not go unnoticed, and neighbours alerted the police. As America was at war, the concerned parties contacted the Office of Naval Intelligence, which decided to investigate. Agents set up an observation post on the fifth floor of the Holy Family Hospital, diagonally across the intersection from Beekman's bordello. It soon became clear that Beekman was supplying his wealthier clients with fit young servicemen. But what most interested the ONI was the fact that many of the clients were foreigners – German born, Nazi sympathizers and, probably, Nazi agents. They plied their young partners with booze and asked questions about manoeuvres; as ever, pillow talk was a good source of secrets.

On 14 March 1942, naval intelligence officers and plainclothesmen from the New York Police Department's Eleventh Division raided the house on Pacific Street. They arrested Beekman, two sailors, other non-military young men and several regular clients, including the composer and critic Virgil Thomson.

The story about the raid on the 'house of degradation' in Brooklyn emerged slowly in the *Brooklyn Eagle* and the *New York Post*. But the idea that it might be a nest of spies was quickly eclipsed by a story that a 'Senator X' had been caught there.

Beekman came under pressure from the ONI and the FBI, who grilled him for hours until he collapsed. Judge Samuel S. Leibowitz announced that evidence collected during the investigation suggested that enemy agents had used Beekman's establishment to entice sensitive information from vulnerable young servicemen. He told Beekman that unless he provided a complete list of clients he would suffer the maximum sentence.

MEDIA INTEREST

On 12 May 1942, the *New York Times* ran the story, saying: 'Gustave Beekman, 55, of 329 Pacific Street, Brooklyn, pleaded guilty yesterday in Special Session

Court, Brooklyn, to a charge of maintaining a house for immoral purposes. . . . He is awaiting sentence also on a recent conviction of a statutory crime, and a Kings County grand jury is investigating the possibility that his home was used for espionage purposes by enemy agents.'

In his gossip column in the *New York Daily Mirror* on 14 May, Walter Winchell wrote: 'The ad-libbers are having fun with the yarn about Brooklyn's spy nest, also known as the swastika swishery. What are the suspects going to claim they were doing there if not spying? Like the gal in the police court who accused the guy of snatching her purse from her stocking. When Hizzoner [His Honour] scolded her for not resisting, she pouted: "I didn't know he was after my money."'

The newspaper reported the flight of a mysterious 'Mr. E.' – 'one of Hitler's chief espionage agents in this country . . . a suave Nazi agent who gave freely liquor and food to sailors'. This was thought to be William Elberfeld, a German national and alleged Nazi spy who the ONI and FBI were trailing. It was alleged that Beekman was not making enough money from his clients to run his establishment so was receiving funds from Elberfeld, who ran a similar establishment in Manhattan.

Elberfeld fell out with Beekman at Thanksgiving 1941 when he told him that Sweden was the next country on Hitler's hit list. In a search of Elberfeld's apartment, a shortwave radio was found (it was an offence for a foreign national to own one at the time). No charges were brought against him, but he was interned on Ellis Island for the rest of the war.

'DOC'

With the 'swastika swishery' making headlines across the country, Beekman decided to tell all. At the head of his list was a man everyone called 'Doc'. One of Beekman's lovers, merchant mariner Charles Zuber, said 'Doc' was a man named Walsh. The assistant district attorney put two and two together and concluded that 'Doc' was David Ignatius Walsh, a 69-year-old senator from Massachusetts. A New Deal Democrat, Walsh was a champion of organized labour. As chairman of the Committee on Naval Affairs, he had been a staunch isolationist – until Pearl Harbor. Now he was fully committed to the war.

Senator Walsh was a lifelong bachelor who lived with four maiden sisters. He told an interviewer that he enjoyed the company of women as 'non-romantic companions'. His closest relationship was with his Filipino houseboy who had been in his employ for 30 years. Walsh stopped off in New York on his train trips between Washington DC and Boston. He usually arrived at Pacific Street around seven in the evening and stayed for an hour or two, taking sailors upstairs.

But although Walsh's description matched those other clients had given of 'Doc', he had not been seen entering or leaving the building. This was because his visits had stopped two days before the ONI began their surveillance – he had, perhaps, been tipped off as chairman of the Naval Affairs Committee. Nevertheless, according to the *New York Post*, Beekman's confession 'Links Senator to Spy Nest'.

Other senators rallied to Walsh's defence. Senate majority leader Alben W. Barkley of Kentucky called the accusations 'undignified, malicious and degrading'. The FBI, he said, had concluded that there was 'not the slightest foundation' that Senator Walsh had 'visited a "house of degradation" in Brooklyn . . . to connive or consort with, or to converse with, or conspire with anybody who is the enemy of the United States'. Barkley condemned the FBI's report as 'disgusting and unprintable' and refused to have it entered into the Senate's official record. Senior FBI agent P. E. Foxworth wrote a memo to J. Edgar Hoover in which he identified the source of 'the homosexual activities of Walsh (in Brooklyn) . . . and a special lead that grew out of a remark that a newspaper reporter had made at the 21 Club a few days ago, to the effect that Hitler was going to win the war, and for that reason he was going to do what he could do for a negotiated peace'. Walter Winchell was a regular at the 21 Club, one of the few reporters who could afford to go there.

Although the *Boston Globe* gave Walsh a clean bill of health, the *New York Times* was sceptical, saying: 'FBI Clears Walsh, Barkley asserts.' The *New York Post* proclaimed that Walsh had been whitewashed. When he ran again for a fifth term in 1948, Senator Walsh was defeated by Republican Henry Cabot Lodge Jr. Meanwhile, enemy interference with shipping in and out of New York had been stopped by Lucky Luciano in co-operation with the ONI. Beekman found he had been swindled. He was convicted of just one charge, sodomy, largely on the testimony of his ex-lover, Zuber, who got off scot-free. Beekman was sentenced to the maximum 20 years, which he served in Sing Sing. Released at the age of 78 on 1 April 1963, he disappeared from history.

CHAPTER 17

PUSSY CAT

In 1949, Mathilde Carré – aka *La Chatte*, 'The Cat' – was sentenced to death for treason. She had worked with the French Resistance and Britain's Special Operations Executive while simultaneously spying for the *Abwehr*, using her considerable charms to survive the war as a double, triple and even a quadruple agent.

AN INTELLIGENT GIRL

Mathilde began her career in espionage with a chance meeting. Born Mathilde Lucie (or Lily) Bélard, in 1908, she was brought up by her maternal grandparents and two maiden aunts. An intelligent girl, she attended the Sorbonne and became a teacher. While at the Sorbonne, she fell in love with a law student named Marc. But when he was sent to North Africa to do his military service, a fellow teacher named Maurice Carré proposed to Mathilde and she married him in 1933.

The marriage was not happy. On her wedding night, her husband said: 'With your free and easy life as a student I should never have believed you were a virgin.'

In her memoirs, she wrote: 'I did not reply. I merely closed my eyes to keep back the tears welling up in them. The whole affair seemed to be false, comic and a complete illusion.'

Maurice and Mathilde lived apart until he was posted to Algeria and she accompanied him. She wanted children, but childhood mumps had left Maurice impotent. Bored, she took one of Maurice's Muslim friends as a lover. When the war came, Maurice was called up, but instead of returning to France to fight on the Western Front, he opted to take a post as a staff officer in Syria. Considering him a coward, Mathilde filed for divorce, but in fact her husband died a hero's death at the Battle of Monte Cassino in 1944.

PREGNANCY

Mathilde returned to France where she trained to be a nurse. During the Battle of France she was a matron at a first-aid post in Beauvais. Unfazed by attacks by the *Luftwaffe*, she remarked to a doctor: 'There's almost a sensual pleasure in real danger, don't you think? Your whole body seems to come alive.'

After the fall of France, she met a young officer named Jean Mercieaux who was serving in the French Foreign Legion. At a seminary outside Cazère-sur-Garonne, they slept in the bed in the bishop's cell under an enormous crucifix and made love under the eyes of the Virgin Mary. Mathilde fell pregnant, but miscarried. In her grief, she blamed Jean for her loss and they split up.

Mathilde then met French tank commander René Aubertin, who she would later recruit into the Resistance. In September 1940 she was in Toulouse, where she met a Polish airman named Roman Garby-Czerniawski in a restaurant named La Frégate. According to Garby-Czerniawski, the headwaiter could not find him a table on his own, so seated him at one where two women were already sitting.

One of them was Mathilde, who he described as 'small, and in her early thirties. Her pale thin face, with thin lips, was animated by very vivid eyes. She wore a black, tailored costume of good cut and elegant taste. With my lowered eyes I could see her lovely hands with slim, long fingers, carefully kept. I could hear her voice as she talked to her companion, a slightly older, plumper woman.'

Mathilde told a different story: 'A man was sitting near us alone at a small table and he had smiled at me from time to time.' A flirtatious woman, she invited him to join them.

After dinner the two women stopped at a bar for a drink. Garby-Czerniawski followed them and asked Mathilde, in a thick Polish accent, whether she could give him some French lessons.

'Why do you come to me when there are plenty of other girls around here who are prettier?' she asked. And in broken French, with a serious look in his dark eyes, he replied, 'Because you look so intelligent and gay. You know what I shall call you? My little Spitfire.'

The next morning, they met at the Café Tortoni. According to Mathilde's autobiography: 'As soon as he saw me coming he rushed up, kissed my hand and thanked me for coming. He was a man of about the same height and age as myself, thin, muscular, with a long narrow face, rather large nose and green eyes which must have originally been clear and attractive but were now flecked with contusions as the result of a flying accident. All his teeth were false or crowned. With his dark, sleek hair he could have been mistaken for a tough, excitable Corsican. He was not handsome but he radiated a kind of confidence and the enthusiasm of youth, an intelligence and a will-power which would alternately give place to a typical Slav nonchalance, or the airs of a spoilt, affectionate child.'

They continued to see each other and 'their friendship became intimate'. While admitting that they became lovers, Mathilde insisted 'that there was no serious affair' between them. MI5 did not believe her.

THE FIGHTER PILOT

Roman Garby-Czerniawski was already an important intelligence asset. The son of a wealthy Warsaw financier and a Polish patriot, he had trained as a fighter pilot before the war, but a serious crash left him partially sighted and deskbound. By the time the Germans invaded Poland, he was already an intelligence officer and had written a well-received tract on counter-intelligence. A colleague said he was 'a man who lives and thinks spying'.

Garby-Czerniawski escaped to Romania and then, using forged documents, travelled through Yugoslavia and Italy to France. With the fall of France, the Poles disbanded. Rather than flee to Britain, he went underground, and met a young widow named Renée Borni who let him adopt her late husband Armand's identity.

With France divided into the German-occupied zone to the north and west and the 'free' zone run by the puppet government in Vichy, Garby-Czerniawski travelled south to Marseille to get in touch with the Polish secret service who were already in contact with MI6, trying to get permission to run a spy ring in the occupied territories. In Toulouse, he met Mathilde.

Following her miscarriage, Mathilde was on the verge of suicide. In Toulouse, she had stood on a high bridge over a river, planning to throw herself off. But she changed her mind: 'Instead of throwing myself into the Garonne, I would fling myself into the war,' she said. 'If I really intended to commit suicide, it would be more intelligent to commit a useful suicide.' To celebrate, she went to dinner at Le Frégate.

After three weeks, Garby-Czerniawski admitted to her that he was a spy. His enthusiasm for his occupation was infectious.

'Every time he spoke of the war his eyes flashed,' she said. 'He would not accept that Poland had been defeated.' He asked Mathilde, who he called Lily, to help him set up a multi-cell intelligence network. Together they would 'do great things'. She could not resist seeing herself as the 'Mata Hari of the Second World War'. Indeed, she subtitled her autobiography: 'The Truth about the Most Remarkable Woman Spy since Mata Hari – by Herself'.

CAT-LIKE

While Garby-Czerniawski, codenamed ARMAND, returned to Marseille to report her recruitment as agent VICTOIRE, Mathilde went to Vichy where she contacted the Deuxième Bureau. She told them that she was going to Paris with a Pole to set up a spy network and would be happy to work for them; in exchange, they taught her the basics of spycraft.

Along the way, she picked up her soubriquet – *La Chatte*. She said it was coined by American reporters staying at the Hôtel des Ambassadeurs in Vichy, where she had taken to scratching the leather chairs. Garby-Czerniawski had his own account.

'You know, Lily, you walk, especially in your soft shoes, like a cat – so quietly,' he had said.

'And I can scratch as well if I wish!' she said, raising her slim hands with the long fingers and long nails. 'Some other people have also compared me to a cat.'

'I would rather call you "She-cat" – *La Chatte*.'

'I like it.'

'So "*La Chatte*" in our organization you shall be.'

The pair moved to Paris and lived together in a studio apartment near La Santé prison in Montparnasse, though they continued to have other love affairs on the side. She passed him off as her cousin and explained that he did not speak French well because he had spent his childhood abroad.

THE FAMILY

Garby-Czerniawski believed that the spy ring should be 'inter-allied' – hence the *Interallié* network was born.

Because some French men refused to work for a Polish man, Mathilde took the role of chief recruiter while Garby-Czerniawski collated the information they collected and transmitted it to London.

'In her black fur coat, red hat and small, flat, red shoes she moved swiftly from one appointment to another, bringing new contacts, new possibilities, leaving me free to concentrate on studying the news from our agents and condensing it into our reports,' said Garby-Czerniawski.

Mathilde recruited her one-time lover René Aubertin, along with Monique Deschamps – codenamed MOUSTIQUE (mosquito) – who was described as a 'tiny, chain-smoking firebrand of a woman' and Janusz Wlodarczyk, MAURICE, a former Polish navy radio operator. The network expanded to include members of the Resistance – railway workers, fishermen, gendarmes, criminals and housewives. Calling themselves *La Famille* – The Family – they delivered the intelligence they had gathered to 'post boxes' in Paris, which included the lavatory attendant at La Palette and a concierge on Rue Lamarck 'who received a bayonet thrust in the buttocks when the Germans entered Paris, so it was only natural he should hate them'.

CHAPTER 17

By the middle of 1941, Garby-Czerniawski said that his 'big network composed of French patriots, directed by a Pole and working for England, was now the last stronghold of Allied resistance against Germany'. His aim was to supply the British with a complete picture of the German deployment in France – ammunition dumps, airfields, radar stations, gun emplacements, naval installations, troop movements and defensive positions. He would type up his reports on tissue paper. Every few weeks, a courier codenamed RAPIDE would take these reports to the Gare de Lyon, where he would board the Marseille train. Ten minutes before it was due to depart, he would lock himself in the first-class lavatory.

Above the toilet bowl was a metal sign which read: '*Remplacez le couvercle après l'usage*' – 'Replace the lid after use.' With the screwdriver blade covered with a handkerchief to avoid tell-tale scratches, the courier would unscrew the sign, place the reports behind it and screw it back into place. Once the train had crossed the border into unoccupied France, a member of the Polish secret service would unscrew the sign, remove the reports, and replace them with fresh instructions for *Interallié*. A courier would then take the reports across Spain to Portugal. From there they would be sent to the Polish government in exile in London, who would hand them on to MI6.

Later a shortwave radio the size of a bulky laptop was smuggled into the cccupied zone from Vichy France. It was set up in a top-floor flat near the Trocadero. Garby-Czerniawski's nominal wife Renée Borni, codenamed VIOLETTE, was brought in to encode and decode messages. They became lovers. Mathilde loathed Renée, calling her 'a typical little provincial woman, and badly dressed'. Garby-Czerniawski denied that Mathilde was motivated by jealousy, merely describing her as a 'strange woman, idealistic but ruthless, ambitious, very anxious and highly strung'.

Three more underground radio stations were set up, but they were overwhelmed; reports were up to 400 pages long and often accompanied by maps and diagrams. These were photographed and the undeveloped film was smuggled over the Spanish border, after being packed in such a way that if the container was opened by anyone not in the know the film would be exposed and rendered useless.

So much information reached London that MI6 had trouble handling it. By the time a message giving the planned route of Hermann Göring's personal train was decoded, it was too late for the RAF to mount an attack.

VICTOIRE SWITCHES SIDES

On the night of 1 October 1942, Garby-Czerniawski was picked up by an RAF Lysander and flown to London. There he was debriefed by Colonel Stanislaw Gano, the head of Polish intelligence and introduced to the Polish prime minister in exile, General Wladyslaw Sikorski who awarded him the *Virtuti Militari*, Poland's highest military decoration. Then, at dawn on 8 November, he was parachuted back into France. But all was not well.

'Subconsciously I felt a disturbing uneasiness,' he said later.

The anniversary of the founding of *Interallié* was to take place on 16 November. By this point *Interallié* had some 50 agents, each with two or three sub-agents. That evening ARMAND, VICTOIRE, VIOLETTE and MAURICE gathered at the flat in Montparnasse to celebrate with black-market champagne and sandwiches. At 8 p.m. they gathered round the radio. Following a brief passage of French patriotic music, they heard the announcer say: 'Many happy returns to our family in France on the occasion of their anniversary.'

MAURICE then transmitted the message: 'Against the Germans always and in every way. *Vive la Liberté!*'

On the morning of 18 November, Garby-Czerniawski was woken by a gunshot. Renée screamed. The Gestapo burst in and the couple were arrested. Mathilde and the other members of *Interallié* were rounded up the same day. Mathilde was held at La Santé prison, where she was searched and her possessions confiscated.

MI5 noted later: 'It is difficult to assess the exact moment that VICTOIRE's collaboration with the Germans begins.' Assessing her case, Captain Christopher Harmer of the SOE noted that, in prison, according to her own testimony, she still had a spare pack of cigarettes to give to a Gestapo officer. When she complained about her damp and dirty bedding, it was immediately changed. And the dinner she said she had been given – four slices of meat, vegetables, bread, cheese and ersatz coffee – was considerably more than the bread and water other prisoners received.

Mathilde was interrogated by Hugo Bleicher, the most feared *Abwehr* counter-intelligence officer in France. From an entry in her diary he noted that she was going to meet an agent in the Pam-Pam restaurant that day.

'I will accompany you,' said Bleicher. 'I will be in your organization; you will introduce me as so-and-so, and when this agent has spoken sufficiently I will arrest him. We will work thus, you and I, and if you do not try to double-cross me you can be sure that you will be free from tonight. If you betray me, you will be immediately executed without trial. Save your skin and regain your liberty. You have done quite enough to be shot several times, having hidden this escaped Polish officer and passed him off as your cousin, more than a year's espionage, and certainly crossing the demarcation line clandestinely, and saving English people: all things punishable by death and you know it. You had better save your skin and start to understand that England is beaten. You can do similar sort of work for 6,000 francs a month. England always makes other people do her work for her and doesn't even know how to pay them.'

Mathilde went along with Bleicher's plan. It was, she said, a 'purely animal reaction . . . winning Bleicher's confidence seemed the surest means of one day being able to escape'.

They took a military car to the Pam-Pam restaurant, where she introduced Bleicher as 'a trusted friend'. When they left, Bleicher offered the contact a lift, then told the agent that he was arresting him. VICTOIRE said the normally pallid agent turned green, then said to her: 'What a slut you are.'

Afterwards, Bleicher took Mathilde to lunch.

'You see how easy it is?' he said. One by one, Mathilde gave up all the names of the people in the network.

At dinner that evening, Bleicher made his first advance on her. In her memoirs, Mathilde explained: 'Bleicher spoke German, boasting of his successes and slapping me on the thigh, which only made him appear more repulsive in my eyes. I could not hide my disgust.'

Harmer noted: 'Knowing VICTOIRE, one may be certain that the truth was the exact reverse.'

By the end of the week, more than 60 *Interallié* agents and sub-agents had been arrested, often lured into a trap by Mathilde. There were tragic consequences. The wife of one agent who refused to speak hanged herself in her cell after her children were taken away.

Ostensibly for her own safety, Mathilde moved into Bleicher's house. He had decided to use her. She was to send a message to London saying that ARMAND and VIOLETTE had been arrested, but that she had managed to hold on to one of the radios and could continue sending intelligence from her principal agents who were still at large. It would, of course, be misleading material made up by Bleicher.

THE GREATEST ACT OF COWARDICE

In her MI5 debrief, Mathilde claimed that for the first three weeks Bleicher was the perfect gentleman. A teetotaller, he played the piano for her in the evenings. Inevitably, they became lovers. Elsewhere, she admitted sleeping with Bleicher after one night in the cells.

'I was fully cognisant of the greatest act of cowardice in my life committed on 19 November with Bleicher,' she wrote in her autobiography *I Was 'The Cat'*. 'It was a purely animal cowardice, the reaction of a body which had survived its first night in prison, had suffered cold, felt the icy breath of death and suddenly found warmth once more in a pair of arms . . . even if they were the arms of the enemy. I hated myself for my weakness and as a result of my abasement I hated the Germans even more. That morning under my cold shower I swore that one day I would make the Germans pay.'

Garby-Czerniawski was interrogated and mistreated, but not tortured. The Nazis were confident of victory and Bleicher thought the Polish leader might prove useful (Bleicher had a reputation for his skilful running of double agents).

Six weeks later, Renée Borni was ushered into Garby-Czerniawski's cell. She told him of Mathilde's treachery and the destruction of the *Interallié* network. Nevertheless, she said, the Germans had told her that they admired his methods. Saying that he 'might exploit this favourable circumstance', she implored him not to kill himself as he had been threatening.

Taking her advice, Garby-Czerniawski went above Bleicher's head and contacted the commander of the German forces in occupied France General Otto von Stülpnagel, who was succeeded by his cousin General Carl-Heinrich von Stülpnagel in February 1942.

In his first letter, Garby-Czerniawski wrote: 'No collaboration which might be proposed to me could come about unless I was convinced that I was working for the good of the Polish nation. . . . If the German nation has among its plans the reconstruction of the rights of the Polish nation, in this case alone discussions about my collaboration could take place. Even in this case all conversations could only take place with an officer of the General Staff who knows these problems and who is authorized to discuss them with me.'

In a second letter, he pointed out that since the beginning of the war Britain had made promises of support to Poland that it was not capable of fulfilling. If the Allies won the war, Poland would find itself under the heel of the Soviet Union – 'all things considered, the best solution would be to come under the cultural protection of Germany, since German culture is preferable to the culture of the barbarian'. He offered to become a double agent. If the Germans could smuggle him into England, he would act as a spy for Germany.

His mother lived in occupied Poland. His brother was a prisoner of war. His lover and many of his colleagues from the *Interallié* ring were in German hands. He himself faced the death penalty if prosecuted. However, he said that he would only work for the Nazis for ideological reasons – that it would be for the good of Poland. The Germans believed him and released him on 14 July 1942, confident that if he fed them false information they would be able to spot it and read the British intentions in his messages 'in reverse'.

After regaining his strength, Garby-Czerniawski was taught how to build a radio transmitter, then he slipped over the border into Vichy France with two wireless crystals concealed in the heels of his shoes. He contacted the Polish secret service, who arranged for MI6 to smuggle him out through Spain along the underground route used by escaping PoWs. He was shadowed by Bleicher who had brought along one of his French mistresses to enjoy a free holiday in the South of France.

A ROBUST IDEALIST

Meanwhile, Mathilde had met up with Pierre de Vomécourt, codenamed LUCAS, a French officer who became the first SOE agent to be parachuted into France after the capitulation. When de Vomécourt's radio operator was arrested and shot, he had no way to communicate with London and had no choice but to contact Mathilde.

'I took an immediate liking to LUCAS,' she said. 'He was a clean, robust idealist with a number of good ideas, but without the necessary drive to run an organization, little physical stamina and no knowledge of military information.'

She persuaded Bleicher to let her take the same role in de Vomécourt's organization as she had in *Interallié*; all the intelligence his network collected would be passed by the *Abwehr* before an edited version was sent to London. To complete the Nazi ensnarement, she and de Vomécourt became lovers.

When Mathilde supplied supposedly forged identity cards and passes that turned out to be genuine, de Vomécourt confronted her. She confessed she was working for the Germans. As the *Abwehr* were on to him, de Vomécourt had no option but to flee France. Mathilde managed to persuade Bleicher to allow her to leave with him, so she could continue spying for the Nazis in England. The ruse worked and on the night of 12 February 1942, the Royal Navy sent a motor torpedo boat to pick the couple up from a small cove in Brittany.

Mathilde broke under interrogation by the British, saying that she had intended to switch sides once she was on British soil. However, when de Vomécourt returned to France and was soon arrested, she was of little further interest to the Germans. And when Garby-Czerniawski arrived in London that October, the full extent of her treachery became known and she was sent to Holloway, and then Aylesbury prison. De Vomécourt, who was lucky to have found himself treated as a prisoner of war rather than a spy, spent the rest of the war in Colditz castle, and survived.

Garby-Czerniawski was interrogated by the British and the Poles. At first they accepted the story of his escape. However, after six weeks, he gave Colonel Stanislaw Gano of Polish intelligence a 64-page typewritten document, entitled 'The Great Game'. In it, he confessed to making a deal with the *Abwehr* and spelt out the terms under which he had agreed to take on his mission to London. As proof of his story, he produced the wireless crystals from the heels of his shoes.

Although MI5 were suspicious at first, they recruited him into the Double Cross System under the codename BRUTUS and he played a major part in the Allied deception operation prior to the D-Day landings in Normandy in 1944. He was one of the primary agents passing false information as part of Fortitude South, the deception plan aimed at convincing Germany that the Allies would land in the Pas de Calais area directly across the English Channel from south-east England.

After the end of the war, Poland fell under the control of the Soviet Union. Garby-Czerniawski remained in Britain and, on his death in 1985, was buried in an RAF cemetery.

After six years in British jails, Mathilde Carré was extradited to France in January 1949 where she was charged with treason. At her trial, 33 witnesses condemned her for sleeping with the enemy. She was also condemned out of her own mouth. The entry from her diary from the first night she slept with Bleicher was read out in court. It said: 'What I wanted most was a good meal, a man, and, once more, Mozart's *Requiem.*'

Found guilty, she was sentenced to death, but her sentence was commuted to 20 years. Following her release in 1954 she was contacted by Bleicher, then a tobacconist in Württenberg, who asked her to collaborate on a book with him. But she was finished with collaboration and instead wrote an independent version of her experiences, *J'ai été 'La Chatte'* (*I Was 'The Cat'*) in 1959 – revised as *On m'appelait la Chatte* (*I Was Called the Cat*) in 1975.

She died in 2007, aged 98.

CHAPTER 18

BLONDE POISON

Stella Goldschlag was born in Berlin in 1922, the only child of an assimilated Jewish family. Her background, together with her beauty and ruthless determination, made her an important weapon in the Nazis' underground efforts to track down and capture Jewish people in hiding during World War II.

SCHOOL STUNNER

When Hitler came to power in 1933, Jews were no longer to attend state school, so Stella attended the Goldschmidt School set up by the local Jewish community. Schoolmate and author Peter Wyden, whose family escaped Nazi Germany in 1937, called her the 'traitor of the Goldschmidt School' and the antithesis of Anne Frank. She stood out because what were then thought of as her Aryan good looks.

'Stella was the school's Marilyn Monroe: tall, slim, leggy, cool, with light blue eyes, teeth out of a toothpaste ad, and pale satin skin,' said Wyden. 'She wore her glowing blonde hair in a pageboy bob that seemed to dance whenever she moved. Her posture was so perfect that it required little imagination to picture her atop a pedestal, a monument to beauty, albeit distant up there, silent, sequestered in her private heights – a masterpiece, untouchable, a fantasy for a pubescent boy, and a vision I could never forget.'

Pretty Berliner Stella Goldschlag was one of a kind. She betrayed her own race. In return for an assurance that she and her parents would be spared transportation, she agreed to entice the untergetaucht *or 'submerged' Jews out of hiding in the German capital. They were known colloquially as 'U-boats'.*

Stella's father had fought in World War I and was a loyal German. He worked for Gaumont, the French-owned newsreel company, but lost his job when the Nazis began to purge Jews from positions of influence. On 10 November 1938, Stella was sent home from school early to find that her father had gone into hiding. Terrified, she and her mother spent the night with the lights switched off, creeping around in stockinged feet, with no hot food and fearing to flush the lavatory. *Kristallnacht* – the Nazi pogrom which took place on the night of 9–10 November 1938 – left the streets littered with broken glass following attacks on Jewish shops and businesses. The Goldschlag family tried to flee the country, but were unable to obtain visas.

Opportunities for Jews to make a living rapidly disappeared. Stella earned a pittance posing nude for life classes at the art school where she had enrolled to study fashion design. Fellow student Regina Gutermann said: 'I thought she was so beautiful, such a Rubens figure. Her walk was sexy and it didn't look posed. She had a sweetness in her speech – she was class.'

Naturally, male admirers besieged her life classes.

Eventually Stella found work in an armaments factory. After 16 September 1941, Jews were forced to wear a yellow Star of David stitched to their clothes. Stella only wore it at work; at other times, she risked doing without it.

At the age of 17 she became a vocalist in a band run by her boyfriend Manfred Kübler. Her role model was Josephine Baker, but her musical career was curtailed when the Nazis denounced American jazz as decadent. The Kübler family had already tried to escape. They had been passengers on the 'Voyage of the Damned' when the liner *St Louis* was turned away from America and Cuba and had to return its Jewish refugees to Europe.

Stella and Manfred married in October 1941. By then, the mass deportations of Jews in Europe had already started. Many people committed suicide rather than surrender to an unknown fate. On 27 February 1943, the SS surrounded the factory where Stella and her mother were employed. While the workers were being rounded up, the two women slipped into the cellar to hide. They waited there until the shift changed, then walked out past a sleepy guard, showing him the reverse of their identification cards which did not carry the purple 'J' for '*Jude*'. Stella and her mother were both blond, and the guard suspected nothing.

Tragically Manfred was not so lucky. He was captured, sent to Auschwitz, and never seen again.

U-BOATS

The Goldschlag family then became 'U-boats' – Jews living illegally and secretly in Berlin. One day in the spring of 1943 Stella encountered another U-boat named Guenther Rogoff, an ardent admirer of hers from art school life classes. He had once persuaded her to pose for him in a private lesson, but she refused to take her clothes off. This time, when they met in the street, she agreed to go back to the room he rented under a false name. On the streetcar, she asked: 'Aren't you worried that you're being foolhardy by taking me back to your place?' Rogoff quickly realized the danger he was placing himself in and changed his mind.

Thanks to Rogoff's training as an artist, he could support himself as a U-boat by forging vital document for others. He forged a police identification card for Stella. When his forgeries began to be spotted, he used his well-honed skills and forged documents to make his escape into Switzerland.

Stella then met another handsome Jewish forger named Rolf Isaaksohn, who passed himself off as Rolf von Jagow. They moved in together, living in a flat where another Jewish man was being protected by his Christian wife. Six people lived in the apartment, practising what they called 'noiseless living'. To avoid alerting the neighbours, no more than three of them could be on their feet at one time. This meant that Rolf and Stella spent a lot of time in bed together. Otherwise they would go out to crowded places where they could maintain their anonymity.

After a few months, however, this strategy failed. At lunchtime on 2 July 1943, Stella was waiting for Rolf at a busy restaurant when a Jewish acquaintance of hers named Inge Lustig came in and waved. Stella smiled in recognition – at which point Inge turned and fled and the Gestapo rushed in and grabbed Stella. Inge was working as a *Greifer* or 'catcher' – a Jew who sought out U-boats and identified them to the police.

When the Gestapo checked Stella's papers, they spotted Rogoff's handiwork and figured they would have no difficulty beating Rogoff's whereabouts out of a slender young blonde. Neither they nor Stella knew that Rogoff had already fled the country.

TORTURE

At the local Gestapo headquarters, Stella was held in solitary confinement in a cell where she could neither sit nor lie down as the floor was underwater. She was interrogated and beaten. Until this point, her dazzling good looks had given her power over men, but now she was in the hands of brutes who thought nothing of beating her to a bloody pulp.

At her trial after the war, she said: 'They kicked both of my shins to breaking point and kept beating the same spot on my spine. I was bleeding from my mouth, ears and nose, and couldn't eat for days. They wanted to throttle me. Three times they took the safety off a pistol and put it against my temple. Totally shattered, I lay unconscious on the floor. Then they kicked me with their boots and I gave up on my life.'

When the Gestapo abandoned trying to get her to talk, Stella was sent to a makeshift women's prison near Tempelhof airport. She complained of a toothache and her guards took her to a dentist's surgery where she made her escape from the waiting room. She went to see her parents, who were hiding with friends. The three of them moved to a pension in Kaiserallee which they had been told was safe. It wasn't, and the Gestapo turned up. Stella had been free for less than 12 hours.

She was returned to prison and beaten again, but was saved from being deported to a death camp because she was considered a potential source of information. On the night of 23 August 1943, the Allies began their major bombing campaign against Berlin. The factories around Tempelhof were a target, and the prison in which Stella was being held was hit by incendiaries. Inmates were burnt alive, some of them forced back into the flames by armed guards. But Stella managed to escape, crawling through the rubble with a Hungarian woman. In the chaos, they fled to a nearby park.

Stella's parents were being held in a transit camp based around the desecrated Jewish cemetery on Grosse Hamburger Strasse. She went there and gave herself up. Her parents had been scheduled for deportation to Auschwitz, but on Stella's arrival this was delayed. Stella agreed to help the catchers hunt down Guenther Rogoff in the hope that her parents' lives would be spared.

When the search proved futile, she was accused of lying and all three Goldschlags were listed for Auschwitz. In desperation, Stella used her good looks to beguile the camp commandant *SS Hauptsturmführer* Walter Dobberke and his deputy *SS Rottenführer* Felix Lachmuth: where else would they find a blond, blue-eyed Jewess who would be able to tell them where the U-boats were hiding?

A PACT WITH THE DEVIL

Stella agreed to become a catcher. In return she was given a private room, a pass to leave the camp at any time and permission not to wear the Star of David. Meanwhile, her parents remained at Grosse Hamburger Strasse as hostages.

U-boats known to Stella soon started disappearing and she became notorious, earning the nickname 'the Blonde Poison'. Although photographs of her circulated in the U-boat community, she still managed to hand over a large number, some believe thousands, of Jews. But despite this, the Nazis failed to keep their promise to her. After seven months, she was told that her parents could not be held back from deportation any longer. They were sent to Theresienstadt concentration camp.

By this time Rolf Isaaksohn had also been arrested and, to save himself, had also volunteered to become a catcher. Rolf and Stella married and went on the hunt together. Stella's excellent memory for names, addresses and dates proved invaluable to the Nazis and, despite her parents' deportation, she continued to turn in fellow Jews with great zeal. To amuse herself in her spare time, she would spend weekends with *Wehrmacht* soldiers, unaware that she was committing *Rassenschande* – that is, sexual relations between Aryans and non-Aryans which had been outlawed by the Nuremberg Laws in 1935.

As the Allies advanced on Berlin, Stella knew the end was drawing near and comforted herself with other men at the Jewish Hospital (which was being used as a collection centre). Among them were two brothers named Hans and Heinz. Hans was also sleeping with Greta, the head nurse of paediatrics, who, in turn, was sleeping with Dr Walter Lustig, the director of the Jewish Hospital. Other nurses competed for his favours.

In September 1944, a detainee called Heino Meissl arrived at the camp. He had been living illegally, and when identified by a catcher argued he should not be deported as his mother was full-Aryan, and his Prague-born father only 'half Jewish'. Although other inmates warned Meissl of Stella's infamous treachery, he was immediately attracted to her. She tried to persuade him that she had mended her ways; while he didn't believe her, he hoped that her influence with the Gestapo might save him from the death camps.

The two became lovers, though Stella still shared a room with Rolf. She managed to keep striking Heino off the transport lists and, in return, hoped he would come in useful as a character witness once the Allies arrived. In February 1945, Stella discovered she was pregnant. She said the child was Heino's and that she loved him and wanted to marry him. But Heino wanted her to have an abortion, believing that she only wanted to keep the child because it was thought that Soviet troops eschewed raping pregnant women.

Nevertheless, he helped Stella escape from Berlin and she sought refuge in the market town of Liebenwalde in the woods of Brandenburg. There she gave birth to a daughter, baptized Yvonne Meissl; but when she was arrested, the child was taken from her and raised by a Jewish foster family.

Put on trial by the Soviets, Stella was sentenced to ten years' hard labour and sent to a former Nazi concentration camp. On her release, she moved to West Berlin, where she was put on trial again. She was sentenced once more to ten years, but immediately set free when the ten years she had spent in a Soviet labour camp were taken into account. She tried to establish contact with her daughter, but Yvonne wanted nothing to do with her.

Stella married a further three times, but eventually killed herself by jumping out of the window of her Berlin apartment in 1994, aged 72.

CHAPTER 19

GRAND DESIGNS

Rumours that the famous French couturier Coco Chanel – creator of 'the Little Black Dress' – was a collaborator during the war are well known. At the height of the German occupation, she lived at the Ritz Hotel in Paris although it had been requisitioned by the Germans to house senior Nazis, including Göring and Goebbels, when they visited. She also took as her lover SS officer Hans Gunther von Dincklage, who worked both for the *Abwehr* and the Gestapo.

VENGEANCE

When Paris was liberated in August 1944, vengeance was wreaked on those who had collaborated. Many were beaten and shot. 'Horizontal collaborators' – women and girls who had slept with the Germans – were dragged naked from their houses. They had their heads shaved by angry citizens and some were branded with the swastika.

Coco sought to mitigate her position by offering free bottles of Chanel No. 5 to American GIs. Nevertheless, the street-fighters of *Les Forces Françaises de l'Intérieur*, who were loyal to the leader of the Free French General Charles de Gaulle, took her to their headquarters for questioning. She was released thanks

Coco Chanel was right-wing, homophobic, anti-Semitic and addicted to morphine. She also actively collaborated with the Nazis when they occupied Paris.

to the intervention of Duff Cooper, British ambassador to de Gaulle's provisional government, on the instructions of Winston Churchill who had known Chanel since the 1920s. She then sought refuge in Switzerland, where she was later re-united with von Dincklage.

In 1949, she was called to testify at the trial of Baron Louis de Vaufreland, who was subsequently sentenced to six years for collaboration. Chanel was never charged and in later years was completely rehabilitated. She designed dresses for the wife of the French president Georges Pompidou. The president himself opened an exhibition to her life and work after her death in 1972. That was remarkable enough. However, it was later discovered that not only had she been a collaborator, she had also been a Nazi agent who had undertaken wartime missions for the Germans.

LA COCOTTE

Gabrielle Bonheur Chanel was born in 1883. Her mother died when she was 12, and she was sent to an orphanage where she learned to sew, but she was not content to be simply a seamstress. On leaving, six years later, she supplemented her income earned from sewing by singing in a café frequented by cavalry officers. There she earned the soubriquet 'Coco' – possibly from a ditty she sang, or perhaps as an abbreviation of '*cocotte*', the French slang word for a kept woman.

Coco caught the eye of the wealthy ex-cavalry officer Étienne Balsan and she became his mistress, living with him in his château and, possibly, giving birth to his child. In 1908, she switched her affections to Balsan's friend, the English polo player Captain Arthur 'Boy' Chapel, who installed her in an apartment in Paris and helped her start a business making ladies' hats. When Coco moved into women's fashionwear, he financed boutiques for her in Paris, Biarritz and Deauville. She opened the House of Chanel at 31 Rue Cambon, near the Ritz in Paris, where she registered as a couturière and found fame and fortune during World War I by designing clothing which liberated women's bodies from restrictive corsetry.

As an aristocrat, Chapel could hardly marry a woman of Coco's lowly background. In 1918, he wedded Lady Diana Wyndham, though he and Coco remained lovers. In 1919 Chapel was killed in a car accident, allegedly en route to meet with Chanel. After his death, when *The Times* announced that he had left handsome bequests both to her and to an Italian countess, Coco discovered she had not been his only mistress. Years later, in exile in Switzerland, she told biographer Paul Morand: 'His death was a terrible blow to me. In losing Chapel, I lost everything. What followed was not a life of happiness, I have to say.'

Coco developed Chanel No. 5 with the help of her Russian lover Grand Duke Dmitri Pavlovich, who introduced her to the perfumer Ernest Beaux. To market the fragrance, she set up Parfums Chanel with the Wertheimer brothers, Pierre and Paul, who owned the cosmetics house Bourjois and could give her access to its production facilities and large distribution network.

COURTING THE BRITISH TOP BRASS

Chanel continued her association with the British aristocracy through the well-connected Vera Bate Lombardi, reputedly the illegitimate daughter of the Marquess of Cambridge. Vera was married to Alberto Lombardi, a leading member of the Italian Fascist Party. In 1923 she introduced Chanel to the Duke of Westminster, and the two began an affair which would last for the next ten years. Chanel also numbered among her lovers the Prince of Wales, Lord Rothermere and several French politicians. Mixing in these circles she met the Duke of Westminster's lifelong friend Winston Churchill, and went hunting wild boar at the duke's lodge in Bordeaux.

Churchill was enchanted by Coco. In January 1928, he wrote to his wife Clementine: 'The famous Chanel turned up and I took great fancy to her – a most capable and agreeable woman – much the strongest personality Benny [the Duke of Westminster] has been up against. She hunted vigorously all day, motored to Paris after dinner, and today is engaged in passing and improving dresses on endless streams of mannequins. . . . With her was Vera Bate, née Arkwright.'

Later, Winston wrote to Clementine again, this time from Stack Lodge in Scotland: 'Chanel is here in place of Violet [the Duke of Westminster's second wife] . . . she fishes from morn to night and has killed fifty salmon (sometimes weighing 24 pounds). She is very agreeable – really a great and strong being fit to rule a man and an empire. Benny is very well and I think extremely happy to be mated with an equal. Her ability is balancing his power.'

The Duke of Westminster encouraged Coco to open a fashion house in London. The clientele soon included the Duchess of York, who would later become queen as the wife of George VI. But when the duke invited Princess Stephanie von Hohenlohe to go fishing with him in Scotland, Coco sought consolation with her former lover, the poet Pierre Reverdy, in Paris. She took further lovers among intellectual circles there, her conquests including the artist Pablo Picasso and the composer Igor Stravinsky, an admirer of Mussolini. She also became a user of the then-fashionable drug, morphine. Chanel eventually broke up with the Duke of Westminster, because of his infidelities, and from Reverdy, because he constantly eluded her.

A CAUSE FOR CONCERN?

Naturally the Sûreté, the detective branch of the French police, kept a watch on prominent supporters of the fascist cause; they therefore monitored the comings and goings of the Duke of Westminster, Chanel, Princess Stephanie, and Vera Lombardi and her husband. German intelligence was already active in France. Baron Hans Günther '*Spatz*' ('Sparrow') von Dincklage had spent ten years as an intelligence officer and earned the friendship of General Walther von Brauchitsch, who Hitler would later appoint supreme commander of the German army. With his English mother and his half-Jewish wife Maximiliane ('Catsy'), von Dincklage was the perfect undercover agent for the *Abwehr* to send to the Côte d'Azur. His charm and good looks attracted both men and women. Meanwhile, Catsy seduced two naval officers – von Dincklage's tennis partner Charles Coton and naval engineer Pierre Gaillard, who supplied strategic information on the French naval base at Cap Blanc, Bizette, Tunisia. The two men would become the cornerstones of von Dincklage's espionage network in the Mediterranean.

In the summer of 1930, Grand Duke Dmitri introduced Chanel to the film producer Samuel Goldwyn who invited her to visit Hollywood. At the time, Coco's creations were becoming fashionable in the United States thanks to enthusiastic coverage by *Vogue* magazine. Chanel wanted her bisexual lover Marie 'Misia' Sert to come with her, but Misia was mired in scandal at the time. Her husband José-Maria had divorced her and run off with Russian Princess Roussadana 'Roussy' Mdivani, the teenage lover they had both shared. The heartbroken Misia had joined Chanel's party on board the Norddeutscher Lloyd liner, SS *Europa*.

A HARDENING ATTITUDE

With its movie stars, drug-taking and sexual debauchery, Hollywood suited Chanel, but she found her design style too refined for the costumes needed in the movies. She returned home on the SS *Paris*, whose manifest included Franklin Roosevelt's mother. Back in Europe, Coco immediately sought the hospitality of the Duke of Westminster who, as a fervent anti-Semite, had stoked the tendency in her. She claimed the Wertheimer brothers, who were Jewish, had swindled her and hired attorney René de Chambrun to sue them.

When Hitler came to power in 1933, von Dincklage was transferred from the Riviera to the German embassy in Paris with instructions to establish a new spy network and produce black propaganda. The following year, Berlin issued orders that the *Abwehr* recruit and train new agents. Meanwhile, the French Deuxième Bureau were taking an interest in Dincklage, his wife and their contacts.

In 1934, Chanel moved to the Ritz, whose back door was just across the road from her salon where she still maintained an apartment. At the time she was having an affair with illustrator and designer Paul Iribe. She gave him the money to run a rabidly nationalistic weekly called *Le Témoin*, which depicted France as the victim of an international conspiracy of Jews. When Iribe collapsed and died of a heart attack in front of her eyes while playing tennis at La Pausa, Chanel's Riviera villa, she was devastated.

With Hitler now seen as a threat, the French intelligence struck out – targeting, particularly, von Dincklage, and naming him publicly as an officer in the Gestapo. Three months before the announcement of the Nuremberg Laws, Dincklage divorced his Jewish wife. He spent the summer with his English mistress and her sister at Toulon, where there was a large naval base. When the details of his espionage activities broke in the press, Dincklage sought refuge in London, though his espionage ring was left intact in France. He even recruited a new member – and lover – Catsy's friend Baronne Hélène Dessoffy, the daughter of a high-ranking naval officer. They returned to France clandestinely, after being expelled from Tunisia for trying to penetrate the naval base at Bizerte. Then, as France mobilized for war, Dincklage sought safety in Switzerland.

ABDICATION AND WAR

Churchill's friendship with Chanel continued into the 1930s. During the abdication crisis, he and his son Randolph dined with Chanel and Jean Cocteau in her suite at the Ritz. Cocteau recalled how Winston got very drunk and, sobbing in Chanel's arms, said: 'The king cannot abdicate.' Soon after this Churchill helped to edit the king's abdication speech. The following year, Edward, then the Duke of Windsor and his bride Wallis Simpson, a loyal customer of Chanel, stayed at a neighbouring suite on their return from meeting Hitler.

At the beginning of World War II, Chanel closed her salon, saying war was not a time for fashion. Some 3,000 women lost their jobs, though it was believed that Chanel was punishing them for going on strike three years earlier. The authorities were on the lookout for spies everywhere. The Duke of Windsor's latest mistress, a French woman, was suspected of espionage and arrested crossing the Channel. Vera Bate Lombardi was being scrutinized by the Italian secret police, even though she had taken Italian citizenship and Italy was not yet at war with Britain. Meanwhile, the newspapers announced that Chanel and Jean Cocteau were about to marry, which amused Cocteau's live-in lover, the film actor Jean Marais. Churchill continued his regular visits to France until he was made prime minister, while those who could do so got out of Paris.

While von Dincklage reported on Switzerland's preparedness for war, Catsy and Hélène's mail was being opened. Hélène was also interrogated by French counter-espionage agents. The two women were arrested, much to the consternation of Hélène's husband Jacques. Swiss counter-intelligence also came to arrest von Dincklage, but he was protected by a diplomatic passport.

Nevertheless, they reported that he kept company with 'women of ill repute, was addicted to morphine and suspected of spying for Germany'.

The government in Bern politely asked von Dincklage to leave the country. When he did so, it was discovered that he had left two agents behind, Hans Riesser and his wife Gilda. Hans was Jewish, but when he was arrested it was discovered that his German passport did not have the obligatory 'J' in it; this omission indicated that he was an agent. He spent four years in a Swiss jail. Gilda managed to escape across the border into France where she continued to work for the *Abwehr*.

Von Dincklage was in Berlin when the Germans drove into the Low Countries. With Paris now under threat, Chanel went to stay at her nephew André Palasse's château in Corbère, near the Spanish border, which was where her first lover Étienne Balsan had retired to. Soon after she arrived, news came that André had been captured and was on his way to a prisoner-of-war camp in Germany. Chanel wept at the announcement of France's capitulation, made on the radio by Marshal Pétain on 17 June 1940. The following day, the BBC carried a broadcast by General de Gaulle from London, telling the French people that the Free French forces had escaped to England and intended to fight on.

The situation grew worse for Chanel when her close friend Winston Churchill ordered the destruction of the French fleet at Mers-el-Kébar, Algeria, lest it fall into German hands. She headed for Vichy where her friend Pierre Laval was acting head of government under Pétain, taking with her the fashion journalist Marie-Louise Bousquet, an intimate friend of Misia. In Vichy, Chanel tried to secure the return of her nephew André who was now ill – but to no avail. So she moved on to Paris, which was now bedecked with swastikas.

PARIS IN WARTIME

That autumn, von Dincklage, now 44, returned to Paris and with other high-ranking Nazis had moved into the requisitioned Ritz. When the 57-year-old Chanel arrived, she found that her things had been cleared away by the porter and her suite had been taken over. Von Dincklage arranged for her to take a smaller suite on the seventh floor in the *Privatgast* (private guest) section reserved for *Ausländer* (foreigners) who were friends of the Reich. The pair were seen everywhere together and other residents said he visited her suite every day.

While ordinary Parisians fought over food scraps, von Dincklage dined at the Ritz or at Maxim's, though he also held more intimate dinners at Chanel's apartment on Rue Cambon. The Serts were now re-united. José-Maria had secured the position of ambassador to the Vatican, though he remained in Paris and had food brought in from Spain by diplomatic bag. He amused guests with tales of British and American spies in Madrid.

The social round in Paris continued unabated as von Dincklage organized white-tie events for German 'guests'. Chanel would dine with the German ambassador and the Vichy ambassador to Paris and was reported to make vicious anti-Semitic remarks. While the Germans and the French elite led the high life, the ration for ordinary people was cut to 1,200 calories a day, half of what the average working man or woman needed to be healthy. The elderly had to survive on just 850 calories. Meat could only be found on the black market at outrageous prices. Even wine was in short supply as 320 million bottles a year were shipped to Germany at fixed prices.

Early in 1941, von Dincklage travelled to Berlin with Baron Louis de Vaufreland. The men had met before the war when von Dincklage had been the lover of Madame Esnault-Pelterie, the wife of a French aviation pioneer. In Berlin, von Dincklage met with Hitler and Joseph Goebbels, who had been his boss when he had been producing black propaganda at the German embassy in Paris in 1944.

De Vaufreland was given an assignment in North Africa where he arranged the arrest of Gaullist resistance fighters in Casablanca. Returning to Paris, von Dincklage was now under the direct orders of Berlin. He was given the title *V-Mann*, which meant a trust agent or go-between. His agent number was F-7667 and his codename PISCATORY. In Paris, he introduced de Vaufreland to Chanel.

The news came that André Palasse had contracted tuberculosis. The *Abwehr* knew Chanel wanted her nephew to be released and told her they could help in return for her co-operation. After all, she had good contacts in Britain, France and Spain. As further encouragement, de Vaufreland suggested he could use his

German contacts to wrest control of Parfums Chanel from the Wertheimers. His boss in the *Abwehr*, Hermann Neubauer, agreed to help Chanel with André's release if she would go to Madrid to do a little spying. She agreed, and the *Abwehr* enrolled her as agent number F-7124, codename WESTMINSTER.

A VISIT TO SPAIN

On 5 August 1941, Chanel and de Vaufreland left Paris by train. The German police at the border crossing at Hendaye in the Pyrenees received a telegram from the *Abwehr* foreign counter-intelligence service telling them to: 'Treat these two passengers with consideration, accord them every facility and spare them any problems.'

In Madrid, Chanel checked into the Ritz. The records of her activities in Spain have not survived, but she attended a dinner party with British diplomat and MI6 agent Brian Wallace, codename RAMON, and his wife, where she described the conditions in France. Chanel and de Vaufreland returned to Paris to find that André had been released. Then de Vaufreland introduced Chanel to the Nazi official in charge of the 'Aryanization' of Jewish property. Before fleeing to the United States, the Wertheimers had given control of Parfums Chanel to the industrialist Félix Amiot who was also making aircraft for the Germans. After the war, Amiot returned the company to the Wertheimers to mitigate charges of collaboration.

In Paris and occupied France, Jews were rounded up for deportation. Laval in the Free Zone also complied. Free French and communist resistance fighters began attacking Germans and French hostages were shot by firing squads in retaliation. Meanwhile, Chanel was hoping that Hitler would prevail and rid her of the Wertheimers forever.

Once America joined the war, *Life* magazine published a list of collaborators which included Chanel's lawyer René de Chambrun. It also referred to Chanel herself as a 'horizontal collaborator'. Chanel's confidence in a German victory was shaken by the American landings in Morocco and Algeria, and by the British streaming westwards out of Egypt after winning the Second Battle of El Alamein in November 1942. That Christmas, German troops moved into the

Free Zone, leaving Vichy powerless. On the Eastern Front, the German army had been halted at Stalingrad and would surrender there in February 1943. In Italy, Mussolini would fall in July of that year.

Still, Chanel was unrepentant. A remark she made at a lunch party on the Côte d'Azur that summer – that 'France has got what she deserves' – was reported back to de Gaulle's Free French intelligence service in London who had marked her down for punishment. The French also had a record of von Dincklage's activities and an *Abwehr* colleague suggested that he seek safety by taking a posting to Istanbul.

But Chanel would not let this happen – she had a plan that involved the two of them travelling to Madrid to seek the help of her old friend the British ambassador Sir Samuel Hoare, who she had met through the Duke of Westminster. Through these British dignitaries, she would send a message to Churchill saying that some leading Germans wanted to ditch Hitler and make peace. At the same time, von Dincklage would communicate with the anti-Hitler faction in Berlin through the German embassy in Spain.

First von Dincklage travelled to Berlin to get *Abwehr* approval for the plan. The damage to the city inflicted by Allied bombers convinced him that Germany was doomed. Other Nazis including Ribbentrop, Canaris, von Papen, Himmler and Schellenberg were also trying to find a way to stop the war, while Claus von Stauffenberg and other *Wehrmacht* officers were already plotting to kill Hitler.

LESBIAN 'VICES'

Making the arrangements with Count Joseph von Ledebur-Wicheln, von Dincklage said: 'The *Abwehr* first had to bring to France a young Italian woman Coco Chanel was attached to because of lesbian vices. The woman was to accompany Chanel on her trips to the Iberian Peninsula and to London. Ledebur would have to furnish passports and visas for Chanel, the girl and Dincklage.'

The girl, of course, was Vera Bate Lombardi who had been interned in Italy. Further investigation by Ledebur with Fern Bedaux, wife of a Nazi agent, revealed that Chanel was a drug addict who 'every evening received Dincklage in her room'.

Ledebur then examined von Dincklage's record and discovered he had been in trouble with the Gestapo because his wife was half-Jewish. He had lived in Toulon with two English girls, one of them his mistress. In 1938, he ceased his espionage work in France because he had been 'burned by the French Deuxième Bureau'. He had then gone to Switzerland to work under *Abwehr* chief Colonel Alexander Waag, who reported: 'I couldn't use Dincklage because he wanted too much money. He lacked a sense of purpose.'

When Ledebur went to visit von Dincklage, then a purchasing officer, he found him living in 'a sumptuous and luxuriously furnished apartment on the avenue Foch' which should have been given to a more senior *Abwehr* officer. Ledebur declined to meet Chanel, and the *Abwehr* withdrew its support for the trip to Madrid. Ledebur later learned that von Dincklage and Chanel had been seen at Hendaye on the Spanish border in January 1944 on a trip arranged by the *SS*. They had been met by SS Captain Walter Kutschmann who had been ordered by Schellenberg to assist Chanel in every way and had delivered a large sum of money to her in Madrid.

Refusing to be thwarted by Ledebur, von Dincklage got his comrade in arms from World War I, Major Theodor Momm, to explore other avenues. Momm managed to contact Schellenberg, and von Dincklage and Chanel were brought to Berlin. They were housed in a guesthouse at Wannsee, where a meeting that planned the systematic murder of Europe's Jews had been held in January 1942. Chanel met Schellenberg at the Reich Main Security Office on Berkaer Strasse, which had been a Jewish nursing home until it was requisitioned by the SS in 1941. At the meeting it was agreed that Vera Bate Lombardi should be released from internment to join what was now being called Operation *Modellhut* – Operation Model Hat.

AN UNEXPECTED TURN OF EVENTS

After the new Italian government signed an armistice with the Allies on 8 September 1943, the Germans occupied Rome. On 12 November, Vera was arrested as a suspected British spy, but thanks to pressure from Schellenberg was released ten days later.

Back in Paris, von Dincklage arranged for Chanel to be issued with a passport, along with a visa for Spain. The passport was issued by the French authorities on the direct order of *SS-Sturmbannführer* Karl Bömelburg, head of the Gestapo in France. Meanwhile, Schellenberg's SD foreign intelligence service made the arrangements for Vera.

In Madrid, Chanel and Lombardi checked into the Ritz. Chanel then met with Sir Samuel Hoare and gave Vera a letter whose contents had been approved by Schellenberg. With the assistance of Hoare, Vera was supposed to take this letter to London and hand it to Churchill. But Vera would not play along and denounced all those involved – including Chanel – to the British authorities as German agents.

To smooth things over, Chanel wrote another letter which she gave to the embassy to be forwarded to Churchill. In it, she explained that it had been necessary to 'address myself to someone rather important' to get Vera freed from internment – that was why her Italian passport had a German stamp on it.

Von Dincklage and Chanel returned to Paris, then travelled on to Berlin to explain why their mission had failed. Vera remained in Madrid and wrote to her friend Lady Ursula Filmer Sankey, the Duke of Westminster's daughter, urging her to get her father to contact Churchill. She said she knew that the British suspected her of being an SS agent because of her involvement in Chanel's mission and she feared they would prevent her from returning to a now-liberated Rome.

Following D-Day, on 6 June 1944, Chanel's prospects looked dire. If the Germans retreated from Paris, the Resistance would be certain to come after her. Von Dincklage was also a marked man. When von Stauffenberg's plot to assassinate Hitler failed, von Dincklage fled. Chanel quit the Ritz and moved back into her apartment on Rue Cambon. As the Allies approached Paris, she contacted Pierre Reverdy, who was by this point with the Resistance, and urged him to seek out de Vaufreland, the one Frenchman able to prove her connection to the Nazis. Reverdy found him and he was imprisoned at the Drancy camp that had been used to house Jews, prior to deportation.

Paris was liberated on 25 August 1944. Two weeks later, Chanel was arrested, but the young Resistance fighters who interrogated her had no record of her secret missions. Returning to her apartment in Rue Cambon, she told her grand-niece Gabrielle Palasse: 'Churchill had me freed.'

Then a message came from the Duke of Westminster telling her to leave France. Within hours she was in her chauffeur-driven limousine on her way to Lausanne. It is thought that Churchill sought to shield Chanel in case she exposed the Windsors as collaborators. This was a sensitive matter. Anthony Blunt, then with MI5, was sent secretly to Schloss Friedrichshof to retrieve sensitive letters between the Duke of Windsor and Hitler and other prominent Nazis.

Fearing for her own safety, Catsy von Dincklage handed herself in to the police and was interned. To secure her release, she provided letters from friends who had worked with her in a black-market operation selling women's underwear. She and her ex-husband were officially banned from France in 1947, though she stayed on in Nice, seemingly working for Chanel.

DYING DAYS

Churchill was recuperating from an illness in Tunisia when Chanel's letter arrived at Downing Street. On his return, Churchill intervened on Vera's behalf and early in 1945 she was allowed to return to Italy. After being re-united with her husband, she wrote to Churchill thanking him.

In the dying days of the war, von Dincklage arranged for the *Abwehr*, now under the command of Schellenberg, to get a German firm to obtain permission for him to travel to Switzerland as their representative. But the Swiss had not forgotten his previous spying mission and refused entry. He then hid out in Germany and Austria, while Chanel sent money via a friendly GI. Then von Dincklage slipped into Switzerland to join Chanel in Lausanne. An attorney made repeated applications on his behalf for the citizenship of Liechtenstein, which would give him the automatic right to enter Switzerland. But this was refused as von Dincklage had been banned from France in 1947. Eventually, he left Lausanne to live in the Balearic Islands.

In May 1946, a case against Chanel was opened at the Palais de Justice in Paris after documents listing the *Abwehr* agent number F-7124 and her codename

WESTMINSTER were found in Berlin. However, while intelligence reports written by de Vaufreland were discovered, there were none on file from Chanel herself. Nor was any connection made between her and Operation *Modellhut*. Questioned about her first trip to Madrid, she said she had met de Vaufreland by accident on the train.

Chanel attended the Palais de Justice in July 1949 to give testimony in the case against de Vaufreland. Her only contact with the Germans, she said, had been via de Vaufreland, who had offered to use his influence to get her nephew released. She denied sworn testimony that de Vaufreland had introduced her to his German handler. The idea that she was involved in a peace mission was patently absurd, she said, and she had received no special treatment by the Germans at the border post at Hendaye.

She also denied that she had asked for de Vaufreland's help to wrest Parfums Chanel from the Wertheimers, and claimed that her trip to Spain had been to obtain raw materials for making perfume. Her second trip to Madrid and her relationship with von Dincklage were never mentioned.

While de Vaufreland went to jail, Chanel returned to safety in Switzerland. However, the court records noted: 'The answers Mademoiselle Chanel gave to the court are deceptive. The court will decide if her case should be pursued.' But other more sensational Nazi war crime trials were being conducted at the time and the de Vaufreland case was ignored by the press.

From Lausanne, Chanel used her millions to buy the silence of anyone who knew of her wartime activities with the *Abwehr* and the *SS*. She provided a comfortable house in Switzerland for the dying Schellenberg after he had been released due to ill health. Von Dincklage also received a handsome stipend.

When Pierre Wertheimer returned to France and took back his perfume business, Chanel was forced to settle with him, knowing that if he sued, her Nazi connections might come out in court. These were swiftly forgotten when Chanel made a comeback in the fashion industry in the 1950s. She was wreathed with honours worldwide. A musical based on her life, *Coco*, starring Katharine Hepburn, appeared on Broadway in 1969.

She took on François Mironnet, who bore a resemblance to the Duke of Westminster, as her young butler. In June 1970, eight months before her death, her client Claude Pompidou, wife of French president Georges Pompidou, invited her to dinner at the Palais de l'Élysée. Chanel died in the Ritz on 10 January 1971. The documents detailing her wartime treachery were only discovered in 1985, by a Soviet researcher working in the German archives.

CHAPTER 20

THE SPY WHO WOULD BE QUEEN

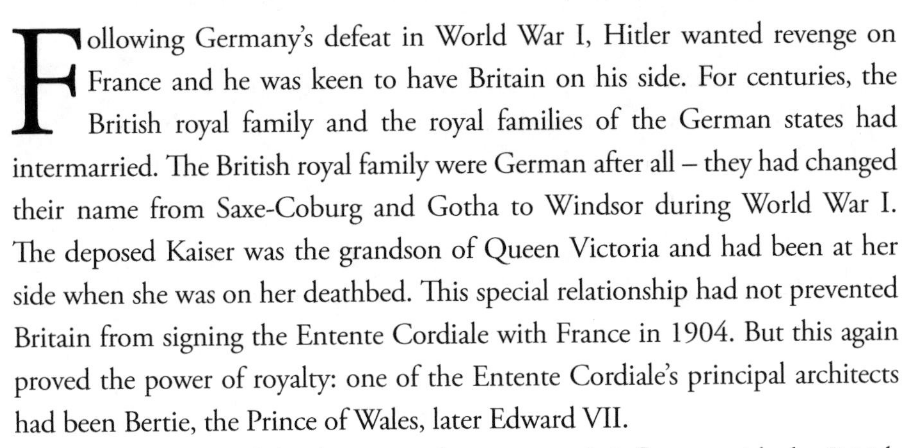

Following Germany's defeat in World War I, Hitler wanted revenge on France and he was keen to have Britain on his side. For centuries, the British royal family and the royal families of the German states had intermarried. The British royal family were German after all – they had changed their name from Saxe-Coburg and Gotha to Windsor during World War I. The deposed Kaiser was the grandson of Queen Victoria and had been at her side when she was on her deathbed. This special relationship had not prevented Britain from signing the Entente Cordiale with France in 1904. But this again proved the power of royalty: one of the Entente Cordiale's principal architects had been Bertie, the Prince of Wales, later Edward VII.

Hitler was aware of this history and eager to seek influence with the British royal family. When he came to power, the queen consort was Mary of Teck (a ducal seat in the Kingdom of Württemberg). And there was an eligible Prince of Wales, who would go on to reign briefly as Edward VIII in 1936. Clearly it would be an advantage to Germany if, like his father George V, Edward could be persuaded to marry a German princess. Before World War I intervened, there had been talk of his marriage to Princess Karoline Mathilde of Schleswig-

Holstein. It was only after changing the royal family's name in 1917 that George V let it be known his children and heirs would be allowed to marry their British subjects rather than foreign royalty.

HITLER'S PREFERENCE

For Hitler, the most promising candidate was Princess Friederike, the daughter of Duke Ernest Augustus III of Brunswick and Duchess Victoria Louise of Prussia, the only daughter of Kaiser Wilhelm II. As daughter of the head of the house of Hanover, she was nominally 34th in line to the British throne had not the Titles Deprivation Act of 1917 been passed, which stripped members of enemy nations of their British ranks and titles.

Hitler was especially encouraged by the fact that her father, Duke Ernest Augustus, was a prominent donor to the Nazi Party and often wore the brown uniform of a storm trooper. Her brother, also Ernest Augustus, was in the *SS*, while Friederike herself was a member of the *Bund Deutscher Mädel* – the League of German girls, the female branch of the Hitler Youth. At school she was known as a committed Nazi and nicknamed the 'Prussian sergeant'.

Her parents had met Hitler and discussed rapprochement with Britain. But it was Hitler alone who decided to offer Friederike's hand in marriage to the Prince of Wales. Ribbentrop was sent to deliver the good news. However, Friederike's parents, who had just returned from visiting George V and Queen Mary in England, were shocked by the suggestion, as Edward was 22 years older than their 17-year-old daughter – the duchess herself had been a candidate for his hand.

'My husband and I were shattered,' she said. 'Something like this had never entered our minds, not even for reconciliation with England. Before the First World War it had been suggested that I should marry my cousin [the Prince of Wales], who was two years younger, and it was now being indicated that my daughter should marry him. We told Hitler that in our opinion the great difference in age between the Prince of Wales and Friederike alone precluded such a prospect, and that we were not prepared to put pressure on our daughter.'

Princess Friederike with her parents, Duke Ernest Augustus III of Brunswick and Duchess Victoria Louise of Prussia.

Though this attempt to bring the Prince of Wales into the Nazi fold had failed, Hitler didn't stop trying. Meanwhile Friederike met Paul, Crown Prince of Greece, at the Berlin Olympics. Even though he was 16 years her senior, they married two years later. It has been suggested that if the Prince of Wales had married Princess Friederike, World War II might never have happened. But by 1934, when the plan was afoot, Edward was already involved with Wallis Simpson.

ROYAL AFFAIRS

The Prince of Wales was not quick to embark on affairs of the heart. He described the prostitutes he saw posing naked in a Calais brothel he visited during World War I as 'perfectly filthy and revolting'. It was not until the age of 25 that he took up with a Parisian courtesan and socialite named Marguerite Alibert, known in the demi-monde as Maggie Meller. The affair petered out with the end of the war and his return to England. Marguerite went on to find fame by killing her husband, the Egyptian aristocrat Ali Fahmy, at the Savoy Hotel in London. Thanks to the robust defence presented by her celebrated lawyer, Edward Marshall Hall, she was acquitted of murder at the Old Bailey. At the trial her husband was portrayed as 'a monster of Eastern depravity and decadence, whose sexual tastes were indicative of an amoral sadism towards his helpless European wife'. To ensure that the Prince of Wales' name was not mentioned as part of the evidence, the judge conveniently prohibited any mention of Marguerite's own sexual history.

Back in England, the prince began seeing Lady Sybil Cadogan, but was soon in love with Marian Coke, a married woman 12 years older than him. He would regularly have affairs with married women; one of his long-term lovers was Freda Dudley Ward, the wife of a Liberal MP. She was half-American and they had met during a Zeppelin raid when she ran to a house where he was having dinner to take cover. The affair lasted several years, though there were many others along the way.

The Prince of Wales was attracted to Americans: he visited the United States several times and set his cap at Audrey James, the daughter of an American industrialist. She rebuffed his advances while single but, once she had married, she succumbed.

Next came Lady Thelma Furness, the daughter of an American diplomat. When the prince met her, she was a divorcée who had remarried. At the age of 16, she had eloped with an older man, but the marriage hadn't lasted. Once she was free of her first husband, she had married Viscount Furness who was famous for his love of brandy and women.

In 1930, Lady Furness accompanied Edward on safari in Kenya. There, she said, she felt 'as if we were the only two people in the world'. In her diary she recorded: 'This was our Eden, and we were alone in it. His arms about me were the only reality; his words of love my only bridge to life. Borne along on the mounting tide of his ardour, I felt myself inexorably swept from the accustomed moorings of caution. Every night I felt more completely possessed by our love.'

The affair came to an end when she had a fling with Prince Aly Khan, a racehorse owner and leader of the Ismaili Muslims. Afterwards Thelma openly complained of Edward's poor sexual performance, scandalizing society by calling him 'the little man'. Others had noticed this deficiency in the unfortunate prince. While at Osborne Naval College, the other cadets joked that he should be called 'Sardines' rather than 'Whales'.

Rumours such as this, and of his possible bisexuality, abounded. The writer and critic Lytton Strachey tried to pick him up once at the Tate Gallery, only to flee when he realized who he was. Later, Strachey wrote rueing what might have been.

WALLIS SIMPSON

It was while Edward was attending a house party at Burrough Court, the country seat of Viscount and Lady Furness, that he was introduced to Wallis Simpson and her husband Ernest. Of Virginian stock, Mrs Simpson had been born in Baltimore. Her first husband, navy flier Lieutenant Earl Winfield 'Win' Spencer Jr, had been an alcoholic and a sadist who liked to tie her to the bed and beat her. He had enjoyed numerous extra-marital affairs with both men and women. Wallis, for her part, launched herself on the diplomatic scene in Washington DC, and had affairs with both the Italian ambassador and a senior Argentine diplomat who was said to be the best tango dancer in town.

In a belated honeymoon, Win took Wallis on a trip to the Far East where together, and separately, they visited the brothels of Shanghai and Hong Kong. In these famous 'singing houses', Wallis was said to have learned the ancient erotic arts of Fang-chung shu. This is a method of sexual union which involves, among other things, massaging hot oil into the nipples, stomach and inner thighs of a partner. Only when the partner is totally relaxed are the genitals addressed. Those adept at Fang-chung shu are said to be able to arouse even the most passionless of correspondents by concentrating on the nerve centres and delicately brushing the skin.

Despite Wallis' growing abilities in the erotic arts, her marriage to Win foundered. This left her free to practise her new-found techniques on a string of other men, including a young American called Robbie and the Italian naval attaché, Count Galeazzo Ciano, who would go on to marry Mussolini's daughter and become Italy's foreign minister. Around this time, it is rumoured that Wallis suffered a botched abortion which left her unable to bear children.

She met her second husband, the Anglo-American shipbroker Ernest Simpson, in New York. Simpson was born in the United States, but naturalized as a British subject when he joined the Coldstream Guards during World War I. Like Wallis he was married, but the couple quickly divorced their respective partners, married each other and moved to London.

After her introduction to the Prince of Wales, Wallis and he were often seen with Wallis' husband and Mary Raffray, Ernest Simpson's mistress. In 1934, the prince holidayed with Wallis in Biarritz. As her husband could not join the party, Wallis was chaperoned by her Aunt Bessie.

In February 1935, the prince was photographed with Wallis leaving a lingerie shop in Kitzbühel, near where they were enjoying a skiing holiday in the Austrian Tyrol. In May, the gossip came home to London that the prince had danced with Mrs Simpson at his parents' silver jubilee ball.

NAZI NEIGHBOURS

While the press barons managed to keep stories about the affair out of the British newspapers, they were widely published abroad; this presented Hitler with another opportunity. He would have known of the Simpsons' political leanings, and Sir Oswald Mosley, leader of the British Union of Fascists, was a frequent visitor to their apartment at Bryanston Court where they could be observed by Hitler's favourite spy, their neighbour Princess Stephanie von Hohenlohe who lived in the same block.

Both the king and the prime minister were growing concerned about the prince's activities, so they called in Scotland Yard. Consequently, Superintendent Albert Canning, a veteran of Special Branch, was instructed to keep an eye on Wallis Simpson. He maintained that Wallis was two-timing the prince with a Ford car salesman named Guy Marcus Trundle. With Princess Stephanie also on hand, MI5 were concerned that Bryanston Court might be harbouring a nest of Nazi spies, one of whom was Wallis Simpson herself.

Princess Stephanie moved in the same circle as the Prince of Wales and Wallis Simpson. She was vociferous on the subject of the Treaty of Versailles, saying it was unjust and that the natural borders of Germany should be restored. She also argued that Germany should be able to build up its armed forces, unrestricted by the treaty, in the face of the Soviet menace. Her principal aim was to convince the prince himself – Hitler wanted a pro-German king on the British throne, and it would be even better if he had a pro-Nazi consort by his side.

Lady Emerald Cunard regularly invited the Prince of Wales and Wallis Simpson to dinner. Nancy Astor condemned Emerald for encouraging the pro-Nazi leanings of the Prince of Wales, even though Lady Astor was an admirer of Hitler herself. Emerald was also one of the principal patrons of Princess Stephanie.

Hitler sent Ribbentrop to join the fray. At a dinner hosted by Lady Cunard, the American society diarist Chips Channon noted: 'Much gossip about the Prince of Wales' alleged Nazi leanings; he is alleged to have been influenced by Emerald Cunard who is rather *eprise* [in love with] Herr Ribbentrop through Mrs Simpson.' He added: 'Emerald had been intriguing on behalf of the German cause, inspired by Herr Ribbentrop's dimple.'

Another of Wallis' favourites, the German ambassador to Britain, Leopold von Hoesch, organized a dinner for Ribbentrop and the prince. The evening went well, with the prince speaking German fluently. As a youth he had enjoyed frequent visits to the country where many of his family still lived.

'After all, he is half German,' Ribbentrop telegrammed Hitler.

The prince disagreed. 'Every drop of blood in my veins is German,' he told Diana Mitford, the wife of Oswald Mosley and a friend of Hitler. Edward also professed to admire National Socialism because it had done so much to improve employment and housing opportunities in Germany, and these were causes close to his heart during the Great Depression of the early 1930s.

The prince was said to have little time for France, which he thought a weak and degenerate country, and he was a staunch opponent of the Soviet Union because the Bolsheviks had murdered his godfather Tsar Nicholas II and his family. He told the Austrian ambassador: 'We are in great danger from the Communists here. I hope and believe we shall never fight a war again, but if so we must be on the winning side, and that will be German, not the French.' Any war between Britain and Germany, he believed, would give victory to the Soviets.

The prince also sought to emulate his grandfather, Edward VII, who as Prince of Wales took a role in shaping British foreign policy. And perhaps he had further ambitions. Chips Channon was not the only one to observe that the prince was going 'the dictator way and is pro-German. I shouldn't be surprised if he aimed at making himself a mild dictator – a difficult enough task for an English king.'

TABLE TALK

At dinner, Ribbentrop paid special attention to Mrs Simpson. Afterwards, he began sending her a bouquet of 17 carnations every day. Ambassador von Hoesch was puzzled by the significance of the number 17. The prince's cousin, the Duke of Württemberg, an opponent of the Nazis who became a Benedictine monk, said that 17 was the number of times they had slept together. He also said the prince was impotent and only the oriental arts practised by Mrs Simpson could satisfactorily gratify his sexual desires. How the duke knew these facts is a mystery, but Hitler later questioned Ribbentrop about the nature of the affair between Edward and Wallis.

Mrs Simpson's friend Oswald Mosley supported the liaison. A dedicated monarchist, he used the prince's name when canvassing for financial support among the upper classes. In the summer of 1935, his fascist-leaning January Club reformed as the Windsor Club.

Bruce Lockhart, a British secret agent who had been a diplomat in Moscow during the Bolshevik revolution, arranged a meeting between the prince and the Kaiser's grandson, Prince Louis Ferdinand. Lockhart noted: 'The Prince of Wales was quite pro-Hitler and said it was no business of ours to interfere in Germany's internal affairs either re Jews or re anything else and added that dictators are very popular these days and that we might want one in England before long.'

At their dinner meeting, Ribbentrop had suggested that Anglo-German relations might be improved if there were exchange visits between former soldiers. The prince took up the idea, telling veterans at a British Legion meeting in the Albert Hall in June 1935: 'I feel there would be no more suitable body of men to stretch forth the hand of friendship to the Germans than we ex-servicemen.'

The exchanges went ahead, but the prince got a dressing down from the king for interfering in foreign affairs. Wallis' cousin was staying at Bryanston Court at the time, and reported that, on his return from Buckingham Palace, the prince was 'wearing a German helmet and goose-stepping around the living room, for what reason I can't imagine'.

THE PRINCE BECOMES KING

Meanwhile, Edward continued to share his opinions. He supported the Italian invasion of Abyssinia, now Ethiopia, on the grounds that fascist efficiency would improve its medieval economy.

George V's silver jubilee in 1935 saw a huge influx of German royalty, many of whom were Nazi Party members. Some returned the following year for the king's funeral. Hitler watched the arrangements being made by the new king, Edward VIII, on the newsreels and noted that Mrs Simpson was standing in the background. He also spotted her in a newsreel that documented the couple's Mediterranean yachting holiday.

At the king's funeral, Edward's cousin, Carl Eduard, Duke of Saxe-Coburg and Gotha, marched behind the coffin in full Nazi uniform and wearing a storm-trooper's helmet; Hitler organized a memorial service for the king in Berlin. A childhood friend of the new king, Carl Eduard was president of the newly formed Anglo-German Fellowship which was decidedly pro-Nazi. Soviet spies Guy Burgess and Kim Philby joined the AGF to conceal their earlier communist leanings. When Carl Eduard broached the subject of talks between Hitler and Prime Minister Stanley Baldwin, Edward said: 'Who is king here? Baldwin or I? I myself wish to talk to Hitler and will do so here or in Germany.'

Ambassador von Hoesch noted: 'We should be able to rely upon having on the British throne a ruler who is not lacking in understanding for Germany and in the desire to see good relations established between Germany and Britain.'

For the British, there were worries about security. At Fort Belvedere, Edward VIII's country house, government boxes went missing and top-secret papers were left lying around for Wallis to read. The Foreign Office had information that the secret codes used by British embassies had been compromised. Edward discussed everything with Mrs Simpson and showed her state papers. According to the under-secretary of state for foreign affairs, Lord Vansittart, she was 'in the pocket of Ribbentrop'. Sensitive information was leaking and the finger of suspicion pointed at Wallis. Vansittart's junior at the Foreign Office, Ralph Wigram, wrote a top-secret memo saying: 'Mrs S is very close to [Ambassador von] Hoesch and has, if she likes to read them, access to all Secret and Cabinet papers.'

Robert Worth Bingham, the US ambassador to London between 1933 and 1937, reported to President Roosevelt: 'Many people here suspect that Mrs Simpson was in German pay.' Meanwhile, Wallis' dressmaker, Anna Wolkoff, was sending stolen intelligence to the Nazis through a go-between in the Italian embassy.

On 7 March 1936, five weeks after George V's funeral, Hitler sent German troops into the demilitarized Rhineland in violation of the Treaty of Versailles. The British response was muted, and Edward was given the credit for this. Ribbentrop told Hitler that the king had sent 'a directive to the British government that no matter how the details of the affair are dealt with, complications of a serious nature are in no circumstances to be allowed to develop'. The architect Albert Speer, one of Hitler's favourites, recalled that the *Führer* let out a sigh of relief. 'At last,' he said. 'The king of England will not intervene. He is keeping his promise.'

According to the press secretary at the German embassy, King Edward called Ambassador von Hoesch and said: 'I sent for the prime minister and gave him a piece of my mind. I told the old so-and-so that I would abdicate if he made war. There was a frightful scene. But you needn't worry. There won't be a war.'

The German ambassador did a little jig and said: 'I've done it. I've outwitted them all. There won't be a war . . . we've done it. It's magnificent. I must inform Berlin immediately.'

Nerves were further calmed by another visit by Carl Eduard, and on 20 April 1936, Hitler's 47th birthday, Edward sent the *Führer* his best wishes by telegram. Then, when Irishman Jerome Brannigan brandished a loaded revolver at the king when he was riding on Constitution Hill, Hitler sent a telegram congratulating Edward on surviving an attempt on his life.

A RIGHT ROYAL SCANDAL

When Ernest Simpson decided he wanted to marry Mary Raffray, he discussed the matter with the king, who said that he wanted to marry Wallis. It was agreed that the Simpsons would divorce. Wallis was shocked when she heard the news – and so was the British government.

Prime Minister Baldwin told the king that, as head of the Church of England, he could not marry Wallis because she was a divorcée. He would either have to give her up or abdicate. With the support of Ribbentrop, who was desperate to keep Edward on the throne, Princess Stephanie suggested a morganatic marriage but her proposal was rejected. Ribbentrop tried to send the king a message through the pro-German Lord Clive, saying that the 'German people stood behind him in his struggle'.

Under British law at the time, it was not possible for a couple to divorce unless one of the partners was caught *in flagrante*. Ernest Simpson therefore arranged for a private detective to discover him with Mary Raffray, alone in a hotel bedroom. Wallis then sued for divorce, telling Chips Channon that the divorce was 'at Ernest's instigation and at no wish of hers'.

The course was now set. Once the news broke in the British press on 3 December 1936, Edward decided to abdicate. Wallis begged him not to, then fled to France to avoid the torrent of salacious gossip that was certain to follow. She was right to do so, as acquaintances were only too willing to offer their lurid accounts.

Bloomsbury Group hostess Lady Ottoline Morrell, for example, noted in her diary that the king 'had injections to make himself more virile and they affected his head and have made him very violent. Poor little fellow, they also say he has been drinking all these last weeks and has signed two abdications and torn them up.'

There was speculation about why a man would consider giving up the throne for a woman, and a commoner at that. Alan Don, chaplain to the Archbishop of Canterbury, said he suspected Edward was 'sexually abnormal which may account for the hold Mrs. S. has over him'. Others speculated that the hold over him was the 'Shanghai Squeeze' or 'Singapore Grip' that she had learned in the Far East. One cheap joke suggested that while match girls could pick up pennies that way, Wallis was so proficient that she could pick up a sovereign.

Later on, Edward VIII's official biographer, Philip Ziegler, noted that: 'There must have been some sort of sadomasochistic relationship . . . [Edward] relished the contempt and bullying she bestowed on him.' Apparently, she would rap him on the knuckles like a naughty schoolboy. Further rumours suggested he was a foot fetishist, and that Wallis ruthlessly exploited this weakness. She also acted as his dominatrix. One day, in front of friends, she turned to Edward and said: 'Take off my dirty shoes and bring me another pair.' To everyone's amazement, he did.

A butler resigned after finding Edward on all fours, painting Wallis' toenails.

There was talk of elaborate nanny–child scenes enacted between them. Freda Dudley Ward commented on this side of his nature: 'He made himself the slave of whomsoever he loved and became totally dependent on her,' she said. 'It was his nature; he was like a masochist. He liked being humbled, degraded. He begged for it.'

The king would not be swayed by idle gossip. On 10 December, he signed the Instrument of Abdication and the following evening made the famous radio broadcast abdicating the crown, saying: 'I want you to know that the decision I have made has been mine and mine alone. This was a thing I had to judge entirely for myself. The other person most nearly concerned has tried up to the last to persuade me to take a different course.'

While his brother, the Duke of York, succeeded to the throne as George VI, the newly styled Duke of Windsor left for Austria. It was thought best for the couple to remain apart until Mrs Simpson's decree absolute came through in May 1937. As a royal duke, Edward was shackled politically. He could neither stand for election to the House of Commons nor speak on political matters in the House of Lords. On news of the abdication, 500 blackshirts from the British Union of Fascists gathered outside Buckingham Palace, giving the fascist salute and shouting: 'We want Edward.'

Oswald Mosley's loyalty was unwavering and he condemned the strongarm tactics used to hustle Edward off the throne. His newspaper, the *Blackshirt*, carried the headline: 'Let the King Marry the Woman of his Choice.' There was even talk that he was drawing up a list of Fascist ministers to form a government under a Fascist king.

Although the king had departed, the British government had not lost interest in his consort. Detectives watching Wallis' activities in the South of France reported that she intended to move on to Germany – and Edward was sure to follow.

As Unity Mitford predicted, Hitler was upset by the abdication – particularly as Ribbentrop had told him that the Conservative government would be defeated and Edward would stay on the throne as a friend to Germany. Naturally, his abdication had been the fault of the Bolsheviks, Jews and Freemasons. Hitler even came to believe that Churchill, who supported the king's marriage to Wallis Simpson, had only done so in order to oust him. The prospect of Anglo-German affiliation was now over.

The Duke and Duchess of Windsor meet Adolf Hitler as the climax to their tour of Germany, 1937.

DISPOSSESSED

Although he had left the country, Edward still tried to influence his brother by letter and phone. Eventually George stopped taking his calls. Meanwhile, there were some in the Duke of Windsor's old circle who maintained that the new king was not up to the job – he was not glamorous and outgoing, as Edward had been, and he suffered from a stammer. But the British establishment was utterly opposed to Edward's return to any role in public life. One of Prime Minister Neville Chamberlain's keys advisers, Sir Horace Wilson, wrote of Mrs Simpson: 'It must not be assumed that she has abandoned hope of becoming Queen of England. It is known that she has limitless ambition, including a desire to interfere in politics; she has been in touch with the Nazi movement and has definite ideas as to dictatorship.'

Eventually it was decided to give the duke an allowance of £25,000 a year – £1.7 million/$2.2 million in today's money – which would be forfeit if he returned to Britain without the king's express permission. Edward was furious, but George would not be moved. There would be no officially sanctioned wedding and it would not be announced in the Court Circular. No member of the royal family was allowed to attend and the Church of England prohibited any of its clergy officiating, although a rogue priest did step in. George informed Edward that his wife would not be entitled to share his title or rank. Mrs Simpson was never to be 'Her Royal Highness'.

When her journalist cousin, Newbold Noyes, published articles in the United States gleaned from their conversations, Wallis decided to sue. She hired Parisian lawyer Armand Grégoire who was described by the French secret service as 'one of the most dangerous of Nazi spies'. She eventually dropped the suit. Meanwhile, Edward sued the publishers of a book called *Coronation Commentary*, which implied that the couple had been intimate before they were married. The case was settled out of court with the duke receiving substantial damages.

The wedding took place on 3 June 1937 at the Château de Candé, which was owned by Franco-American businessman Charles Bedaux. After his German companies were seized in 1934, Bedaux leased a schloss in Berchtesgaden and set about ingratiating himself with the Nazi leadership. He was a personal friend of Göring and was thought to be a Nazi intelligence asset. He became an economic adviser to the Vichy government in France and was designated by the sabotage branch of the *Abwehr* to command a cover mission to capture a refinery in Iran, prior to a German invasion. But after the battles of El Alamein and Stalingrad, the operation was cancelled. In 1943, Bedaux was apprehended in Algeria, allegedly supervising the building of a German pipeline. Flown to the United States, he committed suicide while awaiting trial for treason and trading with the enemy.

The Duke and Duchess of Windsor honeymooned at Schloss Wasserleonburg, a country house in Austria. As the duke grew restless and wanted to return to Britain to take up an official post, Beaverbrook's *Daily Express* campaigned for the couple's return. But the British royal family regarded Wallis as a fifth columnist and she was generally regarded as a Nazi spy. Edward's pro-Nazi views also began to grate with the British public.

CONSORTING WITH THE ENEMY

The Windsors decided they would visit Germany. Bedaux contacted the leader of the German Labour Front, Robert Ley, to arrange the trip. The deal was concluded when the duke met Princess Stephanie's lover, Fritz Wiedemann, at the Ritz Hotel in Paris. The arrangements were made in secret.

Meanwhile, there were attempts to persuade the duke to become a peace campaigner. IBM executive Thomas J. Watson agreed to sponsor a US tour for the Windsors. The German government was IBM's second-biggest client. Watson had met Hitler, attended a Nazi rally and been awarded the Order of the German Eagle.

When the Windsors' German visit was announced, Churchill and Beaverbrook travelled to Paris to try to dissuade them, but they were unsuccessful. The British royal family was in consternation, fearing that Edward was planning a comeback with the help of his pro-Nazi friends, but there was nothing they could do to stop the trip.

When the Windsors arrived at Friedrichstrasse station in Berlin on 11 October 1937, they were met by Robert Ley, who was accompanied by the third secretary of the British embassy (senior staff had been advised to stay away). The place was bedecked with Union Jacks, alternating with swastikas, while the band played 'God Save the King' and the crowd cried: 'Heil Edward.'

Guarded by members of the *SS*, the Windsors were driven to the Hotel Kaiserhof where they were greeted by Nazis singing a song written by Joseph Goebbels. They were then taken to Göring's country estate, where they were greeted by Benito Mussolini, the Nazi-sympathizing pioneer airman Charles Lindbergh, and former US president Herbert Hoover, as well as Göring himself. Göring's wife remarked afterwards that Wallis would have cut a good figure on the throne of England.

The duke and duchess were given tours of Munich, Nuremberg, Stuttgart and Dresden, and visited an apparently empty concentration camp which they were told was a meat store. They met Himmler, Rudolf Hess and Goebbels, and the duchess was reunited with Ribbentrop. Carl Eduard, Duke of Saxe-Coburg and Gotha, and the rest of the German aristocracy also turned out for a gala dinner at the Grand Hotel in Nuremberg.

Greeted by a guard of honour of the SS Death's Head Division at a training school in Pomerania, the duke gave a Nazi salute. He gave a second salute when he met Hitler at the Berghof on 22 October. Everyone, including Hitler, addressed the duchess as 'Your Royal Highness'. She said she was struck by the 'inner force' of the German leader.

The duke had a private conversation with Hitler which lasted 50 minutes. Then they had tea. Afterwards Hitler escorted them to their car and once more exchanged salutes with the duke. When they had driven off, Hitler remarked that the duchess would have made a good queen.

A *New York Times* reporter observed that the duke 'demonstrated adequately that the abdication did rob Germany of a firm friend, if not indeed a devoted admirer, on the British throne'. The trip was judged a triumph and confirmed that the duke admired Hitler and was a Nazi sympathizer.

SIDELINED

Flushed from this success, Charles Bedaux planned another tour, this time of the United States, including a visit to the White House. The aim was to launch the duke as an ambassador for world peace, but it was simply a cloak for Nazi ambitions. Bedaux said that Hitler was a man of genius, the whole world was going fascist, and the Duke of Windsor would be recalled to the British throne as a dictator.

However, Bedaux did not realize the extent of his own unpopularity in the United States. When he started to make arrangements, there were protests. To avoid trouble, Bedaux slunk out of the country and the tour had to be cancelled.

As Europe moved inexorably towards war, the Duke of Windsor was sidelined, while the Duke of Kent became the unofficial peace envoy between Britain and the German aristocracy. War broke out on 3 September 1939. The following month, a rumour circulated in Germany that George VI had abdicated, and Edward was back on the throne calling for peace. But it was wishful thinking.

The Windsors were living in a rented villa on Cap d'Antibes when the war broke out. They arranged to travel back to England on the destroyer HMS *Kelly*, which had been laid on by Winston Churchill, now First Lord of the Admiralty. In London, Churchill gave the duke a tour of a secret room in the basement where the positions of the British and enemy fleets were recorded hourly. Lord Balniel was aghast at the presence of the duke, saying: 'He is too irresponsible a chatterbox to be entrusted with confidential information which will be passed on to Wally at the dinner table. That is where the danger lies . . . he will blab and babble out state secrets without realizing the danger.'

The duke was assigned to the British Military Mission in France as liaison officer. The French had been sensitive about the defences and refused to let the Allies inspect the Maginot Line. However, everything was open to the duke, who spotted the inadequacy of the antitank defences in the Ardennes.

Occasionally Edward would return to London without the knowledge of the king. He still believed that he could lead an international peace movement, until it was pointed out to him that, as Britain was at war, this would constitute high treason.

He was frustrated that none of his reports on the French defences made any impression. However, the Germans somehow got hold of the information and altered their invasion plans to send their Panzers through the Ardennes. It became clear that the Windsors could have been the source of this vital military intelligence. Charles Bedaux regularly had dinner with the couple and was still in touch with Ribbentrop and Nazi agent Otto Abetz.

Bedaux also made frequent trips to his offices in The Hague where the German ambassador Count Julius von Zech-Burkersroda identified the source of the military intelligence he was providing to Berlin as the Duke of Windsor. Bedaux told Hitler that, at dinner parties, the duchess would pass on classified military information she had gleaned from her husband.

Wallis made no secret of her sympathies. When the *Luftwaffe* were strafing English coastal towns, she told her friend Clare Boothe Luce: 'After what they did to me I can't say I feel sorry for them – a whole nation against one lone woman.'

According to an FBI report, the duchess was still in constant contact with Ribbentrop. 'Because of their high official position, the duchess was obtaining a variety of information concerning the British and French government activities that she was passing on to the Germans,' it said.

As the German army overran northern France, the Windsors returned to the south, only to face an Italian invasion of the Côte d'Azur. With no Royal Navy ship available to evacuate them, the couple had to make their way by car across Spain where the duke risked internment. However, the Spanish newspapers were reporting that the Duke of Windsor had been returned to the British throne and was making peace in Europe. Churchill was so concerned that he threatened to have the duke arrested if he ever returned to the UK.

In a conversation with General Juan Vigón, chief of the Spanish general staff, Hitler suggested that Nazi Germany 'would have a substantial interest if the duke and duchess could be delayed long enough for secret contacts and peace talks'. However, this conversation took place three days before the Windsors left their home in France, indicating that there was a spy in their camp telling Berlin of their plans.

Ribbentrop telegrammed the German ambassador in Madrid, asking him if he could persuade the Spanish government to delay the duke and duchess by making them wait a couple of weeks before issuing exit visas. Following the

British evacuation from Dunkirk, the Germans seemed confident of victory and believed they might use the duke to head a collaborationist government like that of Marshal Pétain in France. The German foreign ministry considered Edward 'the only Englishman who Hitler would negotiate any peace terms with, the logical director of England's destiny after the war'.

During the Windsors' stay in Madrid, the duke contacted the German and Italian embassies, asking them to protect property they had left behind in France. Talking with pro-Fascist Spanish aristocrats, he made it clear he believed that Britain faced defeat, and this fate could only be avoided by suing for peace with Germany. The couple expressed similar sentiments to the US ambassador. Their words reached the Spanish government, which conveyed them to Berlin.

OVERSEAS POSTING

Despite all this, on 2 July the Windsors were allowed to leave Spain. They drove to Lisbon where a telegram from Churchill awaited them. It informed the duke that, as he was in military uniform, he was to obey orders and return to Britain as soon as possible. Furious, Edward wrote a draft reply, resigning – but Wallis stayed his hand. His eventual response complained, ironically, of Churchill's 'dictator methods'. The duke only communicated with the British embassy in Portugal by courier, fearing that he would be arrested if he put a foot inside. The couple stayed with a businessman, Ricardo Espírito Santos Silva, who was loyal to the Portuguese dictator António de Oliveira Salazar and friends with the German ambassador, Baron von Hoyningen-Huene.

At last Churchill devised a way to prevent the duke and duchess from doing any more damage.

He appointed Edward as governor of the Bahamas; this way, the troublesome pair would be out of the way on the other side of the Atlantic. Churchill left the Windsors to make their own travel arrangements. Meanwhile the Germans tried to lure them back to Spain, even telling them that the British government was plotting to assassinate the duke in Portugal.

Edward delayed travelling to the Bahamas. Baron von Hoyningen-Huene reported to Ribbentrop: 'He is convinced that had he remained on the throne war could have been avoided and describes himself as a firm supporter of a peaceful compromise with Germany. The duke believes with certainty that continued heavy bombing will make England ready for peace.'

In the meantime, the Windsors planned to return to their home on Cap d'Antibes to collect their possessions. When it was pointed out that this would be dangerous, they cancelled their trip. But the duchess insisted that she would need her favourite Nile-green swimsuit in the Bahamas, so a US consul was sent to fetch it in what was known as 'Operation Cleopatra Whim'.

While the Germans endeavoured to delay their departure, the Windsors made plans to travel to the Bahamas via the United States. However, the British feared that they would disrupt the US election and threatened the duke with a court martial. Edward at last agreed to go directly to the Bahamas. In a last-ditch attempt, Hitler sent Walter Schellenberg to Portugal to apprehend the couple – kidnapping them, if necessary. Hitler told Schellenberg to win over the duchess. 'She has great influence over him,' he said.

First Schellenberg tried bribery and when that failed he told the duke he faced assassination in the Bahamas. A delegation from Britain then arrived and warned the Windsors that the Germans planned to kidnap them. When they were told the dire warnings of assassination, the British delegation organized bodyguards from Scotland Yard to travel alongside the Windsors. They sailed on an American Export Lines passenger liner on 1 August 1940, while Schellenberg watched though binoculars from the German embassy.

In the Bahamas, the duchess was snubbed while the duke still received secret correspondence from Germany via Ricardo Silva in Lisbon, who British intelligence assumed was a Nazi agent. Bedaux was also in touch. The European head of General Motors, James Mooney, who had also been awarded the Order of the German Eagle, visited the Windsors on board a yacht belonging to GM's pro-Nazi chairman Alfred P. Sloan, who was a financier of the anti-Semitic group Sentinels of the Republic. Mooney was also involved in former MI6 employee Sir William Wiseman's backchannel peace initiative with Germany.

SPYING ALLEGATIONS

FBI director J. Edgar Hoover considered Wallis to be a possible Nazi spy. FBI Special Agent Edward Tamm was assigned to keep an eye on her and he described how the British had prevented her from 'establishing any channel of communication with von Ribbentrop'. It was feared that she was hiding messages in the clothes she sent to New York for dry cleaning.

Tamm also reported that the Windsors were friendly with Axel Wenner-Gren, another suspected German agent of interest to the FBI. When the duchess needed specialist dental treatment in Miami, the Windsors were allowed to sail there on board Wenner-Gren's yacht *Southern Cross*. The duke had joined President Roosevelt for lunch on board the USS *Tuscaloosa* when he was cruising in the Caribbean. They talked about fishing. But the US president's aide, Harry Hopkins, told Churchill that Edward's recent yachting trip with a violently pro-Nazi Swede had not created a good impression.

Back in the Bahamas, the duke told the editor of *Liberty* magazine and undercover FBI agent Fulton Oursler: 'There will be no revolution in Germany and it would be a tragic thing for the world if Hitler were to be overthrown. Hitler is the right and logical leader of the German people. It is a pity you never met Hitler, just as it is a pity I never met Mussolini. Hitler is a very great man. . . . You cannot kill eighty million Germans and since they want Hitler, how can you force them into a revolution they don't want?'

If the United States didn't intervene, the duke warned, the war could go on for 30 years. If Roosevelt offered to broker peace, the Duke of Windsor would issue a statement supporting him. Again, this was tantamount to treason.

Fulton Oursler had a school-aged daughter named April. When he told Roosevelt what the duke had said, the president replied: 'When little Windsor says he doesn't think there should be a revolution in Germany, I tell you, Fulton, I would rather have April's opinion on that than his.'

Roosevelt then spoke of Wallis Simpson's dalliance with Ribbentrop, the red boxes left open at Fort Belvedere and the duke's casual attitude to secret plans when he was employed as a liaison officer in France. 'I have nothing to prove what I am going to say,' Roosevelt said, 'but I do know that there were nine shortwave wireless sets in Paris constantly sending information to the German troops, and no one has ever been able to decide how such accurate information could be sent over these wireless stations.'

Though he talked of being an emissary of peace, the duke surrounded himself with Nazi sympathizers and anti-Semites. He was now a poster boy for American isolationists.

When the *Liberty* article was published, Goebbels noted that the duke appeared to have given up on any possibility of a British victory. But he instructed his propaganda ministry not to make use of the information lest it undermine the duke's credibility in the eyes of the British people. Clearly, Goebbels was still focused on the possibility of Edward returning to the throne.

Churchill grew increasingly annoyed about the duke's behaviour, warning that his Swedish friend Wenner-Gren was a 'pro-German international financier with strong leanings towards appeasement and suspected of being in communication with the enemy'. It was believed he had just set up a bank in Mexico to channel money to the Nazis. Churchill blocked a visit the duke was intending to make to the United States, even though it was at Roosevelt's invitation. The interview in *Liberty*, Churchill said, was 'defeatist and pro-Nazi and approving of the isolationist aim to keep America out of the war'.

Despite these strictures, the duke was unable to keep his views to himself. He told the American socialite Frazier Jelke that the United States should stay out of the war, saying: 'It is too late for America to save democracy in Europe. She had better save it in America for herself.'

Worse, it was suspected that the duke and duchess were conspiring with American industrialists who wanted to overthrow democracy in the USA and supplant it with fascism. When they were allowed to make another private visit to Miami, the couple were followed by the FBI, who taped their phone calls at the Everglades Club, Palm Beach. Hoover reported to Roosevelt that he had been 'advised that the Duke of Windsor entered into an agreement which in substance was to the effect that if Germany was victorious in the war, Hermann Göring through his control of the Army would overthrow Hitler and thereafter install the Duke of Windsor as the King of England'. The idea that the duke was to be placed back on the British throne if Germany won the war was confirmed by numerous sources.

A CHANGE OF HEART

Eventually the duke and duchess were allowed to make an official tour of America, where they met pro-Nazi industrialists, including Henry Ford. The British ambassador Lord Halifax chafed at the expense of the duchess's shopping sprees and the cost of transporting up to eight pieces of luggage.

The attack on Pearl Harbor changed everything, especially after the sinking of the battleship HMS *Prince of Wales*, which had been named after Edward. The duke dropped his defeatist talk and arguments for isolationism. Soon the Bahamas would play host to US and British training bases for aircrew.

There were now fears that a Nazi raiding party might kidnap the duke and duchess. Churchill sent 200 Cameron Highlanders to protect them and the US beefed up reconnaissance and intelligence operations in the surrounding waters. Meanwhile, Axel Wenner-Gren found himself on a US blacklist.

While the Windsors were no longer seen as a threat – dining with Roosevelt and attending Congress to hear Churchill speak – their correspondence was still censored by the Americans. Nevertheless, in Washington, Hoover gave them a tour of FBI headquarters.

'I begin to think I'm Mata Hari,' commented the duchess.

Although other more prestigious postings were suggested for the duke, the Windsors remained confined to the Bahamas. Only in September 1944, when the prospect of a German victory had receded, did Churchill allow him to resign as governor. The duke and duchess only left the island on 3 May 1945, the day after the surrender of the Berlin garrison.

After the war was over, George VI launched a series of secret missions in Germany to recover letters, diaries and documents, including Ribbentrop's file on the Windsors. When it was recovered, the duke requested an audience with his brother. This was granted, but still no official position for the duke was forthcoming. Meanwhile, the British government asked the United States to destroy or hand over a microfilm copy they held of the Windsors' file, later saying that the Foreign Office had destroyed the only other copy. US Secretary of State James F. Byrnes refused to destroy the file, but said 'the Department of State will take all possible precautions to prevent any publicity with respect to the documents in its possession relative to the Duke of Windsor without prior consultation with the British Government.'

Other officials at the State Department accused the British of altering the historical record by destroying documents pertaining to the duke and duchess. This was particularly sensitive given that much of the evidence at the forthcoming Nuremberg Trials in November would come from the German files.

When the State Department set about publishing the captured German documents in their possession, the British made every effort to have the Windsor file excluded – or at least 'weeded' before publication. In 1953, Churchill was back in Downing Street; he wrote to his friend President Eisenhower asking him to stop publication of the file, saying: 'The historical importance of the episode is negligible, and the allegations rest only on the assertions of German and pro-German officials in making the most of anything they could pick up.'

While Eisenhower agreed, leading historians did not; nevertheless, publication of the documents was delayed. But the French had found other files, and the newly formed Federal Republic of Germany – West Germany – was asking for its archives back. Britain agreed to return the documents, provided they could retain the Windsor file.

In 1954, some papers concerning the Windsors' activities in 1940 were published. The duke dismissed them as 'quite untrue'. By the time the Windsors' file was published in 1957, it had been upstaged by the posthumous publication in the previous year of Schellenberg's memoirs and the duchess's self-serving autobiography *The Heart Has Its Reasons*. The Foreign Office convinced the press that the duke was plotted against, rather than plotting. And the duke himself declared the documents implicating him were 'part complete fabrications, and in part gross distortions of the truth'.

The Windsors settled in Paris where they kept company with Sir Oswald and Lady Diana Mosley. The duchess and Diana continued to believe that there would have been no need for the Holocaust if Hitler had been allowed to deport all Germany's Jews to Britain and America.

CHAPTER 20

UNDER HER THUMB

To the end, the Duke of Windsor was Wallis Simpson's lapdog. Sexual scandal continued to follow the couple for the rest of their lives. By the 1950s, rumours spread that Wallis had grown tired of his cloying love and was seen about town with much younger men. It was alleged that she took up with Woolworth heir Jimmy Donahue, a homosexual who Wallis was apparently trying to convert. He boasted of participating in oral sex with her. But others claimed the duke was the one who was sleeping with Donahue.

Noël Coward, who moved in the same circles as the Windsors after the abdication, explained the situation. 'I like Jimmy,' he said. 'He's an insane camp but he is fun. I like the duchess; she is the fag hag to end all fag hags, but that's what makes her likeable. The duke . . . well, although he pretends not to hate me, he does because I'm queer and he's queer. However, unlike him I don't pretend not to be. Here she's got a royal queen to sleep with and a rich one to hump.'

Lady Cynthia Gladwyn also observed the ducal couple. 'She spends all her time with effeminate young men staying in nightclubs until dawn and sending the duke home early: "Buzz off, mosquito." What a way to address the once king of England,' she said.

When Wallis spoke, the duke did what he was told. As veteran courtier Ulick Alexander said, the former king was driven by the 'sexual perversion of self-abasement'.

At a birthday party thrown for Wallis by the duke in the South of France after the war, the duchess announced: 'Once my ambition was to be queen of England.' After 1936, that appeared only to be in Hitler's gift – which was, perhaps in her eyes, a good enough reason to spy for the Nazis.

BIBLIOGRAPHY

Bhaney, Jennifer Bowers, *Betrayer's Waltz: The Unlikely Bond Between Marie Valerie of Austria and Hitler's Princess-Spy*, McFarland & Company, Jefferson, North Carolina, 2017

Bloch, Michael, *The Duke of Windsor's War*, Weidenfeld and Nicolson, London, 1982

Bloch, Michael, *The Secret File of the Duke of Windsor*, Bantam Press, London, 1988

Carré, Mathilde-Lily, *I Was 'The Cat': The Truth about the Most Remarkable Woman Spy since Mata Hari – By Herself*, Souvenir Press, London, 1960

Clough, Bryan, *State Secrets: The Kent-Wolkoff Affair*, Hideaway Publications, Hove, East Sussex, 2005

Cochran, Charles B., *Showman Looks On*, J.M. Dent & Sons, London, 1941

Dallek, Robert, *John F. Kennedy: An Unfinished Life 1917-1963*, Allen Lane, London, 2003

Dodd, Martha, *My Years in Germany*, Gollancz, London, 1939

Farago, Ladislas, *The Game of Foxes*, Hodder and Stoughton, London, 1971

Farris, Scott, *Inga: Kennedy's Great Love, Hitler's Perfect Beauty, and J. Edgar Hoover's Prime Suspect*, Lyons Press, Guilford, Connecticut, 2016

Fromm, Bella, *Blood and Banquets: A Berlin Social Diary*, Geoffrey Bles, London, 1943

Galante, Pierre, *Mademoiselle Chanel*, Henry Regnery Company, Chicago, 1973

Garby-Czerniawski, Roman, *The Big Network*, George Ronal, London, 1961

Gerwarth, Robert, *Hitler's Hangman: The Life of Heydrich*, Yale University Press, New Haven, 2011

Görtemaker, Heike B., *Eva Braun: Life with Hitler*, Alfred A. Knopf, New York, 2011

Hamilton, Nigel, *JYK: Reckless Youth*, Random House, New York, 1992

Hayward, James, *Myths & Legends of the Second World War*, Sutton Publishing, Stroud, Gloucestershire, 2003

Haste, Cate, *Nazi Women: Hitler's Seduction of a Nation*, Channel 4 Books, London, 2001

Hersh, Seymour, *The Dark Side of Camelot*, HarperCollins Publishers, London, 1997

Hutton, Robert, *Agent Jack: The True Story of MI5's Secret Nazi Hunter*, Weidenfeld & Nicolson, London, 2018

Kahn, David, *Hitler's Spies: German Military Intelligence in World War II*, Da Capo Press, Boston, 2000

Knopp, Guido, *Hitler's Women – And Marlene*, Sutton Publishing, Stroud, Gloucestershire, 2003

Larson, Erik, *In the Garden of Beasts*, Transworld Publishers, London, 2011

Lepage, Jean-Denis G.G., *An Illustrated Dictionary of the Third Reich*, McFarland & Company, Jefferson, North Carolina, 2014

Macintyre, Ben, *Double Cross: The True Story of the D-Day Spies*, Bloomsbury Publishing, London, 2012

Mazzeo, Tilar J., *The Secret History of Chanel No. 5: The Intimate History of the World's Most Famous Perfume*, HarperCollins, New York, 2010

Merrilees, William, *The Short Arm of the Law: The Memoirs of William Merrilees OBE*, John Long, London, 1966

Moon, Tom, *Loyal and Lethal Ladies of Espionage*, iUniverse.com, Lincoln, New England, 2000

Morton, Andrew, *17 Carnations: The Windsors, the Nazis and the Cover-up*, Michael O'Mara Books, London, 2015

Morton, Andrew, *Wallis in Love: The Untold Passion of the Duchess of Windsor*, Michael O'Mara Books, London, 2018
Murphy, Sean, *Letting the Side Down: British Traitors of the Second World War*, Sutton Publishing, Stroud, Gloucestershire, 2003
Norden, Peter, *Madam Kitty*, Abelard-Schman, London, 1973
O'Connor, Brian, *Operation Lena and Hitler's Plots to Blow Up Britain*, Amberley Publishing, Stroud, Gloucestershire, 2017
Paine, Lauran, *Mathilde Carré, Double Agent*, Robert Hale & Company, London, 1976
Perret, Geoffrey, *Jack: A Life Like No Other*, Random House, New York, 2002
Richelson, Jeffery T., *A Century of Spies: Intelligence in the Twentieth Century*, Oxford University Press, Oxford, 1995
Root, Neil, *Twentieth-Century Spies*, Summersdale Publishers, Chichester, 2010
Schad, Martha, *Hitler's Spy Princess*, Sutton Publishing, Stroud, 2004
Schellenberg, Walter, *The Memoirs of Hitler's Spymaster*, André Deutsch, London, 2006
Seale, Adrian, *The Spy Beside the Sea: The Extraordinary Wartime Story of Dorothy O'Grady*, The History Press, Stroud, Gloucester, 2012
Sergueiev, Lily, *Secret Service Rendered*, William Kimber and Co, London, 1968
Singer, Kurt, *The World's Greatest Women Spies*, W.H. Allen, London, 1951
Stephenson, Jill, *Women in Nazi Germany*, Pearson Education, London, 2001
Tate, Tim, *Hitler's British Traitors: The Secret History of Spies, Saboteurs and Fifth Columnists*, Icon Books, London, 2018
Theoharis, Athan, ed., *From the Secret Files of J. Edgar Hoover*, Ivan R. Dee, Chicago, 1991
Tommasini, Anthony, *Virgil Thomson: Composer on the Aisle*, W.W. Norton & Company, New York, 1997
Tremain, David, *Double Agent Victoire: Mathilde Carré and the Interallié Network*, The History Press, Stroud, Gloucestershire, 2018
Vaughan, Hal, *Sleeping with the Enemy: Coco Chanel, Nazi Agent*, Chatto & Windus, London, 2011
Weinstein, Allen and Vassiliev, Alexander, *The Haunted Wood: Soviet Espionage in America – the Stalin Era*, Random House, New York, 1999

Weitz, John, *Joachim Von Ribbentrop: Hitler's Diplomat*, Weidenfeld and Nicolson, London, 1992

West, Nigel, ed. *The Guy Liddell Diaries: MI5's Director of Counter-Espionage in World War II, Volume 1 1939–1942*, Routledge, Abingdon, Oxfordshire, 2005

Wighton, Charles and Peis, Gunter, *Hitler's Spies and Saboteurs: The Sensational Story of Nazi Espionage in the United States and Other Allied Nations*, Tandem Books, New York, 1972

Wighton, Charles and Peis, Gunter, *They Spied on England: Based on the German Secret Service War Diary of General von Lahousen*, Odhams Press, London, 1958

Willetts, Paul, *Rendezvous at the Russian Tea Rooms: The Spyhunter, the Fashion Designer and the Man from Moscow*, Constable, London, 2016

Wilson, Jim, *Nazi Princess: Hitler, Lord Rothermere and Princess Stephanie von Hohenlohe*, The History Press, Stroud, 2011

Wyden, Peter, *Stella*, Simon & Schuster, New York, 1992

Young, Gordon, *The Cat With Two Faces*, Beacon Books, London, 1958

INDEX